Praise for *Narrow Dog to Carcassonne*

"A smart comic telling of an adventurous undertaking by man, wife, and their narrow dog, Jim (a whippet) ... Darlington has a barge full of opinions ... and dares to voice them as energetically as he dared to make this trip ... [and] to the end maintains what is no façade but an enviable, raucous joy of living."
— *Boston Globe*

"The style echoes the author's clear zest for living in the moment. Frequent flashes of wit and poetic prose capture poignant emotions."
— *Publishers Weekly*

"Hilarious ... engaging and intelligent ... Adding dimension to the experience are countless references to lines of music, literature, movies, etc., familiar to Darlington (and most readers), gleaned over the course of a lifetime in the 20th century.... Figuring out the sometimes obscure references becomes a game embedded in the reading."
— *Fredericksburg (VA) Free Lance-Star*

"Destined to become a travel classic." — *Observer* (UK)

"A richly atmospheric journey ... The writing is as muscular and lean as its canine hero, conjuring up dawn mist or giant catfish in prose haiku before moving on to the next killer one-liner.... A rich and winning comic debut, destined to become a classic."
— *Sunday Telegraph* (UK)

"Boat enthusiasts will appreciate the insider terminology about locks and dock life."   —*Kirkus Reviews*

"Hilariously, brilliantly written…Sheer joy in every sentence…You don't want the journey, and thus the book, to come to an end."   —FetchDog.com

"Dry Brit wit and often poetic descriptions power the quirky memoir."   —*National Geographic Traveler*

"If you want to read about a real dog adventure, check out *Narrow Dog to Carcassonne.*"   —*Dayton Daily News*

"Written with the author's glorious sense of humor, this is one of those journeys you never want to end."

—*Good Book Guide* (UK)

About the Authors

TERRY DARLINGTON was brought up in Pembroke Dock, Wales. He moved to Staffordshire, where he founded Research Associates, an international market research firm, and Stone Master Marathoners, a running club. Like many Welshmen, he is talkative and confiding, ill at ease with practical matters, and known to linger in pubs. He likes boating but doesn't know much about it.

MONICA DARLINGTON's father was a gardener and her mother a housemaid, or perhaps it was the other way around. She was beauty queen of Brecon and Radnor, Wales, has a first-class degree in French, has run thirty marathons, and leaps tall buildings in a single bound. She quite likes boating.

Brynula Great Expectations (JIM) is sprung from a long line of dogs with ridiculous names. Jim can run at forty miles an hour. He is cowardly, thieving, and disrespectful, and he hates boating.

Visit their website at www.narrowdog.com.

NARROW DOG TO INDIAN RIVER

Terry Darlington

DELTA TRADE PAPERBACKS

NARROW DOG TO INDIAN RIVER
A Delta Trade Paperback / May 2009

Published by
Bantam Dell
A Division of Random House, Inc.
New York, New York

Book design by Steve Kennedy

Library of Congress Cataloging-in-Publication Data
Darlington, Terry.
Narrow Dog to Indian River / Terry Darlington.
p.   cm.
Includes bibliographical references.
ISBN 978-0-385-34209-4 (pbk.)
978-0-440-33851-2 (e-book)
1. Southern States–Description and travel.   2. Southern States–History, Local.
3. Darlington, Terry–Travel–Southern States.   4. Darlington,
Monica–Travel–Southern States.   5. English–Travel–Southern States.
6. Whippet–Biography.   7. Travel with dogs–Southern States.   8. Intracoastal
waterways–Southern States.   9. Canal-boats–Southern States.   10. Southern
States–Social life and customs–Anecdotes. 1. Title.
F216.2.D37   2009
917.5096'93–dc22
2008039205

Printed in the United States of America

www.bantamdell.com

BVG 10 9 8 7 6 5 4 3 2

To
Lucy and Richard
Clifford and Katherine
Georgia and Mark

with our love

I've come on Floridas you won't believe—
Arthur Rimbaud, 'The Drunken Boat'

Contents

NARROW DOG TO INDIAN RIVER

One

THEIR GODS ARE NOT OUR GODS

Staffordshire

The Limey Queen of Greenwich Village – Covered Thinly with Maple Syrup – The Marine Terminal – A Thread of Silver – Captain Rob – The Wayfaring Stranger – Their Gods Are Not Our Gods – Farewell Party – Mum and Dad – Summerstreet Lane – The Small Green Ones with the Spotted Bellies – Pork Cracklins – Mantovani – Jesus Ears – Derek and the Alligators

THE TROUBLE WITH YOU IS YOU ARE OBSESSED with the USA, said Monica. The GIs gave you too much gum in the war and you read too many comics and saw too many films—too much Captain Marvel, too much Tarzan, too much *Terry and the Pirates*, too much Alan Ladd. But America will crush you like it always has. Remember after the New York Marathon, when that gay fireman went off with you over his shoulder? If I hadn't come along you would be Tits Magee now, the Limey Queen of Greenwich Village.

I was in a bit of a state, I said. He was trying to help—he was very nice.

What about when you opened an office on Madison Avenue and lost us a fortune *twice*? Now you want to sail down the Atlantic Intracoastal Waterway. It is eleven hundred miles long. There are sea crossings bigger than the English Channel. There are flies. There are alligators. There are winds that blow at two hundred miles an hour. Ten thousand people drowned in Galveston and look what happened to New Orleans. And you want to sail down it in a canal boat six feet ten inches wide.

There's no such thing as a wind of two hundred miles an

hour, I said—the air would catch fire. And Galveston and New Orleans are somewhere else—they are on the Gulf of Mexico.

But that's where you want us to go, isn't it? A narrowboat on the Gulf of Mexico, and you have conquered the US or died in the attempt. And Jim has to die with us. You and me are seventy; we've had our lives, but Jim's only five. He knows you are going boating again—the way he looks at us and shivers. This isn't the Trent and Mersey Canal, it's not the Thames at Henley, it's not the Rhône—this is a bloody wilderness, halfway round the world.

You could stay at home, I said.

You would never come back. Your bloated corpse will be found in some deserted bayou, half eaten by alligators, with three times the permitted alcohol level.

We'll go over and do a recce—check out both ends of the journey: Virginia and Florida. Trust me—I would never do anything to upset my Mon. Slightest problem, we'll stay at home.

How about rednecks and bikers, are they a slightest problem? How about gun nuts and gangsters? How about snakes and poison ivy and rip tides? How about hip-hop and preachers on the radio for a year? How about you have always buggered it up in America and now you are going to do it again? I knew there was something funny about you from the start—just because you went to Oxford and liked poetry I thought you were OK. In fact you are a bloody lunatic, and I don't know what I ever saw in you.

It was my pilgrim soul, I said, and my commanding presence, and my wild, careless laugh.

I could have married that Frenchman, said Monica. He looked like Yves Montand.

• • •

HALFWAY UP THE EAST COAST OF THE USA, Chesapeake Bay reaches a hundred miles towards Washington.

At the mouth of Chesapeake Bay you turn south into the Elizabeth River. On the left is Norfolk, and on the right, Portsmouth. From our hotel room over Norfolk we looked down the river, a quarter of a mile wide. The Atlantic Intracoastal Waterway begins here, and follows the river for seven miles, and then sets out across the Great Dismal Swamp. We didn't know much about the Great Dismal Swamp, but we were not sure we liked the sound of it.

Over the river a US Navy aircraft carrier, and nearer to us a ferry crawling between the two cities; wood and rails, its false paddle-wheel turning. The sun came up quicker than in Stone, and the river went to flame then deepest blue.

There were seventeen breakfasts in the hotel, and lots of African-American waitresses who said y'all all the time. We knew most of the breakfasts, except for the biscuits and gravy. The biscuits were scones, and the gravy was a salty white sauce. There were funny little sausages and hills of crispy bacon. So that's what happened, I said, to the crispy bacon we used to have before the war.

If you stood at the buffet an African-American gentleman would cook you a waffle, and you could have sauce made from fake cherries, or syrup made from fake maples.

We'll get fat, said Monica. And we are already fat after sailing through France.

No doubt, I said, but what can you do? The North American continent is blessed with the riches of nature, and covered thinly with maple syrup.

• • •

DAVE, THE OPERATIONS MANAGER OF ATLANTIC
Containers at Portsmouth Marine Terminal, was a nice man
with a beard. So that's a narrowboat, he said, looking at a
photograph of the *Phyllis May*. Never seen one before–my
God she's thin.

Most of the canal boats in England are like this, I said–the
locks on the main system are only seven feet wide. The original barges were seventy feet long, ten feet longer than the
Phyllis May. They were pulled by horses. The boating families
lived in the little cabin at the back. It was a culture of its own
and it died out when the railways and lorries took over. Then
in the nineteen fifties people started making narrowboats out
of steel as leisure boats.

How much does she weigh?

Seventeen tons. Ten-millimetre flat bottom: paving stones
for ballast. Draws two feet–on a wet day you can sail her up
Stafford High Street.

What's she like to steer?

You stand on that counter at the stern, and hold the tiller
behind your back. She has no bow thrusters but I can do
most of what I want if there are no big waves or winds or currents.

There are big waves and winds and currents on the
Intracoastal, said Dave.

He took us round the terminal. Containers in piles, and
machines a hundred feet high with two legs that pick up the
containers between their knees and roar about and put them
down somewhere else. Yachts on trolleys, and lorries and he-

licopters and tanks, waiting for the fifty-thousand-ton roll-on roll-off container ship that will carry them off around the world.

This is your crane, said Dave–the little one. We call him Clyde. He's only two hundred feet high. I guess you will want to be on your boat when we drop her in.

Yes, said Monica, he will, and Jim and I will stay on the wharf.

I tried to take a photo of Clyde but I couldn't get far enough away.

Dave introduced us to the ladies in the Portsmouth Marine Terminal office. We can't wait to meet Jim, said Nice Amy. We have eleven dogs between five of us. Tell Jim that we will have several bags of pork skins waiting when y'all arrive–are they the same as pork scratchings?

In June, I said, Jim will give us an opinion.

DOWN THE INTRACOASTAL WATERWAY AT thirty thousand feet. A thread of silver across the Great Dismal Swamp, which looked like the weather map on the telly when it's raining. Then sunlight on Albemarle Sound, and on Pamlico Sound, both wider than the English Channel. Along North Carolina the chalk line of Atlantic surf, and just inland the silver thread welling into lagoons and swamps and meanders. In South Carolina, past Charleston, and then through Georgia, the coastline is a madman's jigsaw, and it doesn't get much better in Florida. Now Lake Okeechobee is on our right, misty blue to the horizon, and the Everglades draining in endless patterns to the south.

We turn along Alligator Alley, the motorway across the peninsula, hold to the fast lane, and glide into the long slow afternoon of western Florida.

AT THE MARINA IN FORT MYERS THE MILLION-dollar plastic cruisers *Tarpon* and *Gulfstream Rose* lay quietly depreciating. From the rail an egret looked at us with a lemon eye, and trod its spotted foot, hustling for a sandwich. (An egret is a sort of heron, or perhaps it is the other way round.) A lizard trickled between our shoes, changing colour as it went. Four pelicans in the sky, and beyond them a vulture, its turkey head peering for corpses.

In America you pass examinations and then you can be a captain. Captain Rob was a nice man without a beard: fully denimed, blue-eyed, wiry. I would not like to be a fish on the other end of the line from Captain Rob.

You hit Albemarle Sound in North Carolina as soon as you have crossed the Great Dismal Swamp, said Captain Rob. Albemarle Sound is the estuary of the Chowan, and the Pasquotank, and the Alligator Rivers. You have got to cross it to get into the Alligator River on the other side. It is very wide. You are out of sight of land. First time I went over, the wind came round against the current and the waves were six feet high. I turned back, and I was lucky to get in. Pamlico Sound and the Neuse River are no better. But you've got nearly a year—y'all wait for a good day. There is big commercial stuff, so keep out of the way when that comes along. And the powerboats can turn you over—some of the people who drive those are crazy. But you shouldn't get squashed in a lock chamber because there are almost no locks. You are connected to the sea all down the coast.

We went down a canal connected to the sea in France, said Monica—the Rhône à Sète in the Camargue. It kept trying to wash us into the Mediterranean.

Is it going to be very hot? I asked.

Anywhere up the Waterway it can be over a hundred and absolute humidity. The heat could kill you—with you being so old. And watch for the flies. There is a green one—if you knock it off it attacks you again. Then there are the no-see-ums—they burrow into your skin. They are so small you no-see-um.

I got some lotion from the Avon Lady, I said. It's the one the fishermen use against the clegs, the Scottish horseflies. I put some on and as I walked by our kitchen door the varnish peeled off.

Bring some for me, said Captain Rob.

What about the manatees? I asked, don't they get up to three thousand pounds?

Yes, but they are all right unless they lean on you.

What about the vultures, asked Monica, and the alligators?

The turkey buzzards won't attack you until you are nearly dead. People worry about the alligators of course, but they come out in the dark and you can see their eyes shining round the boat before they start to climb in. Have you got a steel front door?

No, said Monica.

There is a new arrival these days, said Captain Rob. It's a monitor lizard seven feet long. They run at thirty-nine miles an hour. They eat dogs.

Jim can do forty, I said.

I guess he'll have the edge then, given a fair run. The hurricanes can be a problem. They are mainly in the summer and the autumn, but last year Wilma didn't come until the middle of October. Sometimes they don't reach the Carolinas and Georgia. But sometimes they do, so they could catch you on the way down.

What happens then?

Hell and destruction. Get the boat out on to the bank and head for the high ground.

What else is there to stop us?

There are the panthers and the bears and the anacondas, and the Red Tide. We don't like to talk about the Red Tide. But even if you sink, or get ill and die—with you being so old—you will have been the first English narrowboat on the US waterways. If you make it to Florida I will pilot you on to the Gulf of Mexico. I'll lead you out in my charter boat or come on the back of your funny boat with you. There will definitely be no fee—it will be my pleasure to help in this grand endeavour.

WE WENT TO IDA'S BON APPITEATERY ON FIRST Street, Fort Myers, to celebrate the end of our research trip. I am not slow to the bar but a thin grey-haired man got there first. I was once a wayfaring stranger myself, he said, and no traveller from overseas buys his first drink while I am around. I have seen sorrow, toil and danger, he added, everywhere I go.

Look, I said, you can't do that—all right I'll have one of those beers that smell of barbecue smoke—a Samuel Adams—and cheers.

And I'll have a gin and dry martini, said Monica, and thank you very much. The barmaid filled a half-pint glass with ice and held it low. Then she took a gin bottle with a spout and held it over her head and emptied it into the glass. She looked at the glass and frowned and opened another bottle, and added another two inches from that. Then she took an aerosol of dry martini and squirted it in the direction of the glass.

I am going outside to shout at the cars, said the Wayfaring Stranger. It's all right—I know most of them. He went outside and sat down at a table and started shouting at the cars.

I turned to the man on the next stool. Would you be an American gentleman? We just love your crazy accent.

My name is Michael, said the gentleman, and I am a fireman. I was born here, and so were my parents and my grandparents but I am an Irishman of purest blood—I observe St Patrick's Day and drink little but Guinness. Empty your glasses at once so I can refill them. What is your name?

They call me Tits Magee, I said, and this is my girl, Gulfstream Rose.

It took more than one sailor to change my name to Gulfstream Rose, explained Monica.

Michael said that our hotel was in one of the older areas of the town and it was dark and we could get murdered so he would walk us back. The barmaid put a lid on Monica's drink so she could take it home for breakfast. On the way out we tried to buy a beer for the Wayfaring Stranger, but he was shouting at the cars.

There was no one around. From what we had seen of the southern USA there was never anyone around. No one in Norfolk, Virginia, day or night, and no one in Fort Myers,

Florida. Just empty streets and the smell of barbecue smoke. We knew that American citizens were to be found in the shopping malls at certain times, and in bars. Where they were the rest of the time we did not discover.

Goodbye Michael—so many thanks. We'll be back.

Goodbye Tits and goodbye Gulfstream—y'all have a great trip now.

IT LOOKS LIKE THE *PHYLLIS MAY* COULD GET down the Intracoastal with a bit of luck, I said next morning over the biscuits and gravy, if we can avoid the hurricanes. We have got June to the following spring—we have to average only an hour's cruising a day. We can choose our weather for the big crossings. We can have some lovely long stops; get to know the towns and cities, where there are any. But what bothers me is that we are not really close in with the culture here. Going down to Carcassonne was dodgy enough at times. And in France the weather is more like ours, the countryside is more like ours, the towns are more like ours. The French are Europeans like us—realistic, cautious, tired. However much you like the US, their people are not our people and their gods are not our gods. You know what they were like when we opened our office in New York—Oh of course you will sell a lot of research reports and make a lot of money, no problem. They have long antennae—they pick up on what you want to hear. They might agree to one of my ideas about boating and we could be sent to our deaths out of politeness. Or something really American could get us that we didn't expect—like a raft of lumber or a water moccasin snake or a venomous hummingbird that kills with a peck. Or we might say the wrong thing about Vietnam or Guantánamo or Jim Reeves or the Civil War and someone will shoot us. They are very excitable, and they all have guns.

You dream up these crazy schemes and when it all gets real you start to lose your nerve, said Monica. Look at Dave and Nice Amy in Portsmouth, and Captain Rob, and the Wayfaring Stranger, and Michael. The Yanks won't shoot us— they will look after us, and Jim too. The pork skins will be waiting in Portsmouth, whatever pork skins might be.

But we must not forget, I said, for eleven hundred miles, that their pork scratchings are not our pork scratchings, and their gods are not our gods.

IN STONE WE ORGANIZED A FAREWELL LUNCH-time party and a lot of people came. Our daughter Lucy made a speech and everyone said it was much better than I would have made. Peter and Karen from Canal Cruising told us they had never seen wiring like the French wiring on the *Phyllis May* and my how they laughed. Peter said he had taken the engine out and serviced it very thoroughly and Karen gave us a silver St Christopher medal for the ignition keyring just to make sure. We talked with our friends of all we did together thirty or forty years ago and agreed it could have been yesterday afternoon. Cousin Ken, who had seen us off to cross the Channel, gave us a bottle of champagne to open if we reached the Gulf of Mexico.

Next day the papers were full of stories from Florida. A lady had been sitting on the bank kicking her feet over the water and they found her arms inside an alligator. A scuba diver had gone down into the canal and not come up. An alligator with one eye had jumped on a jogger and pulled her into the water. There was an 87 per cent chance of a major hurricane, and the hurricane season would begin a fortnight before we arrived. Last year had been the worst year for hurricanes on record.

We must take a positive view, I said—

> How can a man die better
> Than facing fearful odds
> For the ashes of his fathers,
> And the temples of his Gods?

Let's go and see my mum and dad.

DOWN THE SOUTHERN END OF STAFFORDSHIRE is Albrighton, a little town with a church and chestnut trees.

Before our family was broken up in the war we had chestnuts in our drive. The candles were white and the leaves were soft. Then one day the candles went out and the leaves yellowed and frayed and cartwheeled away.

I collected the washing-up liquid from our camper van, and a trowel and a brush and scissors. I walked up the path. The headstone had been infringed by the sod, as if the earth were pulling it in. I bent over and cut into the grass and heaved it away and then I got some water and poured it over the stone and scrubbed it. The letters came up white—*Together again*. I knelt down.

I am not going to ask you any favours, I said, it is a long

time since I visited you and I don't deserve any. I just want to say that I think of you a lot and will think of you however far I go and whatever I do.

They came into my mind as if they were not quite connected with me or with the earth but they were right by me just the same. I felt their sweetness and their specialness, the ways in which they were each themselves and no one else.

It was no use asking them for luck—they did not care about beasts or tempests, illness or accident, breakdown or loss of will. What did it matter to them? Very soon we would be together again.

FROM STONE YOU GO UP THE MODDERSHALL Valley, then turn right into Cotwalton, backing into gateways to let the tractors by, and you park and walk up Summerstreet Lane.

Stiles: a rising path, across fields, into the sky. Look back and there through faintest blue is Shropshire: the Wrekin and Wenlock Edge. Jim swept round the horizon like a second hand, and came back heavy into oxygen debt, staggering and grinning. At the top of the hill, six hundred feet up, the blue-bell wood—annihilating all that's made, to a blue thought in a blue shade.

Monica and I talked about Stone.

In Stone I can pretend I am retired, said Monica, not a full-time manager of crazy expeditions. I can play bridge and visit my children and my grandchildren and go down to Stone Master Marathoners. I don't have to organize a mooring for tomorrow night or send a chapter of our book to

London from the middle of Burgundy on a mobile phone that doesn't work and we don't have to cross the Channel or sail an inland sea in a storm and I am not scared half the time.

There are the brick terraces, I said, and the canal and the river and the pubs, and the Christmas lights and the service at the cenotaph. And the Stone Festival, with the steeplechase and the Dog Derby that you and I invented thirty years ago. In the spring there are daffodils, and in Stonefield Park the primula in heaps of crimson and gold.

It was all so beautiful after London, said Monica. Remember that poem you wrote for our first Michaelmas–

> *The trees trawl the wind*
> *For angels*
> *They stand among the leaves*
> *Gold faces calm*
>
> *At sunset they blow*
> *Across the sky*
> *In shining hurricanes*
>
> *Fighting the dragon*
> *Bearing our pain*
> *Their blood falls*
> *As gilded rain*

Tell me Mon, what are you looking forward to most in the USA?

I can't think of anything, said Monica.

• • •

Attention Kerry Finch, Store Manager, West Marine, .
Norfolk, Virginia
Dear Kerry—In February you kindly helped us choose
our new anchors for the Intracoastal Waterway. This is
to confirm we would like you to get two of 401596 for
us to pick up shortly after June 20th. We will need
chain and rope too.

Kind regards, Terry and Monica Darlington

Dear Terry—Nice to hear from you. For each anchor
you would need about 1 eft of 3/8 chain and perhaps
250ft of rope.

Thanks, Kerry

Dear Kerry—Can you check your last sentence? I
looked up eft, thinking it must be a nautical term, and
it seems it is a newt. Nothing wrong with newts of
course.

Kind regards, Terry

Morning Mr Darlington—Ha ha, I am sorry, the last
sentence should have read 12ft . . . not 1 eft! I agree
nothing wrong with newts!

Kerry

Dear Kerry—The chain and rope sound just right, and
can you get us in a couple of efts? The small green
ones with the spotted orange bellies if you can. And
two jam-jars, please, and some string.

Yip, T

•   •   •

Good heavens, said Monica, it's a parcel of pork scratch-ings—they are from Andrew, the gentleman who does the canal web-log *Granny Buttons*. How nice—he must have sent for them specially. There are two sorts—Kettle Style Pork Cracklins, with Rinds Attached, and Fried Pork Rinds, which are puffy ones. It says they are made in Henderson, North Carolina. This English packet I bought to take with us says—

> If not in good condition and within the sell-by date please return it to us with the wrapper—we will gladly replace and refund postage.

The American one says—

> For God so loved the world that he gave his only begotten Son, that whosoever believeth in him should not perish, but have everlasting life. John 3:16

There's no arguing with that, I said.

I opened the packet of Kettle Style Pork Cracklins and Jim appeared from behind the skirting boards. No, Jim, I said—no pork scratchings at home. These have been sent us for liter-ary purposes, so we can report to an astonished world about American pork scratchings. You can have one or two in the pub tonight.

They look like ours, said Monica, and they are hard like ours, but not quite as crunchy and they taste of maple syrup and barbecue smoke.

I went to the cupboard and got the salt and poured some

into the bag. In England they bang in the monosodium gluta-mate, I said—no messing about. If you are going to eat rub-bish you may as well do it properly.

Jim started to whine. No, Jim, I said, and that's final. I put the bag on the sideboard, right at the back.

Where is that bag? asked Monica later.

We found it under the table, empty.

Jim lay in his kennel—the eyes of Princess Diana, the legs of Sebastian Coe, the mind of Ronnie Biggs.

MANTOVANI, SAID MONICA, *MANTOVANI*! I'M NOT having Mantovani on my boat. They play Mantovani in su-permarkets in Turkey. I know what you will do—put it on loud and drink too much beer and I'll wake up at two in the morn-ing and you will be asleep in your chair with Jim alongside you and Mantovani pouring all over my new carpet like trea-cle.

Mantovani is a serious musician, I said. He was academi-cally trained, and his father before him. His cascading strings were not done with an echo-box—he scored every note. He was enormous all over the world.

He's not being enormous on my boat. And what on earth is this? The first ever British hit parade—the hit parade of nineteen fifty-two! Who wants to listen to a hit parade of *nine-teen fifty-two*?

I do—I was seventeen—it is the soundtrack of my emotional awakening. Nat King Cole is great, and Frankie Laine made a solid job of 'High Noon'. And Jo Stafford sang 'Jambalaya' and she sang 'You Belong To Me'.

All right, but why Johnnie Ray? Who cares about Johnnie Ray the crying crooner? Do we have to keep alive for half a century the memory of a deaf homosexual?

That's a cruel remark, and personal and quite uncalled-for. Beethoven was deaf, and Benjamin Britten was no ladies' man. 'Walking My Baby Back Home' with the Buddy Cole Trio is art at its most high, and 'Let's Walk That-A-Way' with Doris Day is great.

I don't know how you expect me to live with stuff like that for a year in the wilderness, said Monica. In Mid-Wales we had choirs. In London I was under Sir Malcolm Sargent.

So were a lot of ladies—Elizabeth Jane Howard, the enchantress who helped save the waterways, said she had hardly got into the room before Flash Harry had his trousers on the floor. The answer is country music—the American parallel universe where we can both be at home. Johnny Cash and his 'Ring Of Fire', and Crystal Gayle talking in her sleep, and Dolly Parton always loving you, and Kris Kristofferson with your head upon his pillow and Bobbie Gentry—a man could make a fool of himself over Bobbie Gentry. And Glen Campbell in Galveston, where he used to run.

Yes great, but I thought Galveston had been swept away.

They built it again so Jim Webb could write his song.

What about Emmylou Harris, said Monica, telling us that love hurts—the CD you keep under your pillow?

Emmylou was right, love hurts. It hurt me like hell in nineteen fifty-two, but when I met you love became very good indeed.

Smooth talker, said Monica, you can have your Mantovani.

Son of a gun, I said, we'll have some fun, on the bayou.

• • •

JIM LAY ON THE SOFA SIDEWAYS, HIS HEAD AND front legs over the edge, as if he had melted. He looked like Salvador Dalí's watch in that painting *Persistence of Memory*, but this was *Persistence of Whippet*.

Do you remember you used to call him baby names when he was a puppy? asked Monica.

I didn't call him baby names, I said. No point getting soft. He's just an animal. But he was the first dog I had that was mine—the others were yours, or the family's.

You used to call him Daddy's Little Moon-mouse.

I may have called him Daddy's Little Moon-mouse once or twice, when I was feeling sentimental.

Sentimental as an eft. And the kids heard you call him that and they used to come and tell me and we would laugh.

It's not good for kids to make fun of their father, I said—they will grow up rejecting authority.

The kids are over forty, said Monica, and they have always rejected authority and they learned it from you. Look how you got expelled from school.

I wasn't expelled—the headmaster and I came to an agreement. But oh look at Jim, isn't he sweet when he lies like that. Last weekend he could hardly stand. It was the trembling and he wouldn't eat and the vet was shut.

I wondered if he was upset because I had washed him in the bath, said Monica, after he had covered his neck and ears with cowshit. Or if he had realized what was going on. I know what he would think about going down the Intracoastal Waterway.

I was afraid we would lose him, I said. Like our retrievers when they got that infection. They didn't complain, they just died. Jim was worse than them—hopeless and shivering. How can you have *Narrow Dog to Indian River* without a narrow dog? If he died we could get another one but it wouldn't be Jim. I know he is a bugger, but he is our bugger. We might get a whippet that liked boating, and that would be nice, but then there would be nothing to write about. It would be like *Don Quixote* with a hero who was a practical down-to-earth sort of bloke, or *Moby-Dick* about a whale that wasn't very big and was quite fond of people or *Dr Jekyll and Mr Hyde* about a chap who got a bit irritable now and then.

When Jim was nearly better Monica discovered a hole in his throat. When he had rubbed his neck in the cowshit he had become infected.

He realizes we are going boating again and tries to cut his throat, I said.

He's all right now, said Monica, he is practising his sleeping.

Jim had turned over on his back and pushed one leg into the air. His paws quivered and his eyes were part covered by membrane, and he yipped and chased rabbits, cutting them off from their warrens in the sky.

Jesus Ears, I said.

JIM AND I WENT TO ASTON LOCK TO LOOK OVER the edge of the world—*what spires, what farms, are these?* South along the broad towpath, Jim running ahead, sniffing the grass and jumping. The May trees were hung with snow. The wind was perfumed, and the Gulf Stream had softened it and the mountains of Wales had cooled it. I would miss that wind, that coolness, more than anything else. When you are cold you can cosy up to a fire or to a girl. When you are hot there is nowhere to hide.

Derek came towards us, walking from Sandon. I introduced Derek to Stone Master Marathoners thirty years ago. He runs faster than me, and he is older than me, and he is thinner than Jim. Derek crouched and rubbed Jim behind the ears and Jim tried to enter his body by his armpit.

Borrowed your book about France, said Derek, couldn't get into it. When are you off?

In three weeks, 19th June. The boat went off yesterday from the yard in Stone to Liverpool, no problems. When we loaded her in Carcassonne to bring her back from France the crane driver dropped her and knocked the top off the gatepost, but here they are professionals.

There was a programme on telly about alligators, said Derek. In the mating season they leap out of the water and pull you in and twist round and round to tear your limbs off. You are not going to be in Florida next spring are you?

Yes, I said.

If I was you I'd take a gun. Nice little sixteen-bore would be fine. Those reptiles are fast—they bask in the sun and store energy like a battery. You have one shot and if that doesn't work it's the twisting. Their teeth are covered with deadly bacteria so if you get free they follow you round and wait for you to die.

Thanks Derek, but carrying a gun will only encourage violence.

They won't need encouragement, not in the spring. Have a good trip. And watch Jim—to an alligator he would be a pork scratching. When you come back you'll get fit again and I'll race you up the hill in the Outlanes like I always do, and perhaps one day you'll be lucky. I'll be eighty before long and I might start to slow down. I think you can get sub-machine guns in the States for domestic use.

He shook my hand and wished us luck and we said goodbye and Jim and I walked on.

When I looked back Derek was firing an imaginary tommy gun into the cut, braced against the recoil, his face without expression, like Alan Ladd in *The Great Gatsby*.

Two

THE ICE STORM

Virginia

Jim in the Crate – Ziggy Is Immensely Strong – The Virginia *and the* Monitor *– Phyllis May* at Mile Zero *– The Ice Storm – We Have Lost Control Before We Have Started – Desert Boots – Heartworm – The Screaming Eagles – Total Systemic Collapse – A Cruel and Senseless Crime – The Designer Handbag – Farewell Party – The Sopping Air and the Blasting Sun – The Fatal Shore – Something Awfully Wrong*

WE COULD HEAR JIM BARKING BEFORE WE GOT to the door of the luggage terminal. There was his travelling kennel and a huge fan blowing right at it and an overweight gentleman sitting by the fan and Jim barking. We stood there drenched with rain and sweat and Monica gave the gentleman the papers for Jim's release.

Jim had been twelve hours in the crate, because there was no room for the plane to land at Washington and it had flown round and round until it ran out of gas and it had landed at Baltimore and then flown back to Washington. You would think they knew we were coming, said Monica.

All the journey I had worried about Jim. What if they forget to put on the heating and he freezes? What if they didn't pressurize the hold and he explodes? What if they forget about him because he is the only dog on board? Is he frightened? What if he wants to go to the lavatory? What if they lose him? What if he gets stolen? What if he dies?

Stranger, commemorated here
'Tis but a dog you see

And yet, I beg you, do not sneer:
My master wept for me

Wept as the lifeless earth he pressed
Above my lifeless head
And wrote, where now I lie at rest
The words that you have read

Perhaps I am a crank, but then so was the Greek chap who wrote that poem two thousand years ago.

The overweight gentleman let Jim out of his crate and Jim jumped him and licked his face—the gentleman had kept him cool and given him water and watched over him for two hours. Jim had been barking not because he was angry, but because he wanted to say hello.

It took us half an hour to get back inside our hire car and start it up and switch on the lights and the windscreen washers. During these travails the car rang bells and sirens and switched the lights on and off and shut down different parts of itself to remind us that this was America and we were useless.

Next day we drove to Portsmouth, two hundred miles south, trying to drive as the locals do, on the right with all four wheels on the carriageway. The *Phyllis May* had already arrived at the marine terminal but we could not board her without customs papers. We didn't know what the customs people would make of a narrowboat coming from England. Perhaps they would take it to pieces for bombs or drugs, or send it back home as unsuitable for the journey.

• • •

THE WATERFRONT OF NORFOLK, VIRGINIA, IS neat and modern, with a few high-rise hotels and offices. Little remains of the old riverside town, except for the customs building, which is modelled on a Greek temple.

That's a nice dog, said Officer Nagle. That's Jim I guess. Atlantic Containers told me about Jim. Officer Ellis will do your papers. He hasn't done it before but he can come out and ask me if he gets stuck. What does your boat draw and how fast does it go?

Two feet two inches, I said, and seven knots.

Mine draws four inches, said Officer Nagle, and does sixty knots.

Jim yawned and stretched, showing off his four rows of teeth and the coiled and hurdling muscles of his thighs. I guess he can run real fast, said Officer Nagle.

Forty miles an hour, I said.

And you can go after rabbits with him, I suppose, said Officer Nagle.

Yes, I said, he caught a rabbit in the spring, but I don't think it was very well. It gave him fleas.

A real sportsman's dog, said Officer Nagle—I can see that. I had a choice of dog myself. I made a list. It would be a whippet or a Jack Russell or a Chihuahua. In the end there was a Chihuahua ready and it was my wife's birthday so we took him. Of course Ziggy is not as fast as Jim, but he is immensely strong.

I thought Chihuahuas were small, said Monica.

They are not very big, said Officer Nagle, but the strength is there. Underneath the fur a Chihuahua is the same as a whippet. The bone structure is identical. It's the same dog—

the legs, the deep chest. They have Chihuahua races—there is a league. I don't race Ziggy but I could—he would do great. And my cat weighs twenty pounds.

Good heavens, I said.

Officer Ellis came out from behind the filing cabinets carrying a sheaf of papers—Oh that doesn't matter at all, said Officer Nagle, forget about that; let it go—these people are guests of our nation, for Christ's sake. Twenty pounds, he repeated.

Is it a sort of a big or a fat cat? I asked cautiously. Officer Nagle was not a small chap himself.

Fat? Not in the least, said Officer Nagle. That cat is solid muscle. He is a guard cat. When visitors come he threatens them—he growls and he hisses real scary. You know you are safe when Spike is around.

You have mountain lions here, I said. Perhaps he has a bit of cougar in him.

Cougar, now that's very likely. I never thought of that. Cougar. Mountain lion. A wild cat—a sportsman's cat.

Officer Nagle went behind the filing cabinets.

Some time later he came out with a small computer print of a black and white cat, which looked like an ordinary cat except it was very fat, and a dog that looked like a rat.

Very nice, we said.

Officer Ellis appeared. Ah, thank you Officer Ellis, said Officer Nagle—now here are your papers. Y'all have a great trip. We haven't had one of your English narrowboats here before. I may come and see you—I live just north over the water—in Newport News.

That's a funny name for a town, I said—why Newport News?

I don't know, said Officer Nagle—I guess it has always been that.

What do they call the local paper? I asked.

The *Daily Press*.

Of course, I said.

Here are your documents, said Officer Nagle. You can go and fetch your boat and sail away. Y'all have the best trip now. And goodbye Jim—I could have had a whippet like you, but there was a Chihuahua ready and it was my wife's birthday so I took him. He is immensely strong.

IN 1861 THE CONFEDERACY OF SOUTHERN States decided to break away from the Union. The North went to war to stop them and blockaded the East Coast.

On 8 March 1862 a terrible machine came out of the Elizabeth River and sailed into the broad waters of Hampton Roads, at the mouth of Chesapeake Bay. The terrible machine was the rebel battleship *Virginia*. Nothing like her had ever been seen in these waters, or anywhere else. She looked like a 250-foot flat-iron and under the water she had an iron beak. She rammed the Union corvette *Cumberland* and blew up the frigate *Congress* and crippled the frigate *Minnesota* and killed four hundred Union sailors.

Next day another terrible machine came in from the Atlantic. It was the Union battleship *Monitor*. Nothing like her had ever been seen in these waters, or anywhere else. She was a revolving iron turret on an armoured raft, with two eleven-inch cannon. She was much smaller than the *Virginia*. The populations of Norfolk and Portsmouth stood silent on the hills as she set upon the *Virginia* like a terrier.

Shells could not penetrate these machines, because they were the first ironclads. Then from ten yards away the *Virginia* hit the sight hole of the *Monitor* cabin and the captain fell, blinded by powder and blood. Lieutenant Greene, who was twenty-two, took command and turned on his enemy, but she had fled.

In May the rebels evacuated Norfolk and blew up the battleship *Virginia.*

On the last day of the year the little *Monitor* sank off Cape Hatteras, North Carolina, with sixteen of her crew. The *Dictionary of American Naval Fighting Ships* explains her size, low power, and speed and certain design defects limited her to service on protected waters such as harbours and rivers.

TWO LIFETIMES LATER, ONE BLUE DAY IN JUNE, a machine rose into the air at the Portsmouth International Terminal, and dropped into the broad waters of Hampton Roads. It was the narrowboat *Phyllis May.* Nothing like her had ever been seen in these waters before, or anywhere else in the US. She was sixty feet long and six foot ten inches wide, grey and crimson and white, with long windows on the waterline. She looked like a sinking railway carriage. Near the stern, fairground letters a foot high–*PHYLLIS MAY– T & M DARLINGTON, STONE.*

Clyde the crane loosed his grip and the longshoremen drew away the straps under her hull. The *Phyllis May* gunned her engine and to scattered applause reversed from the wharf into the waters of Hampton Roads. The aircraft carriers the other side of the Roads made her look like a weevil. The populations of Portsmouth and Norfolk carried on eating ice-cream in the MacArthur Mall.

On the back counter, holding the brass tiller arm, was a fat man covered in white bristle, wearing a Breton sailor's cap. His blind eye looked nowhere in particular and his good eye a thousand miles down the Atlantic Intracoastal Waterway: through the Great Dismal Swamp, across the terrible Albemarle Sound, along the Carolinas to Georgia and Florida and out on to the Gulf of Mexico.

In the bow stood a pretty woman of a certain age wearing an Australian bush hat. She was looking through the *Phyllis May* binoculars, with which you can see just as plainly as with the naked eye.

On the roof a dog, six inches wide and four and a half feet long, ribs proud through a fawn velvet coat. The sun shone through his ears and his legs and the skin under his belly. His narrow muzzle sniffed the future and he began to tremble, as if he knew that the size, low power, and speed of the *Phyllis May*, and certain design defects, limited her to service on pro-tected waters such as harbours and rivers, and the fools were planning to take the bloody thing across vast estuaries and in-land seas, and he was an artiste and an athlete, the fastest an-imal in the world, and he could see into the future and knew that dreadful things were going to happen, probably almost straight away, and if anyone had any sense or understanding he would be lying on a sofa in Stone now or under a table in the Star with a scratchings packet and there is no end to how he is put upon.

· · ·

THE MARINA AT MILE ZERO ON THE INTRA-
coastal Waterway has a chandlery, a convenience store, a
restaurant, and room for three hundred boats. The Elizabeth
River was wide and the sky was blue and the boats were
white–Tupperware launches and sailing boats. They were
from thirty to a hundred and twenty feet long, and built high,
like geese trying to look over each other's head. What could
be the use of such height? Above some of the fly-decks poles
soared up–fishing rods. What fish must be pulled forty feet
into the air? What sort of a place is this? What goes on round
here?

It was the weekend of the Cock Island yacht race, which
takes place every year off Norfolk. It is the biggest yacht race
on the East Coast so there were a good number of ocean-
going yachts in the marina. Narrow and trembling–grey-
hounds in the slips, their owners distrait, fussing.

By noon it was over ninety degrees and humid and we
could not endure inside or outside the boat. Portsmouth,
Virginia, is the same latitude as Tunis but hotter. We went into
the old town to look for a restaurant. The streets were broad
and shaded with great trees and the houses were square and
pretty and wooden and many had been there before the Civil
War. Behold, a restaurant with a shaded terrace.

On the other side of the terrace a lady was talking into a mobile phone. They resuscitated her twice yesterday, she said.

She came over to Jim. A greyhound puppy, she said. Oh
my Gard, she's beautiful–be still my heart. I'm an artist. I'm
sixty-two. I came home after a relationship broke up and
have been sleeping on my mother's couch for twelve years.
Where are you going–the Great Dismal Swamp? That's
where the first settlers on these shores went four hundred

years ago. The next expedition found a message on a tree—CROATOAN—but no one could understand it and the settlers had vanished into the swamp. Perhaps they are still there, or their descendants—though they would have degenerated a bit by now I guess, all deformed like in the movies. Y'all have a nice trip.

She went back to her table to spread the news about her mother's pancreas.

The mussels had been frozen to remove the flavour and the crab cakes were grass flavoured with castor oil. The waiter was a big chap with a black beard and we left a large tip—we understood this is wise in the US if you want to avoid violence. We walked back along the Elizabeth River, glassy smooth.

You don't get breakers on the Intracoastal, I said to Monica, apart from the big estuaries and sounds like Albemarle Sound and Pamlico Sound, and they are all right if you know the weather. The weather comes across the country for three thousand miles so everyone knows exactly what is on the way. It said on the radio this morning that there will be quiet weather for ten days at least. Ho ho I am beginning to get the feel of this trip. I am Tits Magee, who circumnavigated the globe in red satin, accompanied only by an eft in a jar. I yam der yingle humperdinck. I am the king of rock and roll. I am a little bloody marvel. Stick with me and you will have love, mystery and adventure.

At the marina the yachtsmen were still fussing and the Tupperware men on their cruisers were pointing at the sky. Then the west went black, and a wind arose and tore the river into surf and hooted and screamed and ripped canvases on the boats.

Thunder and zipping lightning. We pushed Jim into his kennel, where he lay staring. The surf ran under the *Phyllis May* and chucked her into the air and the wind flung her against the quay and then started to tear her away from her moorings to send her across a row of cruisers. Half a dozen yachtsmen came running and asked for ropes and we rushed below and found some and the yachtsmen, who were big chaps, knotted them along the grab-rail and heaved on them and secured the boat so she could only rattle and jerk. They seemed to enjoy helping us—You'll never get that knot undone, said one, I made it up to save time.

Another rope there, said another, for when the storm turns round and pulls the other way. It's not a hurricane, it's a tropical storm, and they turn round and pull the other way. You folks being British perhaps you don't know about the turning round and the pulling the other way. Have a nice day.

The wind was like a brick wall and rain came out of pint pots. Lightning and thunder and more wind, and then there was a hammering and a clattering and we looked out and our well deck was full of ice cubes.

Ten minutes later the sky was clear. The mast on the sailboat across the pontoon had snapped and smashed the top of a Tupperware boat. The chairs on the terrace of the marina restaurant were in splinters in the corner and broken glass covered the floor. Is this normal? I asked.

No, said the gentleman who ran the marina.

We heard later that the wind had reached a hundred miles an hour.

I had no idea what hurricanes were like, I said to Monica. It was just stories, and New Orleans was film on the telly. It wasn't real and now it is, and this was only a tropical storm. I am beginning to understand. I don't know what the hurricanes do to the Americans, but by God they terrify me.

They terrify Jim too, said Monica—come out darling. Stop shivering—it's all over.

MIKE WAS ABOUT FIFTY, BOYISH, CONFIDING: A big chap, with shorts and white socks. My God, he said, she's thin.

It's the size of the locks, I explained. Is there enough room?

You may have to rip out the stove, and I'll need a week for the wiring. It will not be cheap.

We have got to have air-conditioning, Mike, or we will die.

The trouble is the unit takes five and a half kilowatts to get moving, said Mike. There is a surge. It all has to be fed in through your system, which is mainly twelve-volt. And you can't just bang any old woodwork into a pretty boat like this—you need to have it built properly and matched. There, there is the place for it—by the sideboard, floor to ceiling.

OK, let's go. When will it be in?

You have to lift the boat to get the water intake fitted and there is no lift here and no carpenters. You must come to Atlantic Yacht Basin, on the Albemarle to Chesapeake Canal. You go down the Elizabeth River and then on to the canal—it's four miles past the entrance to the Great Dismal Swamp. I'll start the electrics on Wednesday and book you into Atlantic. I don't know how long they'll take to do the carpentry—I can't tell them what to do—they don't work for me. But don't worry—one way or another we'll fix you up.

It was July and each day was getting hotter. We were

supposed to leave for Florida next week, I said to Monica. Now we have to go up another canal in the wrong direction and wait for no one knows how long and spend no one knows how much and probably die of heat while we are waiting. We have lost control of our expedition before we have started.

HAVE ANOTHER BEER, SAID GREG—MY WIFE IS IN charge of the beer wagon.

We were at the reception at the end of the Cock Island races, the guests of Portsmouth Marine Terminal. The reception was held on a grassy space that looked out over the water towards Norfolk.

Greg had a naked lady tattooed on his calf. He was six foot two and tanned and his eyes were close together. He was trim for a young American: maybe three stone overweight, with a brush cut. He patted Jim.

Are you a sailor? I asked.

Yes, I work on the airplanes on the flat-tops. Most people are sailors round here. We have the main US naval base and the shipyards and the *Wisconsin* is just over there.

I had seen the *Wisconsin*—the biggest battleship in the US Navy, now on leave at the end of Norfolk High Street. The *Wisconsin* was known for serving in the Gulf War, and for running into one of its destroyers, nearly cutting it in two.

Easily done, said Greg. A moment's inattention and there goes your destroyer.

When we came, I said, we stayed at the Holiday Inn and it was full of people in desert boots. Sand-coloured suede boots with rubber soles and laces all up them and sand-coloured uniforms with enough camouflage marking to complete the style statement. I really fancied some of them, the ladies I mean. One was on crutches and her male comrades were making disrespectful suggestions about how she hurt her leg.

They were sailors, said Greg. Sailors are like that.

I thought sailors were supposed to wear bell-bottoms and little white hats, I said.

We did have bell-bottoms, but now it's uniform like soldiers. We are off to the desert—I can't tell you when.

WHEN JIM WAS A PUPPY I DECIDED, AGAINST INformed advice, that he be left entire. So Jim's character is loyal, loving, lecherous and violent.

To Jim the existence of a cat is an insult. He went headlong for the cat next door and the cat scarred his nose, and it taught him nothing. If he sees a cat when he is on the lead he stands on his hind legs and screams, and people stare at me: a bad owner and a dangerous incompetent.

All male entire dogs are challenged regardless of size. Most of them are bigger than Jim, so from time to time we have to take him to the vet to be stapled up.

Jim has no fur, only a light covering of velvet. When he is in a rage a rough patch appears on his back, and this is somehow more menacing than a crest. The rough patch appeared in Portsmouth, where in the vet's reception there was a male red Doberman puppy, and a fat black Labrador.

I thought I would have to sit on Jim but he was called into the surgery.

He stood on a platform, which rose slowly to table height. He rolled his eyes and looked around. He doesn't floss his teeth properly, said the lady vet, but he's a lovely dog, in the best condition. Here in the US we get a lot of fat dogs—it's like the people. But now this heartworm.

On the wall, posters showed the horrible things that happened when the heartworms set up home in the left ventricle of a dog. I come from Georgia, said the vet, and so many dogs there are sick with the heartworm. It is carried by mosquitoes.

Ah, I said—

> *The invisible worm*
> *That flies in the night,*
> *In the howling storm,*
>
> *Has found out thy bed*
> *Of crimson joy*
> *And his dark secret love*
> *Does thy life destroy.*

I guess so, said the lady vet, very likely. Here, give him one of these pills every month, and y'all look out for the alligators. I don't have a pill for those.

I MET THIS GENTLEMAN CALLED STEVE ON THE quay, I said to Monica. I asked him for coffee and he's going to bring his father.

Norwood Thomas was eighty-four. He had white hair and his eyes were blue and though he was heavily built he moved easily. The *Phyllis May* has six feet four inches' headroom and Norwood Thomas was too big a man for it. His baseball cap carried the badge of the 101st Airborne Division, the

Screaming Eagles. Norwood Thomas was too big a man for most places.

I think we should get out of Iraq, said Norwood Thomas. I'm a Democrat. In the Depression my mother put cardboard in my shoes every morning. I was there during Roosevelt's New Deal.

The 101st Airborne were the first in at D-Day, I said. You dropped behind the beaches. Eisenhower said goodbye to you—with all the forces he commanded that day he chose the Screaming Eagles to say goodbye. He made the decision himself to drop you behind the beaches. He was told to expect 85 per cent casualties. He said to Kay Summersby, his English girlfriend—It's very hard to look a soldier in the eye when you fear you are sending him to his death. She said he was nearly crying.

Yes, he looked serious, said Norwood Thomas. He was in full dress uniform, stiff braided cap. It was late afternoon—we took off that night. He was congenial in a reserved sort of way. He talked to me as an equal—I am not even sure he called me Soldier. Do you have your own parachute? he asked. Do you have it issued like a weapon and look after it? No, sir, I explained, we used to pack our own chutes in training but now the riggers do it.

Most of you got back, I said.

Yes, we lost more people at Arnhem. On D-Day we dropped behind Utah Beach. Our planes got separated in cloud and nearly all our howitzers were lost, but we did our job. We knew what our objectives were and the Germans didn't, so we could take them on or pass by. The worst American losses were at Omaha Beach—we lost more than two thousand soldiers. The beach was supposed to be cleared by our air force but the bombs went too far inland and the German machine guns were still there. Omaha was butchery.

Monica brought Norwood Thomas a cup of tea. Did you spend much time in the UK?

Yes, I love the UK. I loved the people, how they suffered without hate, without profanity—*Jerry was over again last night*—and I nearly married one of you.

And you fought on through Europe? I asked.

Holland, then the Battle of the Bulge. We were surrounded in the Ardennes and they say Patton rescued us—but we were getting supplies and would have fought our way out. Patton didn't rescue the Screaming Eagles, and never let them tell you different.

Norwood Thomas accepted a book from us. I wrote in it *To Norwood Thomas, with thanks and admiration.* I thought afterwards that's not good enough, I should have put *with gratitude and admiration,* and then I thought whatever I put would not be enough to thank that twenty-year-old, going into action for the first time. He had come out to the plane the day before and then the weather was bad and he had to wait another day and now he was in the Dakota with seventeen of his comrades, coming over Guernsey and turning over the Cotentin Peninsula, to land in Normandy just after midnight on D-Day, behind enemy lines, the first in.

In the forties the enemies were evident and atrocious but there were giants in the earth in those days—Dwight Eisenhower and Norwood Thomas. Later the enemies were shadows. Many brave men fought them and there were pigmies and murderers too—Richard Cheney; William Calley.

But I know who the real Americans are, and so do you, and never let them tell you different.

. . .

THE NICE PEOPLE AT PORTSMOUTH MARINE TER-
minal had given us a bag of presents–scratchings for Jim and
a ball of plush and for Monica and me T-shirts for the Cock
Island yacht races. There were also umbrellas and rubber
sleeves called cosies to keep beer cans cool. Later I realized
they were trying to tell us something about the weather. The
summer on the East Coast of the US is a desperate time, and
to compound the situation there was the Luck of the
Darlingtons–*après nous le déluge.* Wherever we go we bring the
worst weather for a hundred years.

Now we struck at the heart of the US government, and
compromised the dollar itself.

Floodwaters wreak havoc across area–reported the *Washington
Post*–*roads, rails, government buildings shut down. This isn't just
water, this is dark, rushing water, cars moving, turning over sideways, rolling over in the current.* A famous tree in the grounds of
the White House, the one that appears on the twenty-dollar
bill, didn't last a week after we arrived. Only the *Daily Press*
found a ray of hope, telling the loyal citizens of Newport
News that *all records and national treasures remained safe and dry.*

By the time I got to the shower block along the pontoon at
six o'clock in the morning my umbrella had blown inside out
and I was running with rain and sweat. Over ninety degrees
my brain doesn't work properly. As for my body–there it was
in the mirror, half destroyed by the heat. I looked like a frog.
My belly had swelled up and even my *sides.* My ankles were
swollen, my watch was tight, and my rings seemed to have cor-
roded on to my fingers. My eyes were sore and rimmed with
red and my ears were full of melted wax and my joints ached.

I stepped into my favourite shorts: the long khaki ones with lots of pockets. They were a bit tight but in these shorts I am Sanders of the River, I am Trevor Howard as Scobie the colonial policeman, Graham Greene's ruined hero in *The Heart of the Matter*, searching for salvation and having a bit on the side with a nineteen-year-old cracker.

A snatching pain in my groin—oh God I am ruptured! It's all over! I'll have to go to the disgraceful North Staffordshire University Hospital, and be carved up by Mr Pinstripe-Git and they'll get it wrong like they did for my friend Stanley and have to do it again and it will be years before I can walk or lift anything. And I have got dropsy and muscular dysfunction and I am going deaf and I am going blind. It's HAARTSC—Hartsee—Heat Assisted Age Related Total Systemic Collapse. Nature has taken its revenge on a fool in his seventies trying to be an adventurer. I shall be the laughing stock of the public houses of Stone—my children will be disgraced, my grandchildren will be bullied, and my publisher will say I always knew the old bugger would stiff before we made a profit—we should have stuck like everybody else with the 24-year-old lookers who were abused by their uncle and married a footballer.

On the way back to the boat my stomach muscles were tight and sore, and my eyes stung. Still the binding pain in the groin, and my legs seemed to be held back by rubber straps.

I won't say anything, I said to myself, I will wait for the agony to localize and then I'll break the news to Mon as gently as I can and then we'll all go home. I'll make light of it but we will have no choice. Jim will be thrilled.

• • •

WHERE'S THAT HUNDRED DOLLARS I GAVE YOU yesterday? asked Monica—it's time to count the money.

In my pocket, here, I said.

Come on then, said Monica, show me. I hope you haven't lost it like you usually do, or spent it on drink or given it away.

I can't find it, I said, it's gone. I had it in my back pocket. It's a mystery. It was there half an hour ago. I have been robbed. It must have been in those terrible food shops—the 7-Eleven or the Food Lion. They all looked like pickpockets in there. One chap brushed against me at the checkout. He had plenty of time—it took me twenty minutes to check through a bottle of water for Jim. They train for years you know—they can take the watch off your wrist; they can take the teeth out of your mouth. There is no defence—it could happen to anyone.

Try your other pockets, said Monica.

They seem to have gone, I said.

What do you mean, gone? How can your pockets be gone?

I say my pockets have gone—they have disappeared, they are no longer there. They have departed. I have been the victim of a cruel and senseless crime. Not content with stealing my money they have taken my pockets too.

You are trying to tell me someone has stolen your pockets?—you must be barmy. Here, let me see. Oh Lord. Oh my God. Terry can I have a word about this whole trip? Do you think we should go on? Are you really the right man to take us a thousand miles on to the Gulf of Mexico? Through the hardships and through all the pain, through the hurricanes and the alligators, across the great sounds and across Lake Okeechobee, where eighteen hundred people were swept

away? Are you sure you are up to it? How can you expect Jim
and me to believe in you and your vision and give you our
loyalty and obedience when you can't even put on your
shorts the right way round?

YOUR CAT PISSED IN MY DESIGNER HANDBAG,
said my elder daughter Lucy on the phone. I wish I hadn't
said I would look after it. You should have had it put down.
It's old, and it's only got one eye.

There's nothing wrong with being old and only having one
eye, Lucy. How are my grandchildren?

They are fine, but your cat pissed in my handbag. It's an
awful cat, and it's as old as God. Its time had come and instead of doing the kind thing when you started wandering
about in your boat with your wretched dog you persuaded
me to take it in and it has repaid me by pissing in my designer
handbag. I thought it had just pissed over the bag but when I
got out my lipsalve and began to put it on I realized the truth.
It's a dreadful creature and will probably think of something
else dreadful to do.

She's grieving, I said, poor soul, she's missing me. No one
would take her from the cats' home because of her eye and
she was small and the other cats had got the food first and
when we got her she was a skeleton inside a ball of fur. She
had forgotten how to eat—she was dying. I fed her on my own
tits for a fortnight. She is very attached to me when we are at
home.

You won't be home for a year, said Lucy, and the girls
won't see their grannie and their grandad and I won't see my
mummy and daddy. Other people in Stone see their parents

like normal families. All we have is a one-eyed cat that pisses in our handbags. It's not right—you know it's not right.

THREE WEEKS MELTED AWAY BUYING EQUIP-ment that didn't work to get us over Albemarle Sound and seeing vets and fighting the heat and the ice storms and keeping out of Mike's way while he did the electrics and staying alive. But at last we arranged a farewell party for our friends from Atlantic Containers, and Portsmouth Marine Terminal, and West Marine, and the travel agency, and the city of Norfolk. We bought fifty pounds of ice and filled the bath with beer cans but you can't ice the whole of Portsmouth.

Our guests stepped into the front deck where the big brass tunnel light looked ahead and came down into the boat and saw the kennel where I put my laptop and saw how I sat on the log-box with my feet on Jim, and how the log-box had *Phyllis May* on the front side and *Kiss Me Again* on the backside.

Why is she called *Phyllis May*? they asked.

After my mother. That's her photo there when she was twenty. She still comes back.

Oh my Gard, oh my Gard, she's beautiful.

They marvelled at the narrowness of the narrowboat and how you could see right down the inside and out the back and they marvelled at the oak and teak panelling and the six-foot-four ceiling and how we cut our own wood for the stove and how it was never really hot or cold where we came from. They looked at the plates and the paintings and the horse-brasses and the lamps and clocks and the hanging tankards and the plaque with the roses and castles and Monica explained how in the old days the boatmen's cabins were decorated to make the tiny space more bearable.

They passed through the galley with its cooker and refrigerator and the bathroom with the shower that worked, and we explained we had a central heating system and carried a ton of water and enough diesel for two hundred miles.

They saw the cabin with the double bed and the engine room that was the drying room as well and they climbed out and stood on the back counter and waggled the tiller arm with the brass frog on it and gazed forward along the roof looking resolute and stepped over on to the pontoon and admired the fairground lettering on the stern and had another beer.

Jim worked the crowd for treats—Oh the little greyhound puppy—isn't she sweet?

Jim is half bald and has a long tongue for panting and was coping better with the heat than we were, and was scoring freely.

We told Sarah from Norfolk City public relations how there had been a second storm yesterday and the wind had torn branches off the trees and strafed us again with ice. You've got the right boat, said her husband Alec, a nice low boat, but try not to be out at sea if it happens again. Are you going across Albemarle Sound? Oh dear.

My nay am is Pay Am, said a blonde girl. She was eighteen and she was beautiful and she came from the Barbie-pink boat alongside. The boat was all sharp end, with lofting curves. It climbed forty feet in ladders and poles.

Pardon? I asked.

My nay am is Pay Am, she repeated.

Pardon? I asked.

Pay Am, she said, Pay Am Rossiter—we come from South Cay Arolina.

Ah, I said—my nay am is Terry.

Pay Am's chap was Chris. He was twenty-two but looked fourteen. He had trouble getting served in bars, which start at twenty-one. He was looking after the pink boat for the owner, who was colour-blind. When you came, Chris, I said, I called to Mon—*The hairdressers are here.*

Chris thought this was very funny.

What is the tower for, I asked, the one on top of your pink boat?

Well sir, said Chris, the tower is for the tarpon—it is a tarpon tower. They feed on the surface and splash around. You can see them from a long ways and then you go after them. The big poles out at the sides are so you can run lines out and they don't get snarled. Excuse me, if you don't mind my mentioning your tattoo, ma'am, it's the finest dragon I've seen.

I showed Chris the Maori tattoo on my arm. It means *within my immediate social group, my sexual performance is above average*, I said.

Chris showed me the compass rose tattooed on his shoulder. It means *within my immediate social group, my sexual performance is below average*, he said.

Pay Am showed us her tattoos and so did Dave from Atlantic Containers and so did Kerry from West Marine and so did Mike and Christie, his secretary. Nice Amy from Portsmouth Ocean Terminal had her parents' initials tattooed in colour at the nape of her neck, with the dates of their death. The lady from the travel agency had barbed wire round her ankle. They turned Jim over and admired the tattoos on his naked belly and we explained he had them when he was born and we knew there was a map and a secret message there but his belly is dirty sometimes and when you try to read him he wriggles and gets up.

People came across from the boats nearby. One of them had a shipwreck across his chest, with drowning sailors. Another was illuminated from neck to ankle in full colour. Nice Amy took Monica down into the *Phyllis May* to show her the tattoos on her bum.

WE SAILED AT DAWN. AWAY FROM MILE ZERO and into the Elizabeth River and past the flat-tops, the cruisers, the destroyers, the cranes.

I had imagined a departure of high ceremony, saluted by naval guns and trailing a creamy wake. But it wasn't going to be like that—this was not even a real start to our journey. We had to go to Atlantic Yacht Basin and having the air-conditioner fitted would take at least a fortnight, should we live so long with the temperature pushing a hundred, and the sopping air and the hot wind and the blasting sun. It looked like we would never get started, and if we did we would drown in Albemarle Sound in an ice storm.

An adventure will deliver if it wants to, and if it doesn't, tough luck—You should have stayed at home like everyone else and Who the hell do you think you are?

WE HAVE SAILED MANY A WATERWAY, BUT NONE so dreadful as the Elizabeth River out of Portsmouth. All the smokestacks of Belgium, all the building sites of Paris, all the industrial death of Wolverhampton, could not match this fatal shore. Chimneys and rotting ships and a scabbed and uncertain margin. It was eighty-five degrees at seven o'clock, and the breeze was corrosive and the cranes and rusting towers stood in a foul haze. Monica came along the gunwale to where I held the tiller on the back counter and we kissed–We are under way! But we weren't really and it wasn't very nice.

You said the bridges had a clearance of sixty-five feet, said Monica.

They do, I said–it was in the book.

That one doesn't, said Monica.

The river was three hundred yards wide and the bridge was girdered and threatening. We idled in the stream while I climbed on the roof and took down the generator windmill, and we scratched under the bridge.

You lied to me, said Monica.

No, I said–they must mean they have sixty-five feet clearance when they are up, but this one is down.

While I was climbing on to the roof something dreadful had become clear to me but I did not want to face it or tell Monica.

The next bridge was down too. Monica got out the handheld VHF radio, the one they made her promise at the VHF school never to let me use. The handset squawked and fizzed– *Y'all party on–plenty of room–what boat is that? How long you staying?* Monica told him. *Lovely boat, y'all have a nice trip now squawk squawk.* From an office slung in the girders high above us a shadow and a wave.

Now a few green fields and trees and we began to follow the red triangles set on posts every half-mile or so. You have to keep them to your right or starboard going upstream and to your left or port going down, or perhaps it is the other way round.

One of the posts had a nest on it—white head, hawk's beak, and my goodness two chicks looking out of the nest!

Cheep cheep, they said, cheep cheep, as we passed by and under them.

Ospreys, shouted Monica, ospreys!

A white heron floated over, magnificent, yellow bill with a blue flash—egrets, I've had a few—and here are some gulls with black heads, and swallow-type birds flicked across our path. A wooden landing stage before pretty wooden houses: pines, the water calm.

On the right a creek—we should have been going along it into the Great Dismal Swamp Canal, but we can't—we have to go four miles to the Atlantic Yacht Basin, on the Albemarle and Chesapeake Canal.

A lock. A red light. We started to moor up but a notice said *Go away, there is turbulence, go and moor up back there.* We fastened ourselves as best we could to a post made for an ocean liner.

Hi there—a voice below my feet—someone holding on to our rudder. He was tanned, bearded, with a braided sailor's cap. He looked as if he should have been captaining a destroyer, not sitting in a kayak three inches above the water. Love your boat, he said, where are you going?

We told him. Welcome to our country, he said, and we warmed at his welcome.

The water in the lock rose two feet and took an hour, with much shouting and a lady lock-keeper striding back and forth along its hundred yards, and bells and tannoys. In an hour we can do three locks in England but there are few locks round here and they want to get full value from them.

Ahead of us a great bridge. We moored and waited and a klaxon bellowed and the counterweights as big as houses dropped on to the banks and the great bridge broke in the middle and we sailed under the great bridge into Great Bridge.

ATLANTIC YACHT BASIN, GREAT BRIDGE, Virginia, is on an island of pines. A river port, with workshops, big boats on the wharves, in the air, in the row of sheds, each shed big enough to hold an airship. Many workmen, a few boaters, a simple lounge and an ice machine and a courtesy car. You brought her in nice and easy, said the dockmaster.

A quarter of a mile up the track the main road with shops and takeaways. We walked up towards the shops, through the perfume from the pines.

Monnie, I said, there is something awfully wrong, something important, something that could stop us getting to Fort Myers.

Three

STAND
AND DELIVER

Virginia

Dr Gormley – The Dying Whippet – Passion and Grief – Weather from Hell – A Continuous Plangent Shriek – Young Dr Berger in Apple Green – Your Rat? – Just One More Day – The Cancellation – Rusty the Sheriff – The Jellyfish – It's Just Not Going to Be Me Any More – All the Shadows, All the Memories – You Have Had No Egrets? – Two Hundred and Fifty Beats a Minute – Black Chaps with Spanners – Stand and Deliver

DR GORMLEY WAS THIN AND TALL WITH A
southern voice. His face showed concern, and humour about
the burden of mortality that was so boring when we could
have been looking at photos of the grandchildren. You would
tell Dr Gormley anything, and you would trust him com-
pletely, even if he called you into the back room to take out
your liver with a Stanley knife.

It had taken us only an hour to get to Dr Gormley from
scratch, though it was Sunday and the Fourth of July weekend.
In America the medical profession has a special relationship
with patients—you give them money and they treat you. If you
haven't got any money I suppose it doesn't work so well.

I am going to the UK in a fortnight, said Dr Gormley. My
son is marrying a lady from the UK.

Good move, I said, did it myself.

Yes, you have a hernia. It shouldn't bother you if you are
careful but it could strangulate and kill you at any time. This
is the best man to see—ring him on Monday. He will probably
operate.

That night it was ninety degrees. Jim screamed and yelped
in his sleep.

• • •

I DON'T KNOW IF YOU HAVE EVER GONE TO bed *wet*.

It was over ninety and the air was sodden and the mosquitoes fierce and cunning. The boat had to be left open at night or we would suffocate, so we slept under mosquito nets. Mosquito nets are hot and I tangle with them and pull them down and the mosquitoes bite me through the mesh. Monica slept in the saloon and I lay in the cabin soaking, and my old bites came to life, firing up my whole nervous system.

Many people were taking part in the fitting of the air-conditioner. There was Mike and his secretary and his installer, the site supervisor of the Atlantic Yacht Basin and the ladies from the finance department, the dockmaster, the foreman carpenter, the carpenter and the other carpenter, the paint-shop people, the African-American gentlemen with their little boat who towed the *Phyllis May* around, the operator of the boat-lift, the gentlemen who pushed the boat into the canvas swing of the boat-lift and half a dozen other people with fat bellies and moustaches who came on board and patted Jim and said Owyall doon? and Neat boat, never seen one before, and looked worried.

I never wanted anything more than I wanted that air-conditioning. In fact I never wanted anything half as much that did not involve sex or six figures.

The marina worked on a time-plus-materials basis and relying on forty years of business experience Monica and I set our estimate of the bill at twice the highest figure mentioned in conversation, including any sum mentioned in jest.

Monica transferred funds from the UK. I hope you have not destabilized the pound, I said.

Mike's colleague, the installer, walked out on him after eight years and the timing began to fall apart. We could not leave the boat as we could be needed any time. We waited all day for her to be taken out of the water to have the hole punched under the waterline and no one came.

It got hotter and hotter and Jim was doing his impression of the Dying Whippet, lying on his side gasping, with twitches and moans. Jim is a gifted actor but he wasn't acting this time. Monica was thinly coated in maple syrup, and there were things crawling inside my shirt, pissing themselves as they went.

At breakfast the dockmaster called by. Mike's mother had died. I could hear the high, thin laughter of the mosquitoes.

THE COOLEST SPOT IN THE ATLANTIC YACHT Basin is under the trees by the dockmaster's office. I agree with Winston Spencer Churchill that taking a nap after lunch is a healthy practice, providing of course you get your full night's sleep as well. The low wooden chairs let me lean back and relax and I closed my eyes and the breeze from the water was almost cool.

A voice in my ear—Y'all English? I have a half-brother in Southampton.

I did not open my eyes.

Oh yes, said Monica.

My father was over in the war, said the voice. His English girlfriend got pregnant and in those days they posted you somewhere else right away. Nowadays you can find out about your parents if you are adopted and after fifty-seven years my brother found his mother living a couple of miles away, and then he found his father in America and then he found me.

I don't know if I was asleep or awake.

Goodness me, said Monica to the voice.

Ah well, said the voice, and got up and went away.

Rude bugger, I thought, and me having my afternoon rest. And then I thought of the passion and the grief and the loss and the meetings too late and I felt guilty and I should have been more interested but the voice had gone.

One day the grief and the loss will be gone too, but sixty years will hardly be long enough for that.

HEAVY CLOUDS, FLASHES, THUNDER, RAIN, A tempest of afternoon rain. When it was over Monica and Jim and I went for a walk down the island among the pines. The island is sandy, a few acres, with pontoons, boats and board-walks, and pines. Jim liked the island and so did we. I had bought a special mosquito kit—cloth bands for wrists and an-kles, which I had to soak with a foul oil.

The boardwalks were wet, the grass standing in water, the air like soup. Frogs sang in the puddles. Jim became inter-ested in a stick, offering it to me as he does and then refusing it and growling and running away and frolicking—ha ha ha. Perhaps he is adjusting to the heat, I thought, nice to see him happy. Across the river a heron lowered its bum into the wa-ter, trying to cool down. It flew off, dripping. Dusk fell quickly.

That night I woke and our ship's clock, lit through the

window, said four o'clock. My fancy bug kit had failed me and my legs were ablaze. I scratched and sweated and scratched and grieved and scratched and swore and the hands of the clock froze and the wind blew through the window like the exhaust from a bus engine.

At five thirty it was first light and I took Jim for a walk—perhaps it will help my legs, I thought, and I must look after the poor dog. It will be too hot later and I must put the helpless creature's health above my own convenience and I am really an excellent fellow. The frogs were asleep but it was ninety degrees and all the world—river, grass, trees and air—was poached and sodden. I put my hand over the side of the boardwalk and the canal water was hot.

Jim stopped—he did not want to go for this walk. He tried to pull me towards the little marina lounge, which was air-conditioned, then he sat down. Not want to go for a walk? I said. I get up at dawn for you and you don't want to walk? You ungrateful hound, you don't deserve me as your master. Everything is against me—a whippet that won't take exercise, bug defences that don't work, death, delays, physical collapse, weather from hell.

Back at the boat Monica was in tears—We are getting nowhere—no air-conditioning, and you ill and everything soaking wet all the time and that chap yesterday said the Intracoastal was closed and he was a yacht broker and he should know. It's like waiting in an airport in a tropical country and the windows are broken and you don't know if the plane will ever come and you don't want to get on it when it does. And look at the *Virginia Pilot*—the mosquitoes have started carrying deadly diseases. *People over the age of 50 are at the greatest risk of serious illness, such as encephalitis or meningitis. I don't want people to be afraid but I want them to be aware,* said Dreda A. McCreary, Virginia Beach Mosquito Control Biologist. Thanks Dreda, nice of you to keep us in touch.

Remember in business, Mon, I said, we used to say that anyone can be a star when the orders are coming in and the staff are loyal and the suppliers are delivering on time. You think you are making the money then, but you aren't really. You make the money when there are no sales and the staff have betrayed you and suppliers are letting you down and you can't sleep for worrying and you just hang on and hang on. Anyone can blast across Albemarle Sound on a calm day with a good engine and be a hero. But the real adventure is now. We'll hang on and we'll hang on. But I must mention this lump on my head. I think it might be cancer.

JIM LED ME TO THE DOOR OF THE MARINA lounge and we went in.

I made myself a coffee and turned on the television and fiddled with the remote control and hit one of those programmes about people from trailer parks for the fat. There was a pale woman of immense size, with a long sullen face. She was weeping out of control. She had just admitted to her partner that her baby could have been fathered by another bloke. She wept and wept and her partner wept and wept and the audience wept and wept and the anchorman looked pretty upset. From time to time they showed shots of the baby, who was taking it all very well.

The network had paid for a DNA test to decide the parentage of the baby and, God forgive them, were going to tell us the result on camera. The woman began to scream and her partner began to groan and the audience shrieked and the camera cut back to the baby, who was blowing bubbles.

The baby had been conceived by the partner! The couple fell on each other, rolling on the floor. The audience began to break bits off the chairs. In came the baby in the arms of a sobbing nurse and emotions went into the red zone, with random whirling and throwing movements by all involved and a continuous plangent shriek like a train trying not to run into the WH Smith bookshop on Waterloo Station.

And now the commercials.

Come on Jim, back to the boat. Poor little chap—the gravel is so hot for your paws. But I have to go and see a man.

OVER THE MILLENNIA EVOLUTION FITS US OUT to deal with life, sometimes in funny ways. Since my mid-sixties I have developed a defence against humiliation and risk—my heart races and I nearly faint and I have to sit down. It happens when I feel threatened, as when I am about to set out against informed advice across the Channel in an inland boat, or see a surgeon about an operation that could wreck the plans of two years. I leaned against the wall and tried to regain full consciousness.

The waiting room in Chesapeake General Hospital was small, without windows. In the corner a brownskin boy was asleep with his head on the shoulder of a brownskin girl. Two ladies felt their way in, each twenty years older than Monica and me.

Mr Darlington!

Stand up, don't faint. Into a consulting room and here at once is young Dr Berger, tanned and handsome, in apple green.

This your ECG? Your heartbeat is a bit fast—are you an anxious sort of a guy?

Yes, I have always been a bit of a coward.

Excellent—not the sort to go and do anything silly, eh?

Young Dr Berger pushed a finger into my abdomen. No doubt what's the matter with you. Do you have the problem in your family?

Probably, they are a funny lot.

And you are writing a book—hey that's neat, and you are in a hurry. I will operate on Tuesday.

Do you have any questions? asked Andrea at the admin desk. I wanted to ask What is Winston Churchill's middle name? or What happened to the crispy bacon we used to have before the war? But I made do with a short gibber and Monica took on the paperwork.

Andrea was tattooed from her wrist all up one arm, not the other, in tangerine yellow, and blue, like Chris's compass rose in Portsmouth. She was all flowers and fairies. And joy of joys, the design on her Hawaiian shirt, surfers and fish, matched the frieze on the wallpaper.

Dr Berger is a very good doctor, volunteered Andrea.

I thought—what if she had said old Butcher Berger, Berger the Bugger, Half Blind Berger, the Killer of the Eastern Seaboard. What could I do anyway? But thanks Andrea.

I smiled and nodded—See you Tuesday.

• • •

WHEN WE STARTED BOATING IT WAS AROUND the Potteries, which are near Stone. A canal boat goes at walking pace and walkers often greeted us. Are you all right? they would say, pronouncing it Your rat? as if checking the ownership of a passing rodent.

Yes, we are fine, I would say, how kind of you to ask—we had a bit of trouble with a loose throttle cable an hour or two ago but for once I managed to fix it myself and now she is going like a train.

The walkers would look puzzled and fall back.

I turned to my friend Dave, who was born and brought up in Stoke. You have got it all wrong, he said. The correct answer to Your rat? is Your rat?

From then on when a walker called out Your rat? I would call back Your rat? and the walker would wave and smile and sometimes we would exchange further words, each in our respective tongues. Sometimes I would take the initiative and call out Your rat? and they would call back Your rat? and it was great.

In Virginia everyone we passed in the boatyard or in the shops said Owya doon? And we would reply Hello.

But that is wrong, I said to Monica. The correct reply to Owya doon? must be Owya doon? Owya doon? must be the polite greeting round here.

A gentleman of three hundred pounds, one of the African-American chaps who moved the boats, came towards me.

Owya doon? I said.

We had a rather perplexing time with that trawler over there, said the African-American gentleman—I thought for a moment goodness me I have got the lifting rope caught in the rudder, but in the end we got her out fine. How kind of you to ask.

Perhaps you should try Your rat? said Monica.

ATLANTIC YACHT BASIN HAD FOUND US A mooring by the side of one of the boat sheds, near the carpenter's shop. Behind us a wide creek and on the other side of the tea-coloured water tall trees, lightly egreted.

I had given up trying to sleep on the *Phyllis May* and was sleeping in the marina lounge on the floor and Monica and Jim joined me in the daytime and we listened to the air-conditioner and read paperbacks and looked at the walls. Outside the air came off the water like sheets before they go through the wringer.

Our carpenter, Tim, a melancholy man, became slower and slower. One day, I said to Monica, we'll come on to the boat and find him in the corner, covered with lichen.

Mike came back after his mother's funeral. OhmiGard— they haven't put in the cabinet yet—I can't believe it! I can't believe it! But she had a lovely occasion yesterday—after it I felt calm and easy. Don't worry, I'll keep going, I have got to do something.

Mike, I said, I must have the unit in tomorrow. If I have to sleep on the boat without it when I come back from the hospital I won't last the night.

Tangerine-yellow-and-blue Andrea rang with instructions for the operation tomorrow—where to go, what not to eat. There would be a general anaesthetic but I would be able to come home that night.

Will it hurt? I asked.

Dr Berger is very aggressive with pain control, said Andrea.

I wasn't quite sure if she meant aggressive towards the patients or the pain but I think she meant No, it won't hurt.

Just one more day, darling, I said to Monica—the air-conditioning will be in and my hernia will be done and we can get going—Indian River here we come, the narrow dog is on his way!

HELLO MR DARLINGTON, ANDREA HERE FROM the hospital. Your operation has been cancelled. The anaesthetist looked at your ECG and said he can't possibly anaesthetize you or you might die. Your heart rate is out of control and it is a much worse danger than the hernia. Didn't you know about it? You must come and have cardiac tests. I will ring you tomorrow.

First numbness, then anger, then grief. Why didn't the fools pick it up on the first ECG? And I have known about this heart thing for ages and ignored it. Oh bugger, bugger, bugger.

We have come eight miles, said Monica, and we have got eleven hundred miles to go and the Waterway is shut and there will be hurricanes and you are going to die on the way. What chance have we got of getting to Fort Myers?

I'm not going to die, I said. Five years ago I ran a fourteen-mile hill race. Jim and I walk an hour every day. If they won't fix me we'll go anyway. I'll hold myself together and stay alive and we'll have the boat carried round the shut bit or if we can find a pilot we will go out to sea and go round it. Bloody doctors, only interested in telling you how ill you are, and most of them drink too much and cheat on their wives and raid the drug cupboard and die before you do anyway. Don't cry Monnie, you're upsetting Jim. And Jim, shut up, why do you sit there and whine and look so damn miserable when things are going wrong? You are supposed to be a friend and a comfort but you are a bloody liability.

Jim started to howl.

NICE AMY FROM PORTSMOUTH MARINE TERMI-nal and her husband, Mark, asked us for an evening meal. Their car came to the marina gate. The car was square and black with black windows, like a pumped-up Range Rover just before it burst. Most cars we had seen in the US were like that, apart from the pick-ups, which were the same except they were pick-ups.

Wooden houses, trees, shade, boats on the lawns. Some of the houses had flags outside and some had yellow ribbons. By Nice Amy's house a caravan thirty feet long. We keep our Harleys out back, said Nice Amy.

Inside, a wide room and a miniature pinscher called Shy, who looked like a rat that had been shined up a bit. She was wearing a pearl necklace. Jim and Shy chased each other cheerfully for the rest of our visit.

There was a young daughter, who set up a daybed in a reclining chair and in the manner of teenage girls became the centre of gravity. She handled the levee with restraint, Jim licking her feet obsequiously and Shy sitting on her shoulder like a parrot.

I have got you some Samuel Adams, said Nice Amy.

Mark was a big chap with a moustache. He did not drink— I have done my share, he said.

Mark was a fireman and retiring on 60 per cent pay in a few months. He didn't like being a fireman—Mainly going out to medical emergencies because some fool has cut his thumb, he said, or driving the fire chief around, and watching films. The training is boring after twenty years.

Mark was a chain-smoker, but a master of illusion in that he smoked with the half of him that you did not see—holding his cigarette the other side of the door, or out the car window. So there were two Marks, the one you were talking to, and the other, just to one side, smoking like mad. Sometimes he disappeared for a smoke.

I don't mind, I said, I like the smell.

Amy doesn't, said Mark, dematerializing.

He manifested himself again with another Samuel Adams and then joined himself in the garden for a smoke and I watched the baseball on the TV.

Baseball players are big like rugby forwards, and they hate each other—not in the jocular way that cricketers do, but with bland malevolence. This emotion drives the whole match.

The game takes place in a stadium with sloping sides, in front of many tens of thousands of spectators, who have come to have their dinner. The pitcher throws the ball repeatedly at the left foot of the hitter until in rage and despair the hitter swipes at it and misses three times and then he is out. Sometimes he hits it and then someone catches it in the out-field and he is out. After a lot of this everyone goes home including the spectators, full of hot dogs and saying Jesus that was a good stare Washawski gave Bernstein today, Dad, really fried him, and did you see the disrespectful look that Pileggi gave Slokenbergs?

Time for the meal, said Nice Amy. Would you like some sweet iced tea with the spaghetti?

Monica said that on the whole she would prefer another glass of that excellent wine offered earlier and we all sat down.

The door at the end of the kitchen burst open and a sheriff walked in. He was slim, uniformed, his gun at his hip.

I rose to my feet, my hands in the air—I'll come quietly!

The sheriff backed away.

That's Rusty, explained Nice Amy. He's my nephew. He's only a deputy sheriff. He is nineteen. He is just going on duty to the county gaol. He lives upstairs. He left his gun on the bed once, loaded, and I was really cross. His room is a terrible mess.

Half of Mark was with us and half of Mark was out of the French windows and Jim and Shy chased each other round and round on the lawn.

THE ROOM AT THE HOSPITAL WAS LIT BY A guttering neon tube.

It was too dark to see Drew properly before he grabbed me, but I could smell his aftershave and feel the thick hairs on his arm and as he pressed his cheek against mine I realized he was one of those really bristly guys.

He punched me in the neck—That is your jugular, he whispered. I resisted but he got me turned and hit me in the belly with something hard—one two three.

I lived on the New York gay scene, he said. All my flatmates were gay. Saw some stuff I tell you.

Always rather liked the idea of being gay myself, I said.

Nearly got mixed up in it after the New York Marathon once, but I am crazy about girls, so I never followed through.

Me neither, said Drew. You'll see bruises tomorrow, black and blue.

I think he was smiling. While we struggled he was watching the TV screen above my head.

Three more high on the chest, his fist boring into me, and another one square on my left nipple. There it is, that's the money shot, cried Drew. I am the righteous one, the one who never fails. Now look at that. I bet you have never seen one of those before.

He freed me from his embrace and Monica and I looked at the screen, where a shadowy jellyfish was contracting, its delicate tones changing as it fought to get away.

You have atrial fibrillation, said Drew. Your ventricles, which are the main heart pump, are OK but your atria—the bits that send the blood into the ventricles—are just sitting there quivering. It could mess up the pattern of contraction in your ventricles and drop you in your tracks or the blood could clot and give you a stroke or a heart attack.

Is it serious? I asked.

It is if the blood supply to your heart is bad, said Drew. It depends on the tests you are having next week. But it doesn't look right on the ultrasound.

IN THE EVENING JIM AND I WENT FOR A WALK round the island.

They say that just before you die your whole life flashes in front of your eyes. It's a bit like that if you think you may die

fairly soon. Does it matter now that I was beaten in the Paris
Marathon by Jack Harding? And I shouldn't worry that I re-
fused to fight that soldier in Pembroke Dock over that wait-
ress when I was seventeen—he would probably have killed
me anyway. But I wish I had been nicer to my dad and not
rude to that poor job applicant who worked for Arthur
Andersen—though Arthur Andersen were a bunch of crooks.
In any case if I die the race is not becoming extinct or anything, nor am I the last of the Darlingtons. It's just not going
to be me any more—it's a question of moving over and leaving room. They do the big tests tomorrow and we'll know the
options. But in the end there are no options.

A cairn terrier had turned up and challenged Jim to a race
and by cutting off corners was keeping the game going. It was
good to see Jim run, to imagine the great heart clenching.

You going soon? asked the cairn's owner.

Pardon? I said. Oh you mean the boat! I've got to have a
hernia fixed first.

I've got one of those—I just pushes her back in.

We walked along the island. Atlantic Yacht Basin is the
best marine workshop on the East Coast, said my new friend.
They are nice guys here too.

Always Owya doon Jim, I said, and a joke about the new
air-conditioning unit they put in for me. It was late but my
hernia operation was delayed so it didn't matter too much.
They've done a lovely job—every day they come and varnish
it again and then they have a board meeting about whether
the colour is a match. Looks like a coffin stood on end, but
you would swear it has been there since the boat was built. It
takes fifteen degrees out of the temperature and all the humidity. And it will run backwards and turn into a heat pump

if we get cold further down the track. Sometimes I hug it like a tree.

My new friend was on a sailing boat and he had gone outside the Intracoastal Waterway for most of the way from Florida, right out at sea, and I said he was very brave and he said Oh no and he would have liked to see my boat but he had to go back because they were leaving and I never saw him again and Jim never saw the cairn terrier again.

JIM AND I WALKED ON ACROSS THE BRIDGE from the island and into the northern part of the marina, which is mainly great sheds over the water, held up by wooden rafters like medieval barns. There were ten sheds, full of the tall cruisers they call trawlers: and powerboats and sport-fishers and yachts. Some boats were a hundred feet long, some Tupperware, some steel, some fifty years old in wood and bright varnish. It was dark and silent inside the sheds and the security lighting made a shadowy film-set for adventure and mystery. We walked the pontoons over the black water.

Jim stopped suddenly. I should have expected her. There, over the other side of the shed, under the bow of a great cruiser, was my mother. I shouldn't feel scared when she appears—she is my mother after all, or was—but I always do. She was dressed in her winter coat and one of those felt hats with a bit of veiling like the Queen Mother wore. She was smiling. I don't have much hair but it stood up like the velvet on Jim's back and a breeze passed by like ice.

I wonder why she turned up over there? said Monica back at the boat—she normally appears by the stove.

I think the air-conditioning is a bit noisy for her, I said, and if I was coming back from the dead I would manifest myself in those sheds—all the shadows, all the memories. She was smiling.

That's all right then, said Monica, if she was smiling. Everything will go well with your big tests at the hospital next week.

Perhaps she is smiling because soon we will be together again, I said.

ON THE QUAY NEXT MORNING THERE WAS A thin man with long legs and white hair. He stalked along the boardwalk, stooping slightly, looking into the water. Two or three of those little silvery slippery guys would make a nice breakfast, he said. We love your boat—why is she so thin?

When he was thirty-one Lieutenant Colonel Dr James Marquardt ran a military hospital in Vietnam. I didn't think about the rights and wrongs, said James—we treated people from both sides.

James is now a professor of psychiatry at the University of Colorado. He and Joni have a fifty-foot trawler, a square white vessel with five storeys. It was ninety-six degrees and we all took refuge in their air-conditioned cabin. Jim stayed on the *Phyllis May* because Joni was allergic to him.

We lost more boys in the American Civil War than in both world wars put together, said James. More than half a million. One in a hundred of the population. There were towns in the South with no young men left. The arms manufacturers had discovered that by rifling the gun barrels you could more than double the accuracy of the weapons. You can't send men to charge against rifled ordnance. The suffering was terrible on the battlefields and worse in the field stations and hospitals. You know those legends of the Wild West–those cowboys with six-guns? They were Civil War veterans suffering from post-traumatic stress.

Night fell hot and damp and we patched up a meal from both boats. As we ate, James and Joni told us a heartbreaking story of love and loss.

It was late afternoon on a March day in Georgetown, South Carolina, and it was raining. James was wearing his yellow rain-jacket over his white jeans. He was bare-headed. He was by the boat when a Great White Egret landed on the grass a few yards away. It was a magnificent creature, over three feet tall, and its cheeks along its yellow beak were vivid green. It looked at James from one angle then another and came nearer and then stopped and looked at him again. She was real elegant, said James, real beautiful–she was kinda eyeing me.

The egret appeared again that evening when James and Joni were having dinner. She looked in at the window, gazing at James's white hair, moving her head back and forth.

In the morning Joni was in the galley and she saw the egret striding along the boardwalk, following James. He looked round and the egret came within a few feet, looking at him from one angle then another. The great bird stood and watched him all morning until the boat left.

As they sailed north the egret flew away.

So, I said, she didn't phone, she didn't write, and the relationship was never consummated? You have had no egrets?

I have thought about it a lot from a professional standpoint, said James, and I wonder if she was interested in me because of my yellow jacket or my white hair or my white jeans or because I am tall or because I am thin or because I was looking at the fish from the quay. Maybe one of those elements triggered the mating response. She was eyeing me as if she was looking for something but I didn't quite fit. Perhaps she had become habituated to people or imprinted like Lorenz's geese. The marina owner said he had never seen anything like it before.

She had the hots for you, said Joni.

MONICA AND I GOT INTO OUR HIRED CAR AND headed out twenty miles to Virginia Beach. We didn't talk much.

The first test was the blood test. The blood test wasn't too bad if you don't mind having needles stuck in you and your veins are on the outside of your body instead of inside as they are on normal people like me.

Then the radiographers stuck more needles in me and injected me with radioactive thallium and strapped me to a table and pressed a button and a machine slowly circled me, buzzing and clicking, like in the science fiction movies. Make sure you get my best side, I said, and they laughed. Bet they never heard that one before.

Then they brought me into another room that was brightly lit and full of people. They took off my T-shirt and covered me with patches like plastic tits with wires coming out and put me on a treadmill. I was nervous. I walked and then I ran and ran and the treadmill went faster and faster and steeper and steeper and they all seemed to be shouting because I was doing it wrong and they shouted and shouted and I ran faster and faster and then they stopped the treadmill and helped me off. I didn't feel very good at all. A lot of people came running in—Sit down Mr Darlington.

The doctor was a thin gentleman with grey hair, in a suit. My God, he said, your heartbeat went up to two hundred and fifty. They all agreed they had never seen that before, and ran out to tell some other people, who came in and said they had never seen that before. You must have been pumping air, said the thin gentleman.

Am I going to die? I asked. The fast heartbeat won't kill you, said the thin gentleman, but there could be an underlying problem to do with the blood supply to your heart. We'll know soon.

TWO HOURS LATER THEY STRAPPED ME ON THE table again and the machine began to buzz. You already did this, I said—what's going on?

You have had photos taken of your heart when you are resting, and now we are taking them after you have been stressed, said the radiographer. If there are blockages in the blood supply to your heart they will show up as hot spots where the thallium has sort of stuck. You will get the results tomorrow.

I drove us back to the boat. When will we be free of all this? asked Monica. Here we are moored on the side of a tin shed waiting and waiting, too worried to sleep and never knowing when we can get going to Florida or if you are going to die and when we get going we have to cross Albemarle Sound and it's thirty miles wide and we'll probably drown or the boat will be smashed up in the hurricanes and Jim will be killed or we will be killed and no one will have Jim because he bit Rhiannon on Christmas Day because he was over-excited and he was only a puppy and he'll have to go for rescue and they'll cut his balls off and he'll be neglected and I haven't got my daughters or my son or my friends, just a lot of black chaps with spanners wandering around saying Owya doon and frogs and turtles. Poor Tel, you are having a terrible time with all the doctors and the worry and the tests and they made you feel so bad you could hardly drive us home. And poor Monica, poor me, it's awful—I've had about a bloody nuff.

HELLO MR DARLINGTON—YOUR RADIOACTIVE thallium stress tests were negative—no Mr Darlington, please Mr Darlington, come back Mr Darlington, that doesn't mean you are going to die—it means there is nothing wrong with the blood supply to your heart. You just take the tablet each day that Doctor prescribed and we will go ahead and fix your hernia.

Great news, said Monica—you are not going to die!

Five grand, I said, to be told my heart is irregular. It's been going for seventy years—it's a high-mileage heart. And it speeds up if I am nervous—is that a big deal? Now it's a wait of weeks and weeks for the hernia operation and then six weeks to get better. Monica, we have encountered an advanced capitalist society in full flower. They get a hold of you and never let you go. And they are so nice about it, and so thorough, and so professional. Resistance is futile—stand back and marvel; stand and deliver.

But if we leave before October we could get smashed to

bits in the hurricanes, said Monica. All the other boats are going to wait. They said we would be mad to leave. Remember the ice storm. This is a nice boatyard and there is plenty going on round here—Chesapeake is only one of the cities—there is Norfolk, and Portsmouth, and Suffolk, and Virginia Beach. And over the Roads there is Hampton and Newport News. A million people—we can get around; meet some Americans. We can eat out, go shopping, go to church. We can have a look at the Great Dismal Swamp, and at the marina in Elizabeth City on the way to Albemarle Sound. We can leave in October and still have plenty of time to reach Florida by the spring.

We will become students of American culture, I said, and arm ourselves spiritually for our pilgrimage. Then in October the *Phyllis May* will sail south towards Indian River and Florida. At the helm Tits Magee, the ruptured hero, his heart pounding, his resolve undimmed; the beautiful Gulfstream Rose at his side and his faithful hound shuddering below. We shall overcome—the Curse of Darlington will bring down all who stand in my way.

We kissed and Jim jumped around us and made oogling noises and brought us his frog of plush.

An hour later I was on the floor clutching my stomach and leaning over the side trying to throw up. It's the stress of thinking I was going to die, I said, and running my heart at two hundred and fifty miles an hour. I'll be better tomorrow.

I've had about a bloody nuff, said Monica.

Four

THE VILLAGE
OF THE DAMNED

Virginia

THE GREAT DISMAL SWAMP VISITOR CENTRE
was twenty minutes south, three miles over the South
Carolina border.

The centre was cool and spacious with three ladies. Sure
you can moor up here on your way through in October, if we
are still here, said one of the ladies. Last year they didn't re-
new the budget until someone found some money in another
account. This year we don't know yet.

She looked at me as if I were responsible for the US Army
Corps of Engineers' refusing to maintain the Great Dismal
Swamp Canal, or I should be offering to finance it myself, or
I could do something about it.

When will you know about your budgets? I asked.

Last year they told us in December. Guess you'd better
give us a ring before you come, but don't set out before
October. The hurricane four years ago took down seven hundred trees across the canal and you don't want one of those
across your boat.

I am sure the route along the Albemarle and Chesapeake
Canal is very nice too, said Monica, and I know most people
go that way, but we do want to go through the Dismal

Swamp. It is so old, having been started by George Washington, and so mysterious and it's a real canal not a great river or an estuary and we are shallow enough to get along it easily. If we come can we stay at your quay?

There is always room, said the lady. We hope you will come. The boats can breast up alongside each other. Some people won't but most do. Sometimes they put all the food in together and have a party.

She seemed to have forgiven me for not sorting out her budgets.

Outside, the canal was a hundred feet wide, with tall trees and undergrowth hard on each side. You could see a little way into the water, stained by the swamp into Typhoo, and you could enjoy the different leaves and branches, and the butterflies.

They danced on the grass, their wings wide, almost jagged, colours gentle, with flashes of blue and red and yellow. At times one would rise and float about. Each seemed to be different. There are fifty different butterflies on the Great Dismal Swamp Canal, the lady had said, and gave us a list. I looked at the part of the list titled *Hesperiidae*.

The Poet Laureate could not have done better than that list, and the Poet Laureate before would not have stood a chance, and even John Betjeman would have been sweating.

When reading aloud it is best to deliver the second verse quietly and ascend to a shout on the Roadside Skippers–

> *Silver-spotted Skipper*
> *Southern Cloudy Wing*
> *Confused Cloudy Wing*
> *Juvenal's Dusky Wing*

Horace's Dusky Wing
Southern Skipperling

Clouded Skipper
Delaware Skipper
Duke's Skipper
Hobomok Skipper
Zabulon Skipper
Yehl Skipper
Dun Skipper

Lace-winged Roadside Skipper
Carolina Roadside Skipper
Reversed Roadside Skipper

What is a reversed butterfly? asked Monica.

It's a concept some people find difficult, I said, but reversed butterflies are like reversed type—the letters that are holes in something else. A reversed butterfly is in fact not there at all. When a Carolina Roadside Skipper dies before its time (a cold night, a truck) it returns with the colours the other way round. You can never catch them in a net because they are just a hole in the scenery. It is the same with the blue butterflies you used to see in England—they are bits of sky that have sort of flaked off and you can't catch them either.

Don't talk rubbish, said Monica, let's get on to Elizabeth City. The marina probably won't have us because it says in the book they only take short boats and they are at the start of Albemarle Sound and you are scared of talking to them because you are scared of Albemarle Sound and you have gone off into your world of your own.

• • •

ELIZABETH CITY WAS THIRTY MILES SOUTH. IT was low rise, spread out, and over all before it lay the Pasquotank River a mile wide; green shores and smoky blue water broadening for ever into Albemarle Sound, the terrible Albemarle Sound.

The Pelican Marina had two plaster pelicans and a small chandlery, its door wide open. We got out of the car and there was a scream and a lady in her twenties ran out. We hurried Jim and the lady inside before they fainted from their kisses and embraces in the heat. If we had arrived with a vessel a hundred yards long with a verminous crew of pressed Scousers there would not have been a moment's doubt Pelican Marina would take our boat, providing Jim were on board.

We brought up our website on the marina computer and Jeanie said Is that your boat, oh my Gard, oh my Gard. But see that mark here on the counter under the till—that's where the water came four years ago, and the one below it is the hurricane before that. Don't y'all come too soon, or your lovely boat could finish up in someone's bedroom.

I suppose we could run back up the Dismal Swamp Canal, I said.

Yes, said Monica, with seven hundred chances of getting a tree across the boat.

Albemarle Sound is very calm now, said Jeanie—it has been like that for three days. It's usually like that in late July or August but it may not be like that when you come.

We looked out at the Pasquotank River, glassy, fading into the sound.

The captains rely on the Boo Ease, said Jeanie.

Pardon? I asked.

The Boo Ease.

Oh yes, I said, and thought the Boo Ease must be the booze, or perhaps some sort of drug that sailors take so they don't worry so much, like they chew coca leaves in South America. My word this is a funny country.

They can't do without the Boo Ease, said Jeanie—makes all the difference.

Can you spell that? I asked—I have a bit of trouble with the language.

Sure—B.U.O.Y.S.—the Boo Ease.

WE CAN START STOCKING UP FOR THE JOURNEY, said Monica—time to visit a Wal-Mart.

It was the hottest 2 August ever in eighty American cities. To feed the thundering air-conditioners of Virginia, Baltimore Gas and Electric broke the production records they had set the day before. In New York the Empire State Building was dark. *Après nous le déluge.* Monica and I stepped on to the boardwalk into a hundred degrees, and walked between the sheds and under the boats on stilts in the frying gravel.

When a car has been standing all day in the sun in a hundred degrees you have thirty seconds to get in without touching anything and get the air-conditioning going before you die. It's like swimming underwater, or going back into a burning house to rescue the children.

Up the road from the yacht basin along the canal, under the trees, and into Great Bridge and across the traffic of

Battlefield Boulevard. Cedar Road off the boulevard is a wide carriageway with big houses, apartment blocks, churches, gas stations, restaurants, all on green plots—two, four, twenty acres. Want to buy a plot—put up a restaurant? Take a hundred acres—put up a shopping mall. Plenty of room in America, plenty of room along Cedar Road.

After ten miles, a lake, a golf course. A new church, white with a green roof. Wooden houses spreading over the horizon, all similar, modern and smart, behind a gate.

> You owe it to yourself to experience the home styles and the country club lifestyle, perfect for active adults age 55 and better.
>
> You'll also enjoy peace of mind knowing a gate limits traffic into Eagle Pointe.
>
> Why stay in a house that's too much to handle? Why continue to climb those stairs? The time is now to discover the freedom you deserve at Eagle Pointe.

At Eagle Pointe you won't have to bother to talk to the old poor guys who sit in the pub all day that you knew when they were young, or the lady in the newsagents who has been there since the war, or the dark lads in the Indian restaurant or the window-cleaner Monica tried to teach French to forty years ago and he hid in a cupboard in the classroom. Dave who owns the ironmongery won't remind you how close he ran you in the London Marathon. You won't have a chip shop or a tattoo parlour over the road, and you won't have to avoid the people who hate you because you had a bigger car than them in the seventies, or worry about the chip papers on the street or those noisy boys from the high school or those seventeen-year-old girls who are so graceful and make you feel all funny or the noise on New Year's Eve or the fireworks on your roof.

At one o'clock it's Cookin' Chicks, the Women's Club Group, and Games of Choice. At six o'clock it's Creative Cuties.

You won't have to worry about anything any more—come through the gates of Eagle Pointe, under a searing sky—come and join us in the Village of the Damned.

WAL-MART WAS A SHED WHICH COULD HAVE contained the town of Stone, Staffordshire, and its pubs and boatyards and terraces, and its parks and meadows (the churches would have stuck out the top) but instead contained everything you would find in an English supermarket, apart from most of the interesting things.

I worked out from the shelf space that the good people of Chesapeake drink one glass of wine each a year, which is Californian, and a small amount of American beer. American beer tastes like the piss of the Great Gnat of Newport News, and American lite beers are best not discussed in a book that might fall into the hands of children. Some drinks that they call lagers can be drunk without shame, though they do not put the strength of the beer on the pack, and sometimes after my second bottle of Samuel Adams I get feelings of cosmic understanding.

It seems the only fish the Americans eat in quantity are frozen shrimps. Fourteen types of melon were displayed, few of which could be lifted by an adult male. There were four hundred yards of beef, and Wal-Mart was not scornful of the odd vegetable or those shiny yellow and red cherries. They had galleries and boulevards of canned foods and on the ends of the gondolas there was beef jerky, which is dried and flavoured with barbecue smoke and maple syrup.

Yards of hymns and country music. I bought records by Willie Nelson, Kenny Rogers, Kris Kristofferson, Alison Krauss. A man could make a fool of himself over Alison Krauss, who is a bit cross-eyed but none the worse for that.

It was late afternoon and there were not many shoppers. Most were overweight in an overweight sort of way but some were spherical or worse: their bums cantilevered with fat, their arms hung with fat, their faces swollen and their eyes dull. In England they would be overpowered and rushed to hospital.

The books section was mainly romances, and motivational and religious writings. Most Americans believe that Christ will come to judge the quick and the dead fairly soon, and on that happy day, which they call the Rapture, the virtuous will ascend to heaven and the sinful will not. The *Sun*, a weekly newspaper in the genre of the UK *Sunday Sport*, reported that *100,000 people have already vanished from earth*. A teenage boy had gone missing in Des Moines after beautiful trumpet-playing had been heard, and five fishermen were returning home from Alaska's Kenai Peninsula with a boatload of halibut when a crewman disappeared from his quarters. A picture showed a couple of dozen people in mid-air, looking upwards devoutly: the women in dresses, the men in shirts and trousers, their arms spread, ascending to their reward.

On the shelf was the novel *The Rapture*, by Tim LaHaye and Jerry B. Jenkins. Tim and Jerry have sold sixty million books.

I read *The Rapture* right through. The Devil seemed quite an interesting bloke but the scenes in heaven were like being trapped in a performance of the 'Hallelujah Chorus' at the Albert Hall until after the pubs have closed.

WE WALKED JIM ON THE ISLAND IN THE BAKING dusk. It would not be a bad outcome, I said to Monica. I mean old age is not much fun with hernias and hearts already and incontinence and impotence and going mad as forthcoming attractions, and dying can be a painful and messy business. Why don't we join one of the American religions and get ourselves in on this Rapture lark, and then we could go for a walk one day and rise through the air hand in hand with Jim—we'll all be ready at about the same time—and continue our walk on the fields of heaven. Despite what Tim and Jerry say, I am quite sure there are canals, and public houses with London Pride at very reasonable prices, and pork scratchings from Wolverhampton.

You are getting worse, said Monica, the heat has unhinged you. This Rapture business is ridiculous, a crazy cult. You can't just disappear into the sky like that. Terry, have you seen Jim?

There he is, Mon. Quick, up there!

THE MAN WHO GREETED US AT THE DOOR OF Chesapeake Library wasn't very tall, but his sword made him look bigger. He had a big belly and his hair was shoulder-length and he wore a bandanna and a black T-shirt printed with gothic scenes. His girl had a ragged dress and a bullet hole in her cheek.

We can get sixty people, he said—we won an award. Sometimes we go until dawn. We are part of the library. Tonight it's the *Night of the Living Dead*—1968 version and then the 1990 version. Help yourself to the buffet—it's all free.

We sat down. There were six people in the hall. Two women came in—the bum on one of them weighed more than me, and her friend was half a size smaller. They settled down and started eating. Then a lady came in who looked very straight, like a schoolteacher. She wrapped a blanket round her shoulders and sat down and went to sleep. Three people with long hair, dressed in black, came in and put up camping chairs and sat on them in sleeping bags. A small group of tattooed people came and lay down on the floor. The big women went back to the buffet because they had not been able to carry enough the last time.

The main purpose of the Fantasmo Cult Cinema Explosion, like any film society, is to allow a dick, whose opinion would not normally be sought on any matter, the chance to tell you about the film you are about to see, and why you should enjoy it, and how clever he is, and what was the director's last film and all about the plot and who committed the murder. At Chesapeake Library the sworded one was joined by a thin young man, unarmed, in a black sweater—so it was Double Dick. For a quarter of an hour each dick tried to show he was the bigger dick. Finally they agreed that *Can't Stop the Music* with Valerie Perrine and the Village People was the worst film ever made.

With a wave of the sword, half an hour late, Double Dick retired and we were away.

The films were about the newly dead wandering about eating people. Both films were great. In the first version the girl is a useless dolly-bird, but by the second the culture had changed and she was an heroic military figure, and to tell you the truth a right cracker. You should have seen the bit at the end where she turned on the cowardly bloke who caused all the trouble. Then of course there was the bit with the big explosion and how the zombies came along and ate the people who had been blown up.

It was late and as we left the fat women were finishing the buffet. Ghost films scare me, I said to Monica—won't watch them because if I do I am afraid to go to the lavatory in the night. But no trouble with the horror—it's just a good old laugh really.

At the boat Monica took Jim out for a walk and as soon as they were gone the boat moved again. Someone had come on board, stepped off the quay and on to the front deck in the dark, perhaps more than one, not saying anything, just trying the door, ready to blunder down the boat and sink their teeth into me.

But it was Jim and Monica hurrying out of the heat.

Soon we fell asleep to a gentle rain on the roof. An hour later there was an explosion overhead. The *Phyllis May* rang like a bell and the air was full of blue fire. I jumped up shouting—My God, they are here! The storm flashed and cracked and muttered all night and it rained and rained and next day it was only ninety degrees.

• • •

IT'S A DREADFUL BUSINESS IF A MAN CAN'T GO out with his dog for a pint, but you can't in Chesapeake, Virginia, because dogs are not allowed anywhere they serve food. And bars in America are dark, and there is always a drunk in the corner. In the Home Town Heroes bar on the shopping parade in Great Bridge he was a four-hundred-pounder and the barmaid brought him a large beer every ten minutes without looking at him.

The barmaid was the spitten image of Lindsay Wagner, the Bionic Woman, in her panther prime. And good for her, she came through the encircling gloom with a glass of draught Samuel Adams that could almost have passed for a pint, and made Monica a vodka martini with three olives—you should have seen her shake it up. Then she brought us both a plate of beef ribs and salad and relishes which was the best meal we had in the US, or anywhere else really. It took only ten minutes to prepare, but no doubt Lindsay helped in the kitchen, making those pots fly.

The Bionic Woman was about to run her first half-marathon. Monica gave her some tips on racing and Lindsay was grateful though no doubt she would have struggled through, being largely made of titanium and plugged into the mains all night.

The drunk was a friendly chap. I suppose if you weigh four hundred pounds you can always work on the smile. There were twelve screens above the bar and he explained that the keyboard he was fiddling with was connected to the one asking trivial questions.

Are there any prizes? I asked.

One a year, he said.

Do you compete with other people?

You can if you have friends, but as it happens I am on my own this evening.

Whose last words were—*Let us cross over the river and rest under the shade of the trees?* asked the screen, offering a choice of Stonewall Jackson, or Michael Jackson, or Jackson Pollock, with clues.

My glass had refilled itself again. I guess they hired Lindsay because she can see in the dark, as well as being quick in the kitchen and a good shaker. I could feel the Samuel Adams unknitting my nerves, and began to get feelings of divine immanence.

Who wrote *Gone with the Wind*? asked the screen, offering Jane Austen, Margaret Mitchell and Clark Gable, with clues.

> We hold these truths to be self-evident, that all men are created equal; that they are endowed by their Creator with inherent and inalienable rights; that among these, are life, liberty, and the pursuit of happiness; that to secure these rights, governments are instituted among men, deriving their just powers from the consent of the governed; that whenever any form of government becomes destructive of these ends, it is the right of the people to alter or abolish it . . .

Thomas Jefferson and his countrymen did not believe that the upper orders of English society had the right or the wisdom to boss people about. Having come across some of the upper orders of English society at Oxford I am with the Yanks all the way on that one.

When the war against England was won it seemed to the

American Church that it was no longer appropriate to pray that wisdom be granted to George III and his ministers, if only because previous prayers had been unanswered. So in the prayer book some names of the earthly powers were changed and a few other changes made but not many, because we don't want to be nasty about it do we? The person who explains all this in the foreword to the Episcopalian prayer book was a gentle soul—he was writing in 1789, not a forgiving time.

Now it is the tenth Sunday after Pentecost, centuries later—

I am the living bread that came down from heaven.
Whoever eats of this bread will live forever, and the
bread that I will give for the life of the world is my
flesh . . .

The mood in St Thomas Pentecostal Church in Cedar Road was still gentle—a big congregation: the worshippers in sports jackets, slacks, shorts: ordinary guys, quiet people, couples, grandfathers, angel granddaughters. Unlike English churchgoers they did not sleep during the sermon or sit trying to recall Winston Churchill's middle name. They were listening—and they wanted you to know they were listening. One gentleman of a certain age had his arm round his wife, and they both leaned forward, encouraging each other with the listening and showing they were having a great time.

We had seen the same attentiveness the night before, in Hooters. Hooters is American for tits. Although Hooters was almost full Monica and I were shown to a table right away and two seventeen-year-old ladies in singlets and knickers came and sat down with us—Howya doon? I shifted my chair as another seventeen-year-old sped past sitting on a tray. She crashed into the counter and everyone cheered.

One of the seventeen-year-olds fetched us a gin and martini and a twenty-four-ounce glass tankard of Samuel Adams, ice cold. The tankard, heavily misted, was a joyful sight on a hot night, and would not have dismayed me on a cold one. The other young lady asked about the food and we each ordered a sandwich based on a fish billed as the cousin of a grouper. The cousins of the groupers came at once, the plates piled. A sandwich over here is a Sunday dinner with a bread roll on the side.

A hundred and fifty people having a great time—the restaurant well lit: same sex groups, families, grandfathers, angels. And they wanted you to know they were having a great time: glancing around to say Hey, can you see I am having a great time! Waitresses sped between the tables sitting on trays and young men too, trying to impress the knickered ones.

Every few minutes a yell from the open kitchen where an African-American gentleman put loaded plates on the counter— Hey I've just cooked this and here it is and I'm having a great time!

The plates were heaped and the customers were fat and laughing and shouted and shouted. The cousins of the groupers were superb and we put the half we could not eat in a box for Jim, who was not having a great time because he was still on the boat. They would not have him in Hooters, even on the balcony.

But that was last night—this morning here we are in St Thomas Church and the reading is from Deuteronomy—

For the Lord your God is bringing you into a good
land, a land with flowing streams, with springs and
underground waters welling up in valleys and hills, a
land of wheat and barley, of vines and fig trees and
pomegranates, a land of olive trees and honey, a land
where you may eat without scarcity, where you will
lack nothing . . . You shall eat your fill and bless the
LORD for the good land that he has given you.

The Lord your God has certainly delivered on that one, I
thought.

The gentleman of a certain age with his arm round his wife
leaned forward and a choir of bells on the balcony began to
play and the couples and the grandfathers and the angel
granddaughters all began to sing.

> *Bread of Heaven, bread of Heaven,*
> *Feed me till I want no more;*
> *Feed me till I want no more.*

THE DAY OF MY OPERATION DAWNED BRIGHT
and clear. At least I guess it did because it was half past five
when we left the boatyard for Virginia Beach Hospital and
what with one thing and another I wasn't around when the
sun rose.

Nothing to drink since midnight—no cup of tea. Battlefield
Boulevard and the interstate highways were stiff with brake
lights. I know these people go to bed at nine, but my God
look what time they get up!

Now are you absolutely certain, said Andrea, you have

had nothing to eat since last night? Please sign this, and this, and this, so you know your rights, and agree to give us the money. Now we will take your temperature, blood pressure, and your credit card number. Please sit here and Dr Wilder the anaesthetist will come and explain everything that is going to happen.

Ah, I thought, the bugger who tripped me at the last fence.

I had imagined my anaesthetist would be a frail creature, hovering because of his calling somewhere between life and death, uncertain in his opinions, pale and partly transparent like Jim. But Dr Wilder was fair and sturdy and looked like he might still be playing for the hospital football team. He shook my hand and fixed me with a strong professional stare. Yallreddy forall yorone we heldup, he said.

Pardon, I said, and he repeated what he had said.

You must forgive me, doctor, I said, I have a bit of trouble with the language.

You don't understand me?

I'm afraid not. I'm awfully sorry.

Don't understand English?

Well, yes, but you have to speak slowly.

Young Dr Berger had arrived—This guy doesn't understand English, said Dr Wilder.

He does if you speak slowly, said young Dr Berger, he's a writer—some of these writer guys are pretty smart.

Dr Wilder looked at me hard and said slowly—You understand me now?

Yes, I said.

I forgot what I was going to say, said Dr Wilder. This guy really freaks me—and my grandfather came from Shipley in Oxfordshire. And I have a cottage that is two hundred and fifty years old. It's up on the eastern shore of Chesapeake Bay. It is made out of brick.

Goodness, I said, that must be a very early building.

Yes, it's red brick framed in oak. One of the earliest on the shore.

Goodness, I said.

Nice to meet you Mr Darlington. Is that all clear now?

Perfectly, I said.

See you on the operating table, said Dr Wilder.

I HAVE NO RECOLLECTION OF BEING PUT TO sleep. It was a nothing experience: like Céline Dion, like Melvyn Bragg. I seemed to wake up naturally and Monica drove us back to the boat for breakfast.

That night I didn't have any pain but I think the narcotics were quite strong. When the air-conditioner comes on it croaks and moans and then settles down to a whistle and a noise like the beating of great wings. I opened my eyes and there a few yards away was a giant frog, its eyes staring and its mouth wide open. I screamed and hid my face. It wasn't a frog—it was the brass clock at the end of the saloon and the matching barometer alongside and under them like a mouth the oval roses and castles plaque by Ron Hough that we bought on the Grand Union Canal. But it looked like a frog in the darkness and it kept looking like a frog and it stared and it stared and it gaped and the lights from the marina caught it and from each eye there rolled a giant tear.

Next morning Andrea rang and wanted to know if I was all right and if there was anything they could have done better to please me or make me more comfortable in any way and

Were the narcotics strong enough? It was such a professional thing to do I nearly cried, and I quite enjoyed my first day on the boat as a convalescent, junked out and listening to Alison Krauss.

MONICA AND I SAT WITH JIM UNDER THE TREES by the little marina lounge and looked across the hundred yards of the Albemarle to Chesapeake Canal, smooth and black.

Whose last words were *Let us cross over the river and rest under the shade of the trees*? I asked.

Michael Jackson, said Monica, or Jackson Pollock.

Stonewall Jackson was shot by one of his own sentries, I said, at Chancellorsville up towards Washington. Robert E. Lee won the battle of Chancellorsville for the rebels but lost poor Stonewall. This morning we will cross over the canal and rest under the shade of the trees—it's the first day for months it's been cool enough to walk without dropping dead. We can have a really good look at the banks of the cut to see if we can moor up like we do in England. In some places on our way south there are no marinas for fifty miles. If we can't moor up we may need to buy a dinghy to get Jim ashore, but can you see us getting Jim in and out of a dinghy?

We will take Jim with us, said Monica—he has not had a proper walk in America yet. What a lovely day—it can't be more than eighty-five degrees.

We drove across the bridge and down to the canalside, and there we were, looking at Atlantic Yacht Basin from the other bank.

Along a crackling path of dried brush and needles and

cones and above us the pines. It's just like a real walk, said Monica. Apart from the bamboos we could be walking under the pines on Tittensor Chase in Stone. Now we can start to have a normal life again—it is not much hotter than it gets in England, you are walking properly again, Jim is frolicking; everything is going to be all right. I bet there are butterflies.

Something just bit me, I said, but it is very nice here. We walked back by another way, talking about how nice it was and how everything was going to be all right. The path crunched beneath us—not many people seemed to have walked along it and there was no one around today. There were no butterflies and no birds sang. There was a dragonfly with a face like a monkey.

I got into the car and a white four-wheel drive drove up with *CHESAPEAKE* on the outside and an old guy on the inside. He rolled down his window and spoke to Monica. They carried on talking. Monica stopped smiling and they talked some more. I thought He is some sort of copper or official and we have done something wrong.

Monica got into the car. Oh dear, she said, that's all we need.

What's the matter? I asked.

They are burrowing into us.

Who is burrowing into us?

The Red Bugs. The old guy is a ranger and he came down a fortnight ago to put up a notice here and when he finished dozens of Red Bugs had burrowed into him. He had to rush home and his wife had to wash him all over and put stuff on his skin.

My leg began to itch.

He stopped me to warn us, said Monica. We must go home

at once and shower and then paint the spots where the Red Bugs have burrowed in with nail polish–that's the only thing that works. And wash Jim, because they will have burrowed into him as well.

What happens if we don't?

I don't know–I suppose we will die.

At least let's pick up some ice on the way back, I said, so I can have a cold beer before I begin to die.

At the marina T. J. the dockmaster opened the ice cabinet. T. J., I said, these Red Bugs you have over here, I said–are they fatal?

Red Bugs? said T. J.–never heard of them.

The ones that burrow into your skin–do they kill you?

Oh the chiggers. You can see them where they have burrowed in. They are bright red like a little drop of blood. They itch but you don't die–they do.

Can't you go for a walk here in the US? It's a terrible thing if a man can't go for a walk in the woods with his dog.

Of course you can go for a walk in the US–this is the land of the free, and the home of the brave. It's just the chiggers, and the poison ivy, so best not to go walking except at the right time of year. And the poison oak of course. And the ticks that drop on your head from the pines–they carry deadly diseases. And there are the snakes.

What does poison ivy look like?

It varies a lot.

What is the right time of year?

Well it's not very long, and it depends where you are and what you don't want to come up against, said T. J. Personally I find it best to stay at home. Have a nice day.

Back at the boat I saw a mosquito bite on my leg, but we

couldn't see any Red Bugs so we didn't shower or paint ourselves with nail varnish.

THE NEXT DAY MY ANKLES BEGAN TO ITCH. THEY itched for two days and then at three o'clock in the morning they had swelled halfway up to the knee. I put ointment on them and took anti-histamine pills but that did not stop the itching or the pain so I took some narcotics as well and lay talking to the faces in the wall. In the morning there were five hundred spots, each bright red like a little drop of blood, on each ankle where my socks had been.

The next day it was really hot again and Jim would not go for a walk, even on the island. We checked him over for Red Bugs but couldn't find any.

A week later in the slow watches of the night the spots swelled up on my ankles and hundreds more up my leg. The Red Bugs have burrowed through me and are coming out the other side, I thought.

Anti-histamines, narcotics, cortisone, alcohol—all is sin and pain.

I should have listened to the old geezer. That's always been my problem—tell me to do something and I will do the opposite. It works in the UK, which is full of busybodies and everyone patrols his bit of territory and hates any new ideas, and the only sensible response is Sod the lot of them. But it doesn't work over here—I don't think they know what is going on themselves. Most of the time they don't warn you but if they do they bloody well mean it. Will I ever get better—I could have encephalitis and my head will swell up, or malaria coming back all my life, or lose my leg to gangrene. The creatures are inside me, hundreds of them, chewing, shagging, laying eggs, dying. I will be like John Hurt in *Alien*–they will burst out of me while I am having my dinner and run round the butter dish. The itching, the itching–I can't think of anything else.

It took three weeks for the spots to stop itching, and a year later there were still scars on my legs.

By my troth, said Lancelot, this is a dreadful place.

IT WAS IN THE MIDDLE OF A THURSDAY MORNing when Hurricane Ernesto came up from Florida. His lungs were empty and his petards were blown and all he had left was his rain, which was huge. The water beat on the roof all day and we went to bed and dreamed we were on the Trent and Mersey in a wild night, and in the morning we would turn the boat in Tixall Wide and come back up the Trent Valley, the fields green and brown and the last leaves yellow and rust and the soft rain and the duck-egg sky and the sun dying like a red fish netted in the trees. And here we are in the Star for early doors–A pint of Banks's please and a bag of scratchings and that's a nice fire and has Stanley been in?

When we woke up the boatyard was partly under water. The men in the yard came in and went home. Can't understand it, they said–it has never been this bad, but it will soon go down.

Après nous le déluge. We sat waiting for the flood to go down and it got deeper and deeper.

We have got to get poor Jim on to some grass before we go to bed, said Monica. I will go out and you can pass him over to me.

I can't I said. He weighs thirty pounds. I am Tits Magee, the ruptured hero, forbidden for four weeks to carry more than the weight of twelve ounces of Samuel Adams and a bag of beef jerky.

Monica stood on the gunwale and coaxed Jim up on to the gas locker, where he trembled and stared. Jim does not like jumping when he can't see a landing, and he won't walk in water unless he can see the bottom. He is in some ways a sensible creature. Monica picked him up in her arms and trudged off through the flood like St Christopher.

I am a grandmother, said Monica when they came back. I am seventy years of age. All my life I worka like a dog. I have a rich network of social connections—friends to run with and play bridge with and church friends and children and grandchildren I adore. I have a lovely house with a patio and a forty-inch telly and I can go outside on any day of the year. When I find myself stumbling through gravel in ordinary shoes in the middle of the night in a foot of water fetid with diesel oil and coffee grounds and dead crabs and worse, infested with poisonous snakes and snapping turtles, carrying a cowardly dog that will not jump or walk or swim, with a crippled husband sitting in his armchair covered with red spots, drinking and listening to Mantovani, I say to myself, Monica, somewhere you turned left when you might have turned right.

WE KEEP PUSSER'S RUM ON THE *PHYLLIS MAY* for the hard times, because it is very strong and can be taken at any time of day and has a long nautical tradition.

I hope you were careful and didn't step on any of those little tiddlers swimming over the boardwalk, I said. It's not their fault—they did you no harm. Here darling—for a brave Mon.

The rum reminds me, said Monica, of when we began to live on the boat and sail round England. Our mooring at Hoo Mill was beautiful and England was beautiful and you knew where you were with things. I mean there were adventures, like the Harecastle Tunnel and the Tardebigge Locks, but people had got the measure of them. I don't think the Americans are in control of their country and sometimes they act as if they don't understand it. Have you noticed how they can't name their animals or birds? Their weather forecasts are wrong, their cities get blown up or washed away and they stand helpless—look at New Orleans. They go off to war and then change their minds. They elect liars and fornicators as presidents. There is a looseness, a cog missing, a knot that has come untied or has never been tied up properly. Maybe they know this and that's why they seek security—why they have gated communities like Eagle Pointe, why they have fundamentalist religion and country music, why they fight crazy foreign wars, why they have guns, and television linkwomen with false teeth. That's why they need Tony Bennett, and why they need Engelbert Humperdinck and we don't, and why Andy Williams, dear Andy a hundred years old, is still their Huckleberry friend.

The population is five times ours, Mon, I said. There are so many climates and terrains. It took a terrible war to keep it all together. Maybe there is just too much of it. It's as big as Europe and no one has ever made the slightest sense of Europe. By comparison the Yanks have done pretty well.

I poured Monica more Pusser's and some for myself to be polite.

Poor little Monnie, I went on, you put up with so much–I know I can be useless at times and the dog is a coward, but westward, look, the land is bright. Those sea captains who e-mailed us seem really interested in the *Phyllis May* and if we can persuade them to pilot us across Albemarle Sound and Pamlico Sound we have a good chance of making it to the Gulf of Mexico and being back in Stone next May. Do you remember when Clifford made friends with that old soldier, the Desert Rat, when he was a boy? The one who was captured in Africa and Field Marshal Rommel said to him *For you, Tommy, the war is over*? In May next year for you, Monnie, the war could be over. This is the big one, the last hurrah, the final frontier, the crowning glory. No more expeditions, just the sunny autumn of our days among friends and family in the town we love. Though there is the Loch Ness Monster of course–it wouldn't take us long to chase him down once the *Phyllis May* is chugging up the Caledonian Canal and I've got my echo-sounder up his arse.

Jim was on his back on the sofa, one leg straight in the air. Smiley Broadling, the horizontal hound. Jim had liked being carried. It showed respect to the fastest animal in the world, an athlete, a sportsdog, an artiste.

Bugger the Loch Ness Monster, said Monica.

VOLVO PARKWAY IS TEN MILES WEST OF GREAT Bridge. The Parkway Temple is large and new and low-built, with a white spire, on a ten-acre plot. In the lobby a few dozen people. The Temple was smaller inside than out, with upholstered seats in a semicircle. At half past ten a goodly crowd came out of the woodwork. Some of us were African-American.

There were no kneeler stools and no prayer books, but here was the King James Bible–the turtle not the mock. About thirty people walked on to the platform under the cross, and arranged themselves into a choir, a band, a large tanned man in a large tan sports jacket, and a blonde.

The band struck up and everyone started to embrace everyone else. Monica and I had some space around us and we were embraced only a few times. A teenage boy and I shook hands reluctantly.

The large tanned man, who was the minister, motioned us to rise and the blonde broke into song. The words of the song appeared on three screens above the platform. The song was unknown to us and did not rhyme, but that didn't matter as the tune was easy to follow and the blonde, who looked like Lulu's pretty sister, was singing up a tempest.

We all sang along. The blonde waved her arms and spun around and was so full of the spirit that sometimes she seemed to rise into the air. The African-American lady on her left did rise, jumping vertically like Zebedee, raising an arm to reach higher. The other members of the choir held their hands in front of them, and leaped and twisted. Half an hour passed quickly.

We sat down and the minister told us we should give all we could to the Lord and we would certainly profit from it, though maybe not for some time, and he was going to Romania in the morning. He recommended tithing, though past performance was no guarantee of future performance, and any returns on investment could go down as well as up.

He realized that this uncertainty was a problem for all concerned and he addressed the issue for half an hour.

Then he was calling us forward and the congregation rose and went up to the platform and shouted *Hallelujah* and turned their hands up and shouted praise and fell down and crawled up the steps of the platform and over each other.

Some of you have dreadful problems, shouted the minister, but here you will find comfort.

An old lady put her arms round Monica. I know you have dreadful problems, said the old lady.

Yes, said Monica, and told her all about them. The old lady and Monica wept and wept and a gentleman next to me cried *Hallelujah, hallelujah!*

We were in the service for two hours and it did not seem so long. It was one of the best times we had in the US so far, and Monica did not mention the floods, or Stone, or the Bridge Club, or the Loch Ness Monster for weeks.

JIM AND I WERE COMING BACK FROM OUR morning walk along the island and there was an African-American gentleman sitting on the boardwalk by the bridge–one of the gang who operated the boat-lift. He stroked Jim. I saw her with you yesterday, he said. She was running real fast–she was haulin'.

She's a he, I said. Haulin' is what they are for. The miners in the north-east of England bred them for racing and rabbiting. They are quite a new breed and they are very healthy and have lots of colours and lots of chromosomes. Jim is the original sandy colour–they call it fawn. He is a retro whippet.

He is an inch bigger than the strictest UK standards but smaller than your US whippets, though we have not seen any of those so far.

She was haulin', said the African-American gentleman.

He pulled on a string and from the Typhoo depths came up a wire cage two feet square, half full of crabs. The crabs rattled and fought. They were big, with blue claws.

They look very fine crabs, I said—can I buy some?

Gracious no—I will give them to you.

Monica was breaking out the blueberry muffins when we all arrived at the *Phyllis May*. This is Bob, I said, and these are our crabs.

The crabs were making that scratching noise that crabs make in a bucket—the noise you hear in nightmares when the Things are trying the windows. Bob started putting the crabs in a saucepan. The crabs did not think that was a good idea at all, and attacked him as he was taking them out of the bucket. One broke free and fled sideways across the gas cooker. Jim set about haulin' to the other end of the boat, touching thirty miles an hour as he passed the stove.

They will get you if they can, said Bob—they are real mean.

He poured some Budweiser beer on the crabs and lit the gas. Five minutes later he lifted the lid and the crabs had turned red.

I have often wondered what to do with the Budweiser I bought when we arrived, I said.

We are going to do something a bit dangerous this afternoon, said Monica, but if we are spared we will eat your crabs for dinner tonight with a bottle of Californian Zinfandel. Bob, you are so kind.

Plenty of pepper, said Bob, and get some Old Bay spice for the next lot. At the end of the day I love to relax with a beer or two and pick my way through a stack of crabs.

Why have we got crabs in a river? I asked. Is it salt or fresh water?

Bit of both, said Bob, it varies.

Come on Terry, said Monica, we have a date.

STEVE THOMAS CAME THROUGH ON THE EARphones—Look—there's your boat!

Under us, Atlantic Yacht Basin with the *Phyllis May* a matchstick by the Zeppelin sheds.

Steve turned the plane by laying it over on its side and his weight pressed against me. Like his father Norwood, Steve Thomas is too big for most places.

My seat swayed and bounced and slipped away. I looked through the perspex and felt I was about to drop from the zenith like a falling star, straight into the Albemarle and Chesapeake Canal.

Have a good look, said Steve, then I'll take you to a thousand feet where it's smoother. It's bumpy today but it's clear and you are going soon and you want to see that sound you are scared of.

He pointed the Piper Colt into the firmament and the hundred and eight horses of the Lycoming engine began haulin', the opposed cylinders hardly vibrating.

The Piper Colt had been built in 1962 and was the prettiest plane you ever did see—it had spats on its wheels and a wide wing over the cockpit and a snub nose and you wanted to stroke it and talk in its ear. It was made of spars covered with doped canvas a bit like the balsawood and paper plane my father made for me sixty years ago and there was room for two big chaps like Steve and me as long as you don't get embarrassed snuggling up. It cruised at a hundred miles an hour and Steve had pulled it out of the hangar with one hand.

The hangar was carpeted and fully kitted out for weekends polishing the Piper Colt and cleaning the Lycoming with a toothbrush with the radio playing and a fridge full of Diet Coke and just being together, Steve and his plane.

Higher and higher—a crystal day. Around the yacht basin swirls of blue-collar housing and to the east trees and jungle and standing water—four hundred square miles—the Great Dismal Swamp.

I keep off the swamp, said Steve—not a place for a landing. If the trees don't kill you the snakes will get you.

I thought of the ruined Colt, poor baby plane, its back broken, and Terry and Steve stunned in the cockpit and the slithering, the slithering. There, shouted Steve, you can see it, you can see it, what a day!

And there, fifty miles away, plain in view, the patterns of rivers leading into the terrible Albemarle Sound, which stretched to the end of the world.

When it was Monica's turn to go up I went on to the runway with my camera but Steve managed to land somewhere behind my back and Jim and I thought we were on our own for the rest of our lives, but here was Monica looking for us. What a beautiful little plane, she said. Wasn't it lovely how it swayed around and floated on the bumps in the air? Come on, we are going tomorrow—it's time to get tooled up.

· · ·

IN THE SHOP UNDER THE GREAT BRIDGE IN
Great Bridge I picked up a sub-machine gun. Perhaps a bit
more than we need, I said to the lady sitting at the till.

She was so wide that she enveloped the till—in fact the
whole shop, with all its camouflage singlets and hats and jackets and billycans and guns and knives to kill people with, was
sort of in her lap.

It's to defend ourselves against attack, said Monica.
Everyone has been very nice so far but we are going a long
way and you never know. Our friends in the marina had a
baseball bat. That might be more the level of response, if that
is how you say it in the military.

Yes, I said, do you think bringing out a sub-machine gun
could spoil the atmosphere?

Oh that is an Airsoft gun, said the lady. That belt of bullets
is a fake. See all the little white pellets on the floor—it fires a
stream of those.

A teenager joined us. He was stout and pimpled and
bereted—dressed to set out into the dusk and sort out this ter-
rorist business once and for all. You should see them pellets
fly, he said—and they can hurt. He showed us a red mark on
his wrist like a mosquito bite. It's a bit like paintball, without
the paint, he explained.

How do you know you have hit the other guy, I asked,
without the paint?

It's an honour sport, said the teenager. I am myself the
leader of an Airsoft team—I am well known for my honour.
Have another look at my red mark.

Shut up Jason, said the fat lady. You could have a stun gun,
but you have to get up close and press it against them, and
sometimes they realize. The cops have ones with wires so

they can zap you from a distance. Not difficult to get a licence for a rifle in Virginia but for a handgun you have to go on a course. I advise a pepper spray—it works from twelve feet. This is the easiest—just flip and point and press. We sell a lot of pepper sprays here in Urban Survival. The pepper spray is strong—only time will heal the stinging—you can get wipes but they don't help.

It's been quite a day, said Monica, back on the *Phyllis May*, waving her pepper spray. You promised me action, you promised me something new, and I can't complain about today. I wonder is this thing any good against alligators?

Dear Michele and Brent

Thank you for your kind e-mail—we are pleased you are interested in our boat and our voyage and we would love to welcome you on board the *Phyllis May* when you are next in Virginia.

I feel a bit guilty asking a favour before we know you, but as you are both Sea Captains we wondered if you might be able to help us cross the Albemarle and Pamlico Sounds in October, or perhaps you know someone who could. The only time we really went out to sea was when we crossed the English Channel. You are not supposed to do that in a canal boat, and I think we may have been lucky.

The *Phyllis May* is a traditional flat-bottomed English narrowboat, 60 feet long and 6 feet 10 inches beam. She has a 43 bhp diesel engine and her top speed is 6.2 miles an hour.

We have a Global Positioning System with a four-inch screen at the tiller, a back-up GPS below linked to a laptop, VHF radio, two anchors, life jackets, a life-ring, and flares.

On our website www.narrowdog.com there is a picture of the *Phyllis May* going through the wake of a Channel ferry and, I am pleased to say, coming out the other side. But we don't know how she would handle persistent heavy seas and we are a bit worried about the big sounds in North Carolina.

We do hope you can help or advise.

Kind regards
Terry Darlington (and Monica, and Jim)

Five

THE TERRIBLE SOUNDS

North Carolina

Let's Boogie! – The Great Dismal Swamp Canal – The Return of Tits Magee – We Are Going Down! – Letter from Bethan – The Dirty Grocer – Oversized, Overpriced, and Over There – Down the Long Quay the Slow Boats Glide – White Sails, Tall and Leaning Hard – Blush Chablis – A Failure of the Imagination of Some Importance – A Typhoon of Typhoo – Through the World's Tempestuous Seas

CICELY CAME ALONG THE BOARDWALK AND JIM jumped her and she caught him in her arms and they hugged and kissed each other's ears and she came forward and caught me in her arms and we hugged and kissed each other's ears. Cicely was handsome and, like Officer Nagle's Chihuahua, immensely strong. She was not small, and it was like being on a sofa with a girl and the sofa has decided to join in. Goodbye, I said, darling.

We had said goodbye on her million-pound trawler the night before with Felix, her husband who owned a television station, and Max, a rough-haired Jack Russell who was just like Susan that Monica had when she was a little girl in Radnorshire. We had said goodbye at lunchtime when we had given a Coke and cake and crisps and cashews party for the good ole boys in the Atlantic Yacht Basin and we had said goodbye the night before last after we four went to the Olive Garden for dinner, and we had said goodbye when Cicely came on the boat and showed us the photographs of her paintings and we had said goodbye when I was trying to fix the new compass on top of the boat.

Next day a new morning, a blue morning. Early October,

when leaving Virginia was no longer the act of a madman. We were free—free to try our luck on the Intracoastal Waterway, free to try to cross the terrible sounds of North Carolina. I stepped on to the back counter and Monica stood on the gunwale. Let's boogie! I cried, and reversed into our wooded creek where the blue heron and the white heron hunted, and the turtles paddled and the fish rose and the crabs grappled and I swung the *Phyllis May* round the corner on to the Albemarle and Chesapeake Canal and headed north towards the Great Dismal Swamp Canal and there were people on the quay waving and we felt almost sad because we liked them all so much and Atlantic Yacht Basin was a nice place but Monica was talking to the keeper of the great bridge at Great Bridge on her VHF and he dropped the concrete counterweights as big as houses and the great bridge at Great Bridge lifted and we were under the great bridge and Here we go Here we go Here we go!

Did you call by Cicely and Felix's boat this morning with Jim? asked Monica.

The boat wasn't there, I said, they had gone. Never even said goodbye.

A new morning, a blue morning—the North American fall. Sailing alongside, a few yachts and trawlers, waving and taking pictures. They pulled ahead and we settled down to a roar and I watched the little boat on the four-inch GPS screen at my elbow creep between the electric shores and watched the real shoreline of the Elizabeth River unwind in fields and houses and jetties and woods. An osprey glided down to the water. It picked up an eel between two fingers, and flew into a tree.

After an hour a little boat came towards us and passed us

and then turned around to run alongside. In it were two African-American gentlemen. My Gard, shouted one, what an awesome–er–THING!

THE GUIDEBOOKS SAID THE GREAT DISMAL Swamp Canal was beautiful, but they were wrong. When we had visited in July we had already seen the lot. The trees are a hundred feet high, close packed and filled in with jungle, which reaches out over the water. Now in October all the foliage was dark green. There were no views, and you could barely see the sky. No flowers, no fruit, no butterflies. The canal was straight and but for a single kink you could look out the other end twenty-two miles away. The *Phyllis May* left a small wake, like the bubbles on a good cuppa.

I have come from the Trent and Mersey at Stone, I said to myself, remote and open and green and grey and curving and the locks and the clouds from old paintings shining over the hills and a pub every five miles, and I have travelled three thousand miles at great expense and come to this.

Only Jim enjoyed sailing the Great Dismal Swamp Canal, sleeping on the bow in the shade.

We saw a dragonfly. A bird uttered a hopeless cry. The swamp harbours thirty-seven different snakes–many can swim and many are poisonous, but they stayed where they were, waiting.

We moored at the visitor center. The flies had given up for the season, but no one had warned us about the gongoozlers, which attacked from all sides. I rather like gongoozlers, but these gongoozlers were the type that walk along the jetty and talk loudly as they look through the windows.

One had an English accent—Yes, it's an English canal boat, he shouted into his mobile phone—heaven knows what it is doing here.

I thought why not knock on the boat if you are that interested in what we are doing here and I'll show you round and you can tell us what you are doing here, but don't talk about us as if we were stuffed in a museum, you bastard. I was tired after our first day, and I should have been ashamed of myself.

There were four other boats at the jetty. They were Canadian, and had come down the Erie Canal from the Great Lakes—two yachts, a trawler, a catamaran. Everyone was a foreigner on the Great Dismal Swamp Canal—perhaps the Yanks had more sense and went to Albemarle Sound via the Albemarle and Chesapeake Canal.

The Canadians seemed very pleased to be shown around the *Phyllis May*, though one of them seemed to be a dick— Tomorrow there will be wind, he said—twenty-five miles an hour. If you are going down the Pasquotank to Elizabeth City then watch out. The Pasquotank is a big river, a big fetch for the waves to build up. And Pelican Marina is very exposed. Fuck you, I thought.

I think I was nervous.

Some frogs put up a faint chorus. If they had sung loud the snakes would have got them. The North Carolina night fell like a steel trap.

THE PASQUOTANK RIVER STARTED THE SAME size as the Thames or the Marne. It was heavily wooded, then the woods backed away and the river was a quarter of a mile wide and then half a mile. The water turned blue under a clear sky and the wind kicked up a chop against the current and the tiller buzzed and wriggled.

We are canal boaters, used to a few inches of water beneath our flat bottom. If we fall in we can walk to the side. We can reach out and touch the bridges and the locks and the quays, and often we hit them very hard. It all gives you a feeling of security. You don't get much feeling of security driving into the wind on a river half a mile wide, choppy blue water in front and behind for ever and no other boats for hours and no houses: just woods and jungle. It's unstable, it's nasty, it's wide and uncertain. OK you have a life jacket, but it is a skinny thing that might or might not inflate when you hit the water, and we have not put one on Jim and he is just bones and will sink. The boat with its concrete ballast and steel hull would hit the river bottom with a thud. And we are in the water and Jim gone and the boat gone and what happens then? We drift and splash around and after a couple of hours we reach the bank and we wander through the woods soaking wet and the snakes get us. Oh Lord the banks are going further away!

I had the big chart spread on the roof next to the new electronic compass which cost a fortune and which I hoped would cut out the magnetic bias from our boat. On the GPS screen there was the little ship jerking bravely down the magenta line of the Intracoastal Waterway. But the GPS was wrong—the islands were wrong and all the turnings were wrong—nothing tied in, nothing fitted. And the compass was reading 165 and then 167 and then 164 and what the hell does that mean? If it goes to 193 do we explode? Do we abandon ship on 208? A flashy compass won't help if the wind gets up and we go over. It might help the guys who drag the

Phyllis May up from the depths–Ah, 164, most interesting, explains a lot–take that back to the lab–and don't forget the watch and the dog collar.

Ah now I see what's going on! I was lost because I made an error of scale–I thought I had sailed into the broad river estuary, but I am still right back in the thin wiggly bits. The thin wiggly bits are half a mile wide.

That's better–I can match the shores to the chart, and the GPS is telling me where I am to the metre and I know which way to go round that island and look at the little boat on the screen, what fun. And the *Phyllis May* is riding well and Jim is safe inside and why not be a sailor and go to sea? Ours is an island race, shaped by millennia of adventure–Celts and dreamers, hardened with the warrior blood of the North. My grandfather looked just like a Viking, though he spent his life telling stories and never went anywhere at all except up the pub, and my other grandfather didn't get around much either. But blood will out–sooner or later the corpuscles will carry you kicking to the starting line and fire the gun, and you will know what to do and you will do it. You have no ordinary adventurer here, my man–this is Tits Magee, who circumnavigated the globe in red satin, by the light of his fearless eft Kilroy, the one with the orange belly with spots. Let's screw a few more revs out of the *Phyllis May*–come on, you old trollop, boogie!

The *Phyllis May* slopped into the waves and the river widened another order of blue magnitude and the banks began to sink under the horizon and you could see the arch of the earth. We hammered on, south, south, south, and the sun ignited the spray. Flame, and the flakes of flame.

Monica and the bridge-keeper at Elizabeth City were

squawking at each other—I could hear it on the VHF radio by my knee. I had said something into the VHF yesterday going into the lock at the start of the Great Dismal Swamp Canal, and someone heard me and squawked back. I got nervous and froze up and couldn't remember what button to press or what to say, but after a bit of practice I would soon be spicing up the airwaves with my manly repartee.

The keeper lifted the bridge and we were blown sideways into Pelican Marina by a wind from the south, a wind racing up the Pasquotank from the Albemarle Sound, which opened out before us and went on for ever.

We have reached our first new city on the route, I said to Monica—we are under way, we have begun, we are off, we have done fifty-five miles. We are haulin'– perhaps a rum?

We have over a thousand miles still to go, said Monica— and we are averaging twenty-five miles a month. We'll all be dead before we get there.

ON AN ADVENTURE MUCH OF THE TIME YOU feel rather as you would do at home, perhaps a bit happier at times, a bit more bored at others. But sometimes you are scared—jolted and empty and cold and tasting metal in your mouth. It is not a nice feeling and you don't forget it.

In the dead of night we were woken by screams and the boat pitching and bucking. I looked out of the bedroom window and there was the water right on me, rising up the hull to the window, shining and surging. My God, I thought, where is the pepper spray, where are the life jackets? Someone is being murdered and we are going down!

I tried to put things together in my mind.

The screaming was not Jim, who was hiding in his kennel, preparing for the end. Nor was it Monica. It was coming from outside—Oh heavens it's the wind generator—it's gone into the screaming mode. The bucking is the sea—we are on an outside berth and there is nothing between us and Albemarle Sound and this is some sort of squall—it must be the wind the dick was talking about. Out of the galley window the sea seemed to be in the right place. So how can the bedroom be sinking? Has the back of the boat broken? Can a squall snap a seventeen-ton steel tube? Is it metal fatigue? Poor welding?

I realized it was an optical illusion. From the galley my gaze hit the water ten feet from the hull. But in the bedroom I had to stand right up to the window and look down. The water was right on me, inches away, just through the hull, and it was surging up in the darkness—but then it was falling back to where it ought to be. I sat down but I still felt awful and so did Monica. From his kennel in the corner the backs of Jim's eyes shone green.

We have never had a mooring out at sea before, said Monica—we are not used to it.

I know, I said. We are used to flowery banks in three feet of water in a twenty-foot cut, not the edge of a bloody ocean. It's like when we were driving down the Pasquotank, when I felt I was standing by a precipice. The sea is powerful and cold and frankly, my dear, it doesn't give a damn.

The wind is dropping, said Monica, and I think I'll have that rum. Come out Jim and give mistress a cuddle.

The wind generator dropped to a howl and began to moan and fizz and the boat settled down. I looked out of the cabin window at the waves—*We are very very near, we can scare you any time we want, we can get you any time we want—any time at all.*

The marina lights polished the waves and their teeth flashed and their lips smacked as they washed by.

From now on whenever I went to sleep, I would be underwater.

NEXT MORNING AN E-MAIL ON MONICA'S laptop–

> Dear Granny and Grandad
> How are you? Are you having an exiting adventure?
> We love the picture of Granny carrying Jim through
> the floods!
> We are all fine and missing you.
> > Lots of love from Bethan

Bethan is so sweet, said Monica—but I was hoping to get across these sounds alive and do my exiting some time later. I thought perhaps we were exiting last night, and this wind doesn't look like dropping. We'll have a look around Elizabeth City today and go on that charity walk tomorrow, and meet a few people.

PLEASE SIGN IN, SAID THE YOUNG LADY IN THE Elizabeth City Information Office. Here is a map, and a booklet, and yes there is a grocery store. I am obliged to mention to you that not all grocery stores meet the standards of hygiene that other grocery stores meet.

We must not miss the Dirty Grocer, I said to Monica.

We passed along the waterfront where the dick from the

Dismal Swamp Canal was waiting in his square plastic trawler for the weather and there was a huge building with a short pagoda-like tower—the Museum of the Albemarle. Please sign in, said the lady on the desk. In the main gallery there was a plough and a traction engine and someone seemed to be building a shed.

We headed north for the Dirty Grocer.

Imagine a child has laid out a town on the floor of his playroom, but has put all the buildings in the wrong places and mixed up the kit with another one called *Build Your Own Ghetto* and one called *Small Ugly Sheds of the Late Twentieth Century* and one called *Assorted Builders' Debris* and the layout was much too big so there were not enough pieces to fill the plots.

Next to a fine church or a charming old wooden house a goalmouth of mud and in the middle a mustard cube, pebble-dashed, with rusting windows, or a rotting bungalow. An alley off one of the main streets looked like a murder had taken place there daily for some time. We picked our way along the smashed pavements.

The Dirty Grocer was a big shed with broken Coke machines outside. Like most buildings in Elizabeth City it stood in an oversize plot. There was a smell of drains. I am not leaving Jim outside this place, said Monica.

People were going in and out. I worked out my strategy for when one of them mugged me—Go on, spoil my looks, but don't take any of my money.

Or just smile and treat it as a normal transaction—Certainly my dear chap, now let me see what I have got on me—turned a bit cold don't you find?

• • •

NEXT DAY THE HUNGER WALK. SIGN IN PLEASE, said the man at the desk under the roof in the park, and here is your receipt. Where are you from? Nice of you to support our cause. The walk starts here and goes for four miles.

Dozens of people came to pet Jim and soon off we went, two hundred of us, walking for the Food Bank of the Albemarle. We were young and old, black and white, fat and thin: mostly fat. We all wore trainers except Jim, who dropped into a fluent saunter. You don't need trainers when you don't touch the ground.

Do you have a lot of hungry people? I asked the lady alongside.

Yes, and drugs, particularly in the public housing projects. Half our population is African-American. We try to keep a store of food for when it is really needed. There is nothing here, no industry. Here in the east North Carolina is poor, and then in the middle it is rich, with cities like Charlotte and Raleigh and Greensboro and then it is poor again over in the Appalachian Mountains five hundred miles away. We came here because my husband is a urologist and there were no urologists here and we like boating. Now there is a four-lane highway to Elizabeth City and new building starting up because the military can get from Norfolk in less than an hour.

What about that museum, I said—forgive my saying but it looks to me like a vanity project.

That area was one of the poorest, said the lady. A lot of state and federal money went into the museum. When we saw it going up we all thought My God, look how big it is!

We walked along the waterfront, past the brick or shingle palaces of the rich, and back to the park where the walkers were queueing for free Coke and hot dogs and crisps. I wonder why they do not miss this meal and give it to the poor, said Monica. And instead of the museum they could have bought some pavements.

From the boat we could see the museum crouched dejected across the bay—without detail or delight, its green roof nearly reaching the ground. Oversized, overpriced, and over there.

THE EASTERN COAST OF THE USA IS FLAT AND the rivers are broad. Sometimes several of the rivers come together in estuaries and sounds. The widest of the sounds will be the first we meet—Albemarle Sound, the estuary of the Pasquotank and the Perquimans and the Chowan and the Alligator Rivers. It is thirty miles wide. The Albemarle Sound had frightened me for a long time.

But strangely, though our fear was great, it was not as strong as the longing that came on us in the Pelican Marina before dawn the first morning after the wind had dropped—

> Down the long quay the slow boats glide
> While here and there a house looms white
> Against the gloom of the waterside
> And some high window throws a light
> As they sail out into the night

Monica and I watched them, the plastic sport-fishers and trawlers and sailboats as they left the quay under the museum and passed across the palaces over the river and dwindled into the earliest light on Albemarle Sound, the masts of the sailboats the last to go.

Some events open up instincts and longings—a fish on the line, a kiss, applause, a new baby, your first late cut to the boundary. Yes—this is what I am for, this is one of the reasons why I am here.

Our feelings surprised us both—this longing to sail out into the dawn, this ache to try our courage, to extend our range, to know what we did not know, to be who we were meant to be.

NEXT MORNING I LOOKED THROUGH THE GALley window past the shiny Swedish lamp that I paid too much for and love so much and the Ron Hough roses and castles plaque with the lake and the yachts and there fifty yards away was a real yacht: red hull, white sails, tall and leaning hard, the spray on the window blurring it into an old painting. The *Phyllis May* rushed into the wind, neither pitching nor rolling, foaming at the neck, most like to a swan. She loves it, said Michele, she's beautiful—we'll never get Brent off the tiller now.

No one would know it was Brent anyway—he looked just like me. He had bristly hair and a bristly beard and he even had my funny Burmese eyes. Michele was small like Monica, and neat. Maybe we could go home, I thought, and sit in the Star and make the book up and leave Captain Brent and Captain Michele to finish the journey. They would have a lot more chance of finishing it than we would, and no one would know.

Monica had put her little back-up GPS on the roof and

plugged it into her computer and there on the sideboard was the beetle *Phyllis May*, creeping the magenta line of the Atlantic Intracoastal Waterway, ten miles from shore, right in the middle of Albemarle Sound. Out of the windows on the edges of the sea a hint of darkness, but no land, just the chopping waves and the spray and the rain and the low clouds and boats falling over the horizon and rising behind.

A hundred-foot powerboat hurled up on us, slinging a six-foot curtain of tea left and right. Such insolence, such force. Brent said something into his VHF and it crackled a reply and slowed and the crew took pictures as it tiptoed by.

I stood by the door, watching the spray chucked sideways by our bow, and looked at the grey waves and sought the horizon, which was not there. We were going south—we were haulin'.

Time for my second hour on the tiller. Brent stood with me and told me about missing the crab pots and what to say into the VHF to ask a powerboat to slow down and what to do if it won't and that the crenellation on the edge of the world was the Alligator River Highway Bridge, and tucked in its armpit was the Alligator River Marina.

We went into the Alligator River. As it was four miles wide you couldn't really tell.

We had crossed Albemarle Sound.

ALLIGATOR MARINA IS A GAS STATION ON ROUTE 64, at the approach to the Alligator River Highway Bridge. There was a lighthouse and a wharf and our ropes were taken by a lady of our age with yellow hair and a stern face. Michele said this was Miss Wanda, who was well known on the Waterway and it would be wise if Brent and I went on deck to negotiate as Miss Wanda did not greatly care for ladies. Half a dozen red-faced men in camouflage stood on the quay and watched us–Hunters, said Michele, for deer, even bear.

Even boaters, I thought.

The Alligator River Highway Bridge leads to the North Carolina Outer Banks–the barrier islands that lie out to sea in a bow for two hundred miles and protect the shore from the Atlantic. Along the Outer Banks there are hundreds of wrecks, but there are few inside the Banks. We had met no ocean swell on the Albemarle Sound, just a foot-high chop, and the Banks would shield us for many miles yet.

Come along the quay and I will fill you with diesel, said Miss Wanda, and smiled.

Outside the Alligator Marina store there was a car with *SHERIFF* on the outside and a sheriff on the inside. A notice over the check-out offered smoked alligator. There were T-shirts and plastic lighthouses and plastic fish and plastic pelicans and half a dozen Formica tables and chairs. On the counter fresh coffee and a pot of boiled peanuts–*Fill the plastic cup and take to the check-out.*

I was brought up in the war and can eat anything, and I can eat boiled peanuts, but I would rather not–they were soggy and hot and wet and I couldn't get them out of the shells and they tasted of wet starch. Brent took over–when you bite them the hot water can squirt out of the shell, he explained, over your shirt. He was shucking and swallowing the boiled peanuts with one movement of the tongue. Brent has the skills to survive in the most desperate situations.

I took Jim down to the shore of the sound. The crossing

had been seven hours but after shivering for the first half an hour he had cheered up. I tried to keep him away from the edge of the water and the long grass. I knew about the alligators and the monitor lizards and the snakes and the mosquitoes and the bears and the hunters and the poison ivy but I knew there was probably something else in the grass, behind the scrub, waiting. *Beware the Jubjub bird, and shun the frumious Bandersnatch.*

Dinner in the gas station. Monica and Brent ordered a hamburger and I ordered soft-shelled crabs and Michele had crab cakes. Brent and Michele told us that to be a captain you had to study and have lots of experience and that Brent worked on the ferry to Aurora and Michele used to run a cruise business and they had sailed the Intracoastal twenty-six times and they thought the *Phyllis May* was a very fine boat considering she was never meant to go to sea; and in fact she was a very fine boat without qualification, a sweetheart, and she handled beautifully with a very fine engine that liked going flat out and they would stay with us all the way across these wide northern waters to Oriental on the Neuse River and they looked forward to it.

Like most Americans we had met, Brent and Michele did not drink alcohol with their meals, and ordered iced tea. I went to the counter and ordered a glass of Merlot for Monica and a glass of Chablis for me. Miss Wanda appeared at the table—We do Chablis and we do Blush Chablis. When you ordered the Chablis I could not help wondering to myself why you did not choose the Blush Chablis. To me you look the type of gentleman who would be drawn to the Blush Chablis. Would you like to try the Blush Chablis?

The Blush Chablis tasted like Chablis and cough syrup. I drank it, because I will drink anything. Miss Wanda reappeared—would you like some more Blush Chablis?

She leaned against my shoulder.

AWAY AT DAWN, INTO A HEAVY BLACK CHOP AND a beam sea—the one from the side that tries to turn you over. I was on the tiller.

Brent had suggested we take off the storm deck on the front of the *Phyllis May* because she had ridden so well across Albemarle Sound and he thought closing one of the two exits was not a good idea. As soon as we got a chance we should make the drain-holes—the scuppers—bigger in the front deck because they were made for rain, not waves.

The *Phyllis May* floundered and swerved and the sea flung up each side of the bow. I was scared but at least I was on the tiller and had the illusion of control.

Go under the bridge now, said Brent, and I did, and we were out on the Alligator River, straight at the wind. I could see how wide the river was and now, having crossed the Albemarle, I realized that I had suffered a failure of the imagination of some importance.

I had known there were sea crossings but in my mind, apart from the sounds here in the north, the Waterway had always been a *canal* down the side of the US—There it is, look at the maps, that little thread-like line and those little rivers and estuaries.

But in the nature of things all the rain that falls on the eastern side of the North American continent, a million square miles of deluges, runs downhill until it reaches the Atlantic. So every drop of rain that isn't steamed off flows to the ocean in an estuary or a sound *right across the path of the* Phyllis May.

We have to cross all these great waters without protection— you can't build a canal where the tides pour in from the Atlantic and the wind kicks up the tides and the tropical storms crackle and the tornadoes twist and the hurricanes rush up from the south bringing hell and destruction.

Yes, there are canals, cutting across points and isthmuses, but the rivers and estuaries are immense: huge inland seas, wide, wide, wide, out of sight of help or harbour: a prey to harsh chops and waves and currents. The Albemarle is only the start—the Intracoastal is not a canal, it is not a waterway— it is a *seaway*. America had diddled me again—just like my failed offices on Madison Avenue: just like my botched New York Marathon.

As a businessman I had not begun to understand the money and commitment you need to set up a company in the US—as an athlete I had not begun to understand that the Verrazano-Narrows Bridge was a mountain and if you don't hold plenty in reserve the wind on the Elizabeth Bridge will cut you to pieces and a gay fireman will be waiting in Central Park. And as a boater here I am in another ridiculous and dangerous situation, because of pride, because I let my fantasies take me over, because of hunger for attention, because of carelessness for my safety and the safety of my dear wife and my defenceless dog.

I did not see any canal boats in Atlantic Yacht Basin, among all the hundreds that passed through.

And do you know why you did not see any canal boats in Atlantic Yacht Basin, Terence my son? Do you know why? Would you like me to tell you why? Because there are no canal boats on the Intracoastal Waterway, Terence my son.

THE SPRAY WAS FLINGING UP EACH SIDE OF THE bow and crashing into the foredeck and pouring through the ventilation louvres in the front door and into the boat. We were going into two-foot waves, smash, smash, smash—this is new, this is nasty—we have not had these conditions before—we don't know if the boat can take it.

Monica and Michele were mopping up, and Brent covered up the louvres. Jim was shivering in his kennel, coming out now and then to do a bit of cowering. Cascades of water were coming into the front deck, and against the front window like a rainstorm from hell. Slap, spray, the air full of waterfalls. Outside the windows a maelstrom of blue waves and sunlight and foam. Would the front deck drain, or fill and sink us?

Through the window on the door I watched a spot on the front deck and no standing water appeared—how is all this water getting out through our little drain holes? *You cannae change the laws of physics, Captain.* Another few inches on the waves and the front deck will be overwhelmed and the bow will be pulled down and the front doors will give way and that will be it. I went up out of the engine room and stood on the tiller with Brent, holding on to the grab-rail very hard.

The wide part of the river ends in seven miles, said Brent, and the waves won't get any worse. They didn't and for an hour I arm-wrestled the tiller on the tea-dark sea, musing upon our wreck, which would surely happen sooner or later; it is only a matter of time—and what will they say in the *Star*?

In harmony with my mood the trees had all died on the

distant banks and stood jagged in rows, white bones in the sun. There was a fire, said Brent.

Must have been a hell of a fire, I said.

The breeze was still brisk but the waves were not moving the boat so much. Then the Alligator River stopped.

We sailed into an opening two hundred yards wide and looked ahead and could see straight down the twenty-mile Alligator-Pungo Canal all the way to the horizon, where it opened on the foam of perilous seas, in faery lands forlorn. Grey ivory lay heaped and twisted along the banks and the low trees let in the light from a huge sky. Now and then a powerboat crept by and put the pedal to the metal and fled, brewing up a typhoon of Typhoo.

Monica took the tiller and I went down inside the boat for my afternoon nap and when I awoke we were out of the canal cut and in the Pungo River, nearly as wide as the Alligator.

An hour of light breeze and crystal spray and here we are at Dowry Creek Marina, Brent and Michele's home port, in the forks of the creeks. We moored next to the trawler *Miss Maggie*, where they lived. We had been sailing for eight hours.

Jim, you are a star. You have been so good, and I know you were scared—we all were. Let's go for a walk along the river.

Monica and I walked past the holiday homes on their stilts with their lawns running down to the river. Jim ran and ran, and when he came to a grassy drain across the lawns he jumped, and to celebrate his freedom hung motionless in the air. He did not know that the Pamlico River was next, then the Neuse River, the second widest in America, and he did not know the wind drove the waves down the Neuse a hundred miles from the Outer Banks, or that this could be the most dangerous part of our journey.

TWO MOSQUITO BITES CLOSE TOGETHER MULTI-ply your misery by three, and if I slept at all it was not for long. Anyway on the backs of my eyelids the sea stretched ahead, and powerboats came from the side, and the waves waterfalled into the front deck, and the drain holes couldn't cope and in went the door.

I know what to do—as the front deck fills I'll turn on the taps so the water tank in the bow will lighten and come up. I will stand by the taps and run them at exactly the same speed as the deck is filling. *Where is the captain? Oh, he's on the taps—he won't let anyone else touch them.*

My misery ended at four o'clock as the alarm went off.

Brent and Michele were on the quay—The local weather forecasts are unreliable—we don't want to hang around for weeks—we're taking a chance—we'll go today.

We pushed off, our green and red boiled-sweet navigation lights glowing, and headed into the darkness before creation. Isolated lights far away—then the dawn came up and the darkness comprehended it not. The firmament streamed with lavender and orange, the trees on the bank stark black. The water was so smooth you could have shaved in it.

Ten miles down the Pungo River and five miles across the Pamlico River. The mirror trembled and shimmied along the boat, and then the wind was up and a light chop a foot high. The *Phyllis May* ran on rails into the morning, out of the Pamlico into Goose Creek—lovely, desolate, shining. Watch for the crab pots, said Michele, and look for the daymarks. They are on poles—red triangles on your left and green squares on your right, except when they are the other way round.

Along the narrow Bay River and out into the Neuse. And out, and out and out. I had thought to hug the shore in my little boat that only draws two feet and can sail down Stafford High Street on a wet Sunday afternoon. But no, but no, said Michele—you must follow the daymarks or you will hit a shoal and be stuck until the waves turn you over. Or you will go off up some poisonous bayou or out into the Atlantic as soon as your GPS at the tiller goes down, like it just did. And your electronic compass only works if you hold it ten feet away from the boat and just try doing that in a beam sea.

Out to sea, and out to sea: miles out to sea, stretching my confidence to a thread. As we passed a pole with the red or green daymarks you could sometimes see the next one on the horizon, and sometimes you couldn't. Good practice, said Michele, and the cormorants on the daymarks looked at me out of the corners of their eyes and spread their wings in the sun.

The wind got up and the waves hit us on the left and the boat started to bounce, but it was not taking water over the bow. Powerboats and trawlers came up behind and gave us hundreds of yards of space but their wakes rolled us and inside we bumped and staggered and Jim crouched tight inside his kennel. Shrimp boats on the horizon, their arms out like little children pretending to fly. Will the sea get up? If it does the front deck will start filling, and only the taps can save us.

The *Phyllis May* fought on through the beam sea. We could

have got Brent off the tiller, but I so hate violence. My old flat-water *Phyllis*, my darling, my love, was not happy, but not pitching and hardly rolling–just slightly off balance. Brent was hammering along at nearly six and a half miles an hour. That's fast, but we were on a fifty-mile journey today. You could feel the vibrations through your feet and when you hung on the walls.

It took an hour to reach the corner off Maw Point, three miles from the shore to avoid the shoals, and now at last we could turn on to a smoother course with the wind coming from behind and from the left.

Then an hour later the electric beetle turned again down the magenta line of the Intracoastal on the GPS screen and the *Phyllis May* had the sea dead behind her, heading for Oriental.

We were going to make it; we were going to make it! White blurs and a bridge, and a pretty port with the shrimp boats with their arms over their heads. Go for the man with the blue jumper on the quay, said Monica, holding her VHF radio.

There were two men with blue jumpers, on different quays, and even Tits Magee can't get a boat in with dignity in those circumstances.

But we would have stood no chance of getting to any quay without our gallant captains, who like Jehovah guided us through the world's tempestuous sea, for a hundred and thirty miles, and guarded us and kept us and fed us, for we have no help but thee–asking for nothing in return but a chance to drive an English narrowboat and drink iced tea with its hopeless crew. You don't forget people like that.

Mile one hundred and eighty, out of eleven hundred. We are haulin'. Now we have to cross the four miles of the Neuse River to get to Morehead City, but we might be able to manage that ourselves when we have had a break in Oriental.

Who are these people at the bridge, and why are there so many dogs?

Six

WHY AM I SO COLD?

North Carolina

Jim Goes for the Throat – A Blizzard of Flashes – One Day You'll Find Out Where She Gets It – Breakfast with Eisenhower – A Dying Man Falls into the Boat – Accept Your New Scuppers as a Sign of Welcome – The Seven Lucky Teeth – Why Am I So Cold? – Tennessee Honey – Backwards to Florida

THE POPULATION OF ORIENTAL WAS LEANING
on the rail to the marina and looking at the *Phyllis May* from
five feet away. Not the whole eight hundred—a dozen at a
time, in shifts. Cars would drive up and people would get out
and do a quarter of an hour, and then get back in their cars
and go and buy a disposable camera and come back.

Monica was hiding in the boat. If she looked out they
asked her—Did you sail her across the Atlantic? Did she go in
a container? And then She is the damn cutest boat I ever did
see and What does she draw? and What is her horsepower?
and Where are you headed?

The Tiki Bar was nearby, under a little roof, South Pacific
style. Traffic in Oriental is limited to fifteen miles an hour, explained Bob, and the dogs roam free. The mayor is a dog.

Bob was a boater, like nearly everyone else in Oriental—a
nice man with a beard.

A dog like a teddy bear passed and a dachshund bustled
by. A black retriever arrived and Jim went for the throat and
nearly pulled me off my stool. They were waiting for us when
we sailed in from the Neuse River, I said to Bob, and the dogs
were waiting too. They were lining the quay. The local

reporter was on board before the boat had stopped. Then the lady who does the town website, who looked like Sigourney Weaver, asked me When you get off your narrowboat does the world look very broad? After fifty miles of the Pamlico River and the Neuse I couldn't think of an answer to that one.

It'll be worse when the newspaper comes out, said Bob. Did you sail her across the Atlantic?

WE SLEPT MOST OF THE NEXT DAY, THE GON-goozlers nattering alongside. Some brought their lunch. A narrowboat is almost soundproof if you shut the windows tight and I was fathoms into sleep when someone hammered on the roof. I stumbled to the door and it was a pretty lady of a certain age–Will you come to dinner with us tonight?

Of course, I said.

Never seen her before in my life, I said to Monica.

When Bob came to fetch us the shrimp boats had lit their anchor lights, which shone on their masts and rigging and poles, all folded up like the wings of a dragonfly.

We rushed into the car with coats over our heads, through a blizzard of flashes.

BOB AND BETTY'S HOUSE WAS A MILE AWAY. IT was white-painted cedar, raised, in a large plot, with many windows. It was richly furnished, traditional-style but colourful, and the carpets were deep. Outside the sitting room a lawn and flowers and twenty yards away the river, turning to ink. You couldn't see the other side. I sucked on a bottle of Newcastle Brown that tasted of barbecue smoke and maple syrup. (You can always ask for a glass in America, and sometimes you get one.)

Bob had been in telecoms and Betty was an artist. They had asked Dick and Judy. To me Dick looked like Lyndon Johnson, and Judy like a beautiful spy. I wasn't far out–Dick had been a Washington lobbyist, and Judy in the CIA. I was a prostitute, said Dick–that's all lobbyists are–prostitutes. How long have you been married?

Forty-five years, I said.

My God–most of us are on our third wife and Monica looks so young!

She gets plenty of sex, I explained.

One day you'll find out where she gets it, said Bob, stealing my punchline.

Property here is much cheaper than up north, said Dick, and people who like boating come here to retire–we all know each other. The average age here is sixty-five. There is a small shrimping fleet with some Hispanic workers and the black guys live at the other end of town. We are forty-five minutes from New Bern, and three hours from Greenville. Tomorrow is ladies' night at the Tiki and the next night there are free peanuts on the bar. Then there is gentlemen's night and the next night is the marquee and a band. Saturday is the picking of the roast pig at Don's place and in the evening the rock group from Virginia Beach. On Sunday the croquet and then dinner at my place on Monday. We will come and get you for these occasions, and tomorrow we will see you at breakfast.

AT SEVEN O'CLOCK NEXT MORNING VOICES came across the road into the cabin. Some American gentlemen have a note in their voice which recalls the grinding of steel. Here it is considered a sign of masculinity, but to an effete European it sounds like someone grinding steel and For the love of God turn it down.

I got up and crossed the road to the café. Sitting on the stoop was Gabby Hayes, the bearded guy in braces from the old western films. Bob and Dick were inside at a table, with Clint Eastwood and Ernest Hemingway and Dwight Eisenhower. Sigourney Weaver was on a stool in the corner reading a book, and over there were Larry David and Johnny Cash. They were all looking at each other, like cormorants, from the corners of their eyes. Look, said Bob and Dick, we are having a great time!

One of the few useful things they taught me at Oxford was not to talk at breakfast but I chatted as best I could with my new friends and bought two cups of coffee and a Danish to go and as soon as I could go politely, I went.

THAT EVENING JIM AND I SET OUT INTO THE sunlight and walked under the big trees between the wooden houses, painted and pretty, in their open plots. There were lots of squirrels and they were tame, which is not to the advantage of a squirrel if a whippet is in town. Jim's screams echoed down the leafy avenues and more than once I was tempted to let him slip, but I was not sure what a suburban American would say about havoc on his lawn and a shredded squirrel. For all I know they feed them and give them names and put them in the airing cupboard in winter.

We came to the new marina by the big bridge over Smith Creek and there outside a restaurant was an African-

American gentleman playing upon the organ. Jim lay down on the cedar decking and I ordered a bottle of Samuel Adams and listened to 'Groovin'', and 'Ferry 'Cross the Mersey', played and sung Ray Charles style. You hear many more British songs in the US than you do in England. It is just like being at home, except you don't hear the songs at home, if I make myself clear.

A withered gentleman left his table. Is that a greyhound? he asked.

No, I said, a whippet.

The dog is being bothered by the music, said the withered gentleman. He went up to the African-American gentleman. Can you turn it down? You are bothering the dog.

The musician smiled and turned down the volume.

I have a resolution that when on the waterways I shall think the best and not take offence, and on the whole this has worked well. But I wish I had walked away from the withered gentleman, instead of carrying on talking to the little prick.

My dog died, he said. She was a boxer. She had cancer then she got it again. Cost me ten grand in chemotherapy and radiation in one year. She still died but when they took her away I could look her in the face. We are too far from the hospitals here—it is three hours to Greenville. My wife's got Parkinson's disease and so we will have to move. No one stays here very long.

When Jim and I got back into the boat it was empty but at once a large man with white hair fell into the front deck. I helped him up. Came to see your boat, he gasped. Lost my footing. Jesus what a boat—love it! I'm going to die soon. I've got cancer—it doesn't get much worse than that, does it? Come back to the Tiki Bar and drink with me.

You know Monica, I said later, there is something sinister about Oriental. Everyone has a terrible disease. There are no children. It is three hours to a big hospital—in three hours we can get from Stone to Glasgow. People move here because it is beautiful and because of the boating and because of the property prices but they are bored stiff and getting more and more ill and they are cut off from the world and their families and to ease the pain they drink all the time and smoke all the time and go to each other's parties. They are so sweet and so generous but they seem so needy I am afraid they will eat us up. One night they will be scratching at the windows, grinning, with blood on their teeth.

WE AWOKE ON SUNDAY TO THE GRINDING OF metal. At first I thought it was the breakfast crowd talking, but it was Bob Two cutting holes in the *Phyllis May*. Bob Two looked fit and had white hair and an easy manner as if he were many times a millionaire, which of course he was. He lay in the well deck in a flood of sparks.

This baby is made of the toughest steel I have ever seen, said Bob Two. I had to put the big head on the cutter. The drain hole each side is now six inches by two—she'll come up quick and be ready for the next wave. No, I will not take anything—a handshake is enough for me. Accept your new scuppers as a sign of welcome to Oriental.

Bob's hand shook slowly as he held it out, but he got the gas cylinders back in his truck before I could help him. Do you want to come back to my place and take my car? he asked. Or I'll take you anywhere—just let me know.

Dear Bob Two, I thought. No need to work the taps now.

∙ ∙ ∙

WE WENT TO THE EPISCOPALIAN CHURCH. THE service was led by the ladies who look after things when the minister has put on the whole armour of God and gone to serve with the marines.

There are few public events lower key than an Episcopalian service and this ten o'clock observance was almost invisible. The Episcopalian Church does not worship God so much as show him a certain amount of respect. During the service we were asked, as usual, to greet each other. Peace, said a fairly withered man in a brown sports jacket.

Peace, I replied.

Peace and the love of God, said the fairly withered man, which passeth all understanding. He embraced me—What sort of engine does she have?

On the way out of the church he approached me again. It has been a privilege to have you at our service, he said, to share our Sunday on this God-given morning. What's she like in a beam sea?

They are so generous and kind, said Monica at lunch, laying her teeth by her plate.

Along this coast millions of years ago there were sharks that could snatch the *Phyllis May* and break her back and pick her clean of people and dogs. In the Tiki Bar Monica had made a friend called Bev who had a fossilized shark's tooth seven inches long. Bev had given Monica five little teeth polished to jet—one to protect us each month to Florida.

∙ ∙ ∙

WHY DO I HATE ORIENTAL SO MUCH? WHY AM I
so cold? It seems unfair when everyone is so good to us. I lay
waiting for five o'clock and tried to work it out. Heaven
knows I will take a glass but I hate the relentless drinking—
being summoned to the bar at five o'clock every day—and
their relentless smoking. I hate the contrast between the hostel for the Mexican girls who process the shrimps and the
wooden palaces by the water. I hate the way the streets where
the African-American people live are left off the street map. I
hate the lack of children, the way everyone seems to be playing a role, and people hanging around waiting for the next
trip to the bar or the hospital. I hope I will never be rude to a
gongoozler, but these people have pushed me close—I found
one chap in the bedroom cabin. I hate the way they nearly all
seem to be divorced. Monica and I know what a broken
home is like—our fathers were in the war.

Rich, desperate, sick people, running away from their families and the world—My God, they are a bunch of bloody *ex-
pats*!

I do hope the good and generous citizens of Oriental will
forgive me—four o'clock in the morning is not when the mind
is most clear or the heart most full of love, and of course I was
scared. The captains had departed and to get back to the
Atlantic coast we had to cross Carteret County and to get to
Carteret County we had to cross the Neuse River and the
Neuse River was four miles wide.

Our last solo crossing in the *Phyllis May* had been the Etang
de Thau, the inland sea by the Mediterranean, where we set
out one morning two years ago and nearly didn't come back.
You can see your way round the Etang de Thau, because you

stick to the margins and head for the lighthouse, but you can't see across the Neuse—we had to rely on charts and daymarks.

The makers of charts pour out alphabet soup and photograph it, and the charts are impenetrable even on a table at home. On the top of the boat before dawn, forget it.

Daymarks are poles stuck in a river or an estuary. They have green or red squares or triangles on them. You go to the left of one and to the right of the other, or to the right of one and to the left of the other. Few boaters ever work out why, and none of them managed to explain it to me.

As you steer the *Phyllis May* you can see the beetle boat crawling along the four-inch GPS screen by your elbow, but I was still scared. This was the first crossing in America on our own, and we were leaving at dawn regardless of a poor forecast, hoping to get over the river before the wind came up. We had been here ten days and, overwhelmed by hospitality, had lost too much time.

A BANGING ON THE BOAT—HELLO, HELLO!

On the quay a white beard two feet long. The beard came out of the darkness into the boat and behind the beard a tall thin man with a stocking cap. He had two fruit-preserving jars under his arm full of something golden. I am Tennessee Ronnie, he said, and this is to help you through the winter. And here is a bag of apples.

How wonderful, Tennessee, I said, how generous. Is it honey?

In a way, said Tennessee Ronnie. It's Tennessee Brown— the best there is.

I just don't know what to say, Tennessee—you are from Tennessee?

Tennessee Ronnie's face saddened. No, he said, I was born in Arkansas, but only twenty miles from Tennessee. They are waiting for you at breakfast.

IT WAS STILL DARK BUT THE BREAKFAST CROWD was in—Ike, Sigourney, the lot—Bob and Dick of course.

Owya doon, they cried. They did not know the dark thoughts I had harboured in the night.

Bloody awful, I said, I'm terrified. Haven't slept since midnight. The Neuse is four miles wide and I've never tried to navigate by daymarks before and it's going to be windy.

No trouble, said Johnny Cash—you leave the green ones on the left—follow the magenta track on your GPS screen—I walk the line.

You're telling him wrong you old fool, said Ernest Hemingway. You leave the green ones on the right; it's an estuary. Terry, why is your dog so thin?

I picked up my coffee and muffins and went back across the road to the boat. My stomach didn't feel good and my brain was running without oil, making a grinding noise. Jim was shivering and whining. Monica was setting up the backup GPS on her computer in the galley and looked pale.

I heaved out of the hatch and stood on the back of the boat. The breakfast crowd had come across the road and stood two feet from me and watched me put on my life jacket. You try putting on one of those inflatable life jackets with straps when you are disabled with fear and there are twelve people watching you, making remarks. I put it on sideways, then upside down, then the right way and reached over and shook hands with everyone and dropped into reverse and set out backwards for Florida.

Out of the slip, slowly into the harbour basin, avoiding the shrimp boats and yachts. I might be frightened of going to sea, but I can handle a narrowboat in flat water. I turned in my own length to scattered applause and looked back to wave goodbye. On the balcony of the café a row of people was holding cards a foot square. I could see in the dawn light the numbers 9, 8, 9, 7, 9, 8, 9, 8.

I wonder which bastard gave me a seven. I bet it was that Sigourney Weaver.

Seven

SEA OF GRASS

North Carolina

The Most Wonderful Moment – Tears for Jackie – Half a Dozen Beards on Stools – The Gongoozler's Charter – Jim Began to Shudder – It's Only Us, Said the Dolphins – The Swansboro Scale – Sea of Grass – A Great Deal of Water Rushing About – You Know What You Are, Terence My Son? – With a Wag of His Tail He Was Gone – I Heard It Singing in the Wires – A Fox Jumped Her from the Garden Shed – Jim in the Zone – Rocky Mountain Spotted Fever – Nine People Were Killed – What About the Piranhas? –

Crossing the Cape Fear River – The Brits Started Drinking at Ten in the Morning – I'll Just Die if I Don't Get That Recipe – I Blasted It with a Shotgun – White as Eternity

———

MY NERVES QUIETENED AS WE CAME OUT ON TO the Neuse, and my brain began to tick over. A congregation of cormorants, largely submerged, let us pass. Do they sleep in the water? Every spin of the engine would take us nearer the safety of the other bank, but further from the safety of Oriental. I watched the beetle boat on the GPS screen at my elbow and I watched for the poles with the markers and there they were, nearer and clearer than I expected and they seemed to match the ones on the screen. Past the last one and out into the stream, the beetle pushing nearer to the middle, the southern shore four miles away, the Oriental shore still close.

It was dawn and the wind got up and the *Phyllis May* began to roll, pulling the counter from under my feet—not very nice, but there seems to be no water coming in at the bow. That was a big one—now don't lose control of yourself—keep a firm hold on the tiller and smile in case Monica looks back from the bow. How far is the daymark for the other shore? I can't see it—just the bank a long way off. You can't see the bloody things, you can't separate them from other things on the bank, and when you do you don't know which mark it is, or which side to pass it, or where to go next. But settle down, you old coward, watch the little beetle boat, he won't let you down. The engine, my pride, was clamouring and leaving a white tunnel just under the water and the wake jostled with the chop from the side. Use your weight, Terry, lock the tiller, trust your engine and trust Pete Wyatt at Canal Cruising in Stone who set it up.

We forced on and the banks and the trees came nearer and the waves lessened and we were in the mouth of a great creek. You sailed a perfect course, said Monica—I was checking on my computer screen.

I went and sat in the bow with Jim, who was still shivering. Jim had wanted to settle in Oriental. Everyone loved him and the mayor was a dog, and he could kill squirrels and the black retriever. I put his bed on the bow. He narrowed his eyes and went to sleep, and the creek closed to half a mile wide and the sun came out and the waves became ripples and the water went richest blue.

Terry! Terry! Look!

Two grey bodies, each about three hundred pounds, close together, came out of the water right by us, going at our speed, and flew with us, looking at us, and then slipped back into their own element. I could hear them slap the water, I could hear them breathe, see the muscles working, the water dripping from their skin, feel the power.

In response to this marvel of nature I should have cried out What hath God wrought! or Welcome beautiful creatures to our little adventure! But all I could think of was Bloody 'ell! Bloody 'ell! I shouted. And Bloody 'ell! again as the dolphins encored their joyful flight.

You can see them in zoos God forgive you and you can see them on the telly, or you can watch them from the deck of a cruise ship, or once in your life they will say Can we join you for a moment in your own world right here and now because it would suit us to do so?

And there they are in the sunlight, the water shining on them, your own special creatures from another world come to have a laugh, just with you. It was the most wonderful moment in ten years of boating.

THEY ALL THINK JACKIE WAS LITTLE BUT SHE wasn't, said Becky. She was nearly as tall as John—have a look at the photos. She called me her Cheffette because I cooked on her friend Maurice's boat. She was lovely.

Bob and Becky had met us in Atlantic Yacht Basin in June and now we were twenty feet in the air on top of their trawler at Seagate Marina on Adam's Creek Canal, halfway across Carteret County, mile 194 on the Intracoastal. Bob was a sturdy chap and Becky was small and blonde. They were a bit younger than us.

We were captain and crew for five years for Maurice

Tempelsman, said Becky, and Jackie was there a lot. It was after Onassis—she was very happy with Maurice.

Being a captain is not just sitting around you know, said Bob. You have to plan all the journeys and you have a budget to look after everything. You can't clean a seventy-foot Hatteras trawler in one day, believe me. Have a bit more steak.

Bob and Becky had a stainless steel barbecue that looked like a robot. I chatted with it and said *Take me to your leader* and *Exterminate*, as you do, and they thought that was funny, but they had not heard of Daleks. They gave Monica another large gin and filled their own glasses. I was not drinking much because I was still getting over Oriental.

Becky was crying. She was so sweet, she said. When she looked at me and said—Becky, help me buckle this travel case, I don't think I can do it, then I realized how ill she was. She was so beautiful.

Becky cried some more and Monica put her arms around her. Remember little John-John saluting his father's coffin? asked Bob. Grew up into a bloody idiot. Nearly killed one of his friends. Skin-diving—gave him the bends. Then he flies straight into the sea with his wife and her sister.

JFK must have been a terrible hard act to follow, I said. The Mafia killed him you know. Joe Kennedy gave them money to fix the presidential election then JFK set Bobby on them so they killed him. They may have killed Bobby too. I read a book about it.

There are plenty of books, said Bob, some better than others.

We carried on talking while Becky wept. Perhaps we were being callous, but it seemed all right at the time.

I haven't thought of Jackie for so long, said Becky. She was so beautiful.

NEXT DAY WE WERE NEAR THE OCEAN AGAIN, AT Town Creek Marina in Beaufort, just sheltered by the out-stretched fingers of the Outer Banks.

The city waterfront was big boats, gift shops, old houses. The sort of place you are supposed to visit–the sort of place that bores us stiff.

On the way back to the marina we passed the Ebb Tide Motel. The tide was going out for the Ebb Tide Motel, and looked as if it might not come in again. Opposite the motel, the Handlebar, which looked like a chicken shed. Let's go and have a look, said Monica.

I'm not going in there, I said. It's bikers–they'll rape and eat us.

Come on, said Monica. Jim pulled her across the road. The smell of beer can mean scratchings.

In the Handlebar there were half a dozen beards on stools, with thin men in overalls looking out from behind them. Their eyes gleamed. On draught was Budweiser and Foster's. Monica had a vodka and tonic. The barmaid was blonde, tat-tooed in blue and orange.

At the bar the owner, who had been to England once and liked it. She asked us why we were here and the barmaid gave Jim a biscuit. The beards watched closely, sometimes making loud comments, which we did not understand, and they would all laugh. A large gentleman bought us a round. The beards began to tell us that they were fishermen, and one of them asked me outside into the car park.

He looked like those confederate soldiers you see in old photographs—tall and thin, with a plaid shirt and desperate eyes. He took me just outside the door and stopped. He leaned close and I realized I had forgotten to bring the pepper spray.

I wondered if he was going to knife me or offer me sex but he was speaking in my ear. I was a writer, so he was reciting his poetry. He got through his two short poems smoothly and smiled. The poems were about keeping the planet clean.

Very nice, I said, and we agreed that the most important thing about a poem was the rhythm, and went back inside, where the large gentleman had bought us another round, and the beards were telling Monica about fishing and Jim was getting more biscuits.

We got back to the *Phyllis May* in time for a late dinner. The fisherman had given us twenty pounds of roasted oysters in a bag. We had not bought a drink all night. Come to breakfast tomorrow, they had said, and to the Hallowe'en party in the evening. You missed the transvestite show last night, such a pity.

When we turned up for breakfast the next morning there were half a dozen drinking beer, but our invitation had been forgotten. They all came back to the boat anyway, and the confederate soldier recited more of his poetry to Monica and me, not too much of it, without embarrassment, and the poems had a rhythm that fitted a sunny day and the gulls crying and the pelicans diving outside the window.

IT'S RUNNING OUT OF CONTROL, SAID MONICA. Last night I was lying awake for hours. We can't keep up.

There was the invitation to breakfast, and now there is the free lunch from the posh restaurant over the marina with the English owner. Then tonight there are two Hallowe'en parties—one at the Handlebar and one with the large gentleman who kept buying us drinks. It's Oriental all over again.

I never thought I would see the day when I would dread being asked out for a drink, I said. Perhaps we need a new approach—can we refuse to talk to gongoozlers, keep the curtains drawn? But poor gongoozlers—we paid a fortune to have our vessel carried to a country where they have never seen one before and we can't complain if people take an interest. All they want us to do is talk for hours and accept gifts and lifts and come to parties and meet their friends and join their families and never go home.

Can we do some sort of gongoozlers' charter? asked Monica. They all ask the same questions. Why not write a leaflet—we can stick it on the window or hand it out before they really get a hold of us.

THE *PHYLLIS MAY*–
FREQUENTLY ASKED QUESTIONS

Why are you here? A lot of people bought our book *Narrow Dog to Carcassonne* about sailing through France, so now we are writing *Narrow Dog to Indian River*, about sailing down the Atlantic Intracoastal Waterway from Virginia to Florida.

Why is your boat so thin? Locks in England are 7ft wide.

Why is your dog so thin? Whippets in England are 6in wide.

Did you sail the Atlantic? You think we are crazy?

What are the specifications of the **Phyllis May***?* 60ft long. Steel—17 tons. Draught 2ft 2in. Top speed 6.2 mph. Saloon/galley 25ft long. Headroom 6ft 4in. The flowers on the roof are connected to the main warp drive.

Is there anything that you want to know? What was Winston Churchill's middle name? What was John Lennon's middle name? Who put the bomp in the bomp-a-bomp-a-bomp? (I'd like to shake his hand.)

Is there a website? www.narrowdog.com. Photos, biographies, how to e-mail us.

Thank you for your interest. Tell your leaders we come in peace.

The next gongoozler was a Norwegian from New York. He looked puzzled when I handed him the leaflet, but walked away reading it. In five minutes he was back—What's she like in a beam sea? Do you race your dog? What do you call that sandy colour? What's your freeboard? Where do you live? Where is Stone?

I won't be long, I said to Monica. Bergen is going to show me his sport-fisher. It's fifty feet long. He caught a four-hundred-pound blue shark once. He runs seven lines out of the back. I'll be back for lunch. We can have this pound of shrimps he gave me.

That's very nice, said Monica, but I have just been online. The weather's gone wrong. There are twenty-five-knot winds for days and days—we are trapped. We'll be dead of hospitality before we get away.

• • •

I WOKE AND FRETTED IN THE SLOW WATCHES OF the night, where all is sin and shame. We had done two hundred miles, but it had taken four months, and now we are stuck again, with the gongoozlers closing in. Perhaps we are just not up to the whole thing—we can't handle the boating; we can't handle the social side. Look at this decision about leaving Beaufort—we have to go down the Bogue Sound, twenty miles long and more than two miles wide. I know so little of what we are facing, what it will be like, how suitable is the *Phyllis May*. I know she doesn't like high winds or currents, and can handle small waves if they are head-on, but that's about all I do know. I don't understand the weather forecasts and they are all wrong anyway. What is a twenty-five-mile-an-hour wind like? Are two-foot waves too much for us? We are falling behind again in our journey, but if we go I might be risking losing the boat or even our lives. Poor old Mon, poor old Jim. But we can't stay here until the gongoozlers eat us up and our nerve goes and the port-rot covers us with mould.

I decided to go.

I decided to stay.

I decided I didn't know what to do.

I decided to ring Michele and Brent.

Michele said—Stay where you are, there is a warning out for small boats, then Oh well the sound is not too bad. It's shallow and not much of a fetch for the waves and no swell. Perhaps you shouldn't go really but you will probably be all right.

Jim began to shudder.

. . .

ACROSS THE BAY WAS MOREHEAD CITY AND ON the great mirror of the city harbour it was almost dark, and it was cold, and we were alone, but a pelican passed us gliding inches over the water, and I felt he might be my good luck pelican. We had been studying the alphabet soup for days and some of the daymarks were where we expected.

The fingers of the Outer Banks had slipped from our shoulders but the great waters of the Bogue Sound lay inside barrier islands. The cold wind came from behind and fussed and cuffed and pulled a chain of glittering waves under our stern and along the boat and out ahead but the *Phyllis May* held steady—6.2 miles per hour said the little beetle screen. I held the throttle down—we were haulin'.

We were a quarter of a mile out—houses and hamlets to the west, a low green shore, sometimes a road, always wooden piers, white boats bouncing. The sun had come up on our left as it should, turning the sea, the spray, to jewels and bright crystal—and here were narrow sandbanks and islands, spoil from the channel. Beyond the banks the sound was two miles wide, and the land smoky before the ocean. The wind got up some more.

Black fins sweeping towards us—My God, we are being attacked by sharks! It's only us, it's only us, said the dolphins, and rolled their grey shoulders out of the water, and their bright eyes, and they seemed to smile. The wind was howling now but it was behind us and our sixty feet slithered across the waves without pitching. From time to time a sport-fisher or a powerboat or a trawler came from behind, always slowing and waving, and the wakes rolled us and swung us back.

I went below and comforted Jim—he wanted to come out on the deck, but I could not risk it on this vast water. And he didn't like it when the boat swung about. Peace, my little one—as soon as we arrive a nice walk and lots of new places to sniff and tonight we will bring you some chips. I know it's tough and you are a land dog and a highly tuned athlete and you hate the boat, particularly when it moves, but we love you and you are our dog and we have got a boat so tough luck.

On the spoil banks cormorants and gulls dipped and strutted. We sloshed and thundered along—Monica on the tiller, in her Australian bush hat. The *Phyllis May* was back in business.

FIVE HOURS LATER WE WOUND THROUGH A paisley pattern of islands to Swansboro. The marina gave us leaflets for local restaurants. One of the restaurants said it could quite possibly be the best restaurant in the world.

Most of the works of man have something of style about them. There is a reflection, an interpretation, however dilute, however corrupt, of a place or a time. The humblest French bar has advertising graphics, tubular furniture echoing the thirties, the curve and stain of glasses. The fake English pub, three years old, with thatch and beams and old chairs, is conscious of the traditions it parodies. But this restaurant was style-free. It would have served as a set for a modern play about despair.

The room was big, and the ceiling was low and off-yellow, faced in acoustic tiles—the plastic foam ones with holes. The lighting was dim, as if you were just coming round from a faint. The carpet was congealed blood, in swirls. The tables were Formica, in a dull grain, and they had rims of aluminium. The pictures on the walls had been salvaged from outside the Ebb Tide Motel. It was hardly November but in the corner was a fully decorated Christmas tree.

The restaurant had been there for many years and I imagine it had begun looking like a North Carolina fifties domestic dining room and then slowly slipped into the abyss.

It should be preserved for the nation, and indeed the world, as an example of a nothing, a zero marker, against which all attempts at style or design could be graded. Like the Greenwich Meridian, the Beaufort Scale, the Periodic Table, the *Oxford Dictionary*–the Swansboro Scale could slow our drift to chaos.

The nineteen-thirties Lyon Yacht Club building on the
   Rhône–97
Concorde–94
The Chrysler Building, Manhattan–92
The Albert Bridge, Chelsea–88
A Jean Muir dress–87
The *Star Trek* Feature Films–61
The London Gherkin–49
The Ford Scorpio–13
The Osmonds singing 'Crazy Horses'–6
The MI6 Building, Vauxhall–3
Cap'n Charlie's Swansboro restaurant–0

Back at the boat Jim growled and squeaked and groaned to welcome us and complain that we had left him and to extract from Monica the chips he had smelt as we came along the dock.

Outside the galley window under the boardwalk a Night

Heron stood on a cable, watching the water. Night Herons are stocky with a thick beak and I guess they can see in the dark, or they would all have starved long ago.

We have beaten the weather, said Monica—it is blowing a gale for days but we have made it to the narrow waters. We can move on.

THE GOOD LORD STARTED WTIH LIGHT, AND then he divided the earth from the waters, and then He said Let the earth bring forth grass, and in North Carolina He stopped right there, and moved on somewhere else to do all the trees and stuff, and He forgot to come back to the Intracoastal Waterway.

First the channel, waves flashing and spitting, then yellow grass for ever, standing in water, the wind stroking it, sometimes a creek running away. Seas, seas of grass. Far off, to the east, higher ground before the ocean, then a scrubbed sky and an attenuated cloud ten miles long like the sketch of the first cloud ever. Light, and more light, and blue and yellow and white and a touch of dark in the distance, and air, the first air, a wind that none has breathed.

So it must have been at the dawn of the earliest light.

To set off such purity, such restraint, the Good Lord would have introduced a pelican, floating above the waves, relaxed, but no, He would have the pelican tumbling through the air just like that one—a clownish comma in the poetry of dawn, here on the North Carolina sea of grass.

· · ·

MY TASK WAS TO BRING A NARROWBOAT INTO the quay at Swan Point Marina behind two one-hundred-ton shrimp boats moored side by side and a three-knot current behind me and a twenty-five-mile-an-hour wind against the current, and the quay just the right height to snarl my front fender. It took me three passes and I cannot pretend I knew what I was doing, having not spotted the current, but I did it, or Monica did it, by getting a line off the bow into the hands of the dockmistress, who stood astonished on the quay—My God that's the cutest thing I ever saw!

I had read that the tides on the US East Coast were a few metres and I had assumed we would not notice them. The tides around England can be forty feet, and all the estuaries on our little island empty twice a day, with a great deal of water rushing about. But I had underestimated the tides, as I had underestimated everything in the US—the rise might be modest, but the great sounds leading to the Atlantic take up and lose millions of tons of water, often through narrow channels. This was our first meeting with currents, and the *Phyllis May* does not like currents.

We strapped Jim into his life jacket and handbagged him on to the high quay. He likes it when we do that. The marina was a long way from any shops but it said in the book there was a convenience store.

In the convenience store there were ordinary crisps and crinkle crisps in light and dark: in regular, salt and vinegar, cheese, barbecue or spicy: and in small, large, medium or car-trunk size; and there was a cigarette lighter and some rope—every convenience for a chap who fancied a bag of crisps and a smoke before he hanged himself.

We will eat from a tin tonight, then, said Monica, and have a glass of Tennessee Brown. Tomorrow we pull out the big one—we have a six-and-a-half-hour run to Wrightsville. Six and a half hours is as much as we can handle—we need a quiet night and an early start.

Here, I said, these barbecue dark crinkles are not bad at all.

WHEN YOU HAVE A LONG DAY AHEAD YOU TAKE care—not too much Californian red wine with your dinner, because at the last it biteth like a serpent and stingeth like an adder. You wake in the middle of the night because you are nervous, but try to doze until six, then out with Jim for his first walk, and away at seven with the dawn. It was bright and cold and windy. Here's your tea, said Monica, for the top of the boat—you get us out of the bay.

No probs, I said. Tits Magee at your service. Nothing's gonna stop us now!

I swung the *Phyllis May* from the quay and held the throttle down and made for the first red triangle on a pole in the middle of the bay. I could see a second red daymark a mile away. The water thrashed behind me.

I left the daymark on my right and headed across the bay to the next one—we've got a long way to go, let's rock and roll! A breaker was following me on the right—how strange. A brushing skittering sound and the back counter slowed under me and at full speed I drove the *Phyllis May* aground.

Monica came up on to the bow and looked back at me along the boat with one of her expressions.

I went round the first red mark, I shouted, and I headed straight for the second one—I am innocent. It's a fault in the dredging!

What about that daymark over there? shouted Monica.

A hundred yards to my left there was a green square on a pole with a green light over it.

I had decided weeks ago to follow the red daymarks and ignore the green ones, and this had worked well until now. After all, the *Phyllis May* drew only two feet and you have to cut out some of the bullshit from this navigation business so you don't drown in the alphabet soup.

So why did someone go out in a boat and drive a fifteen-foot pole into the bed of the bay, Terence my son? Why did he nail a big green square to it? Why did he put a light on top? Why did he take a wire all across the bay under the water and wire up the light so it shone lovely and bright? So some brain-dead Brit could come along and pretend it did not exist? No—I will tell you why—he was trying to help the boaters keep to the channel, helping them keep away from that little island of marsh grass about twenty yards from your right-hand side, the one you had edited out of your deranged view of the world. Do you know what you are, Terence my son? You are a fucking idiot, Terence my son, that is what you are.

We'll be fine, I shouted, I'll back her off. I dropped the throttle into reverse and a cataract rushed down both sides of the boat. We seemed to be moving but a quarter of an hour later we were in the same place.

Monica joined me on the back counter so she could give me the expression at close range, the one that can freeze gin. I'll ring Towboat US, she said. She picked up the mike to the VHF and there was a lot of squawking and shouting of numbers—latitudes and longitudes. They are coming, she said, in thirty-five minutes—good job I took out a subscription.

I'll give it another burn, I said, I'll get her off, no trouble. I always do.

Thirty-five minutes later a white dot came into the north of the bay and became a line of foam and an orange inflatable—at the wheel a black dog.

THE INFLATABLE CAME CLOSER AND THE DOG, A German shepherd, passed the wheel to a large young man with a suntan and a baseball hat and white teeth. I thought Towboat US would send out a tug, with a smokestack, and an engine that was immensely strong, to draw us back into the channel with a steady heave and a certain amount of foam, and cheerful nautical shouts from men with Breton sailors' hats and beards—but here was a rubber dinghy, and a red-neck and a dog.

The inflatable was alongside—the dog passed a rope to the young man and he threw it to me and I tied it on. I'm going to dig you off, he shouted.

He shortened the rope to four feet and revved up his two outboards, which said on the back they were both a hundred and forty-seven horsepower. Hold the tiller, he yelled.

I did and he swung the inflatable around the stern of the *Phyllis May* and back around again, his engines bellowing, surf blowing under the boat and along the boat and over my feet. The tiller tore out of my hand. Hold the tiller, shouted the young man again, and the dog barked at me.

Two hours later we were still doing the same thing. We had

been joined by a dozen dolphins, circling round. I don't know if dolphins can laugh, but I would say these dolphins were having a great time. The dog barked at the dolphins and the young man fastened his rope on a new place on the *Phyllis May* grab-rail and revved up and the tiller tore out of my hand again. The wind was strong and I was shuddering with cold. The back counter was covered in sand, the back fenders had come up and were lying on the counter in their chains, and the *Phyllis May* lay dead in the water.

I thought, I have been in some strange situations, but never in the middle of a bay freezing to death with a redneck trying to pull my arms off and a big black dog barking and dolphins laughing at me. And this is not going to work and the young man is getting desperate and he will damage me or the *Phyllis May* or himself or the dog. I think he has already dislocated my shoulder.

All at once the *Phyllis May* heeled over.

She's floating! shouted the young man.

She's sinking! I shouted.

Monica appeared on the bow, Jim in her arms, preparing to abandon ship. Then there was a heave and a slurp and the *Phyllis May* wallowed sideways and settled.

Start the engine! shouted the young man.

I did and dropped into reverse and gave her full welly. The *Phyllis May* didn't want to move, but she crawled off the bank and came back to life. The young man made a gesture of wiping his brow—I thought you had me there, Cap'n, he said.

I thought you had me too, I replied.

The dog barked—he thought we had him as well.

The dolphins had exhausted themselves and had gone

away to tell their mates with those little squeaks dolphins make. I bet they were all squeaking like mad up and down the Atlantic coast and holding on to each other with their flippers.

The German shepherd dropped the inflatable into gear and with a wag of his tail he was gone.

I have been thinking what is the matter with you, Terry Darlington, said Monica, and I have worked it out. There is only one term to describe a person like you and do you know what it is?

Yes, I think I do, I said.

SO IT WAS LATE, GENTLE READER, WHEN WE reached Wrightsville Beach, which is the resort near to Wilmington, the largest city on the North Carolina coast– mile 283 on the Waterway.

Hundreds of cormorants were sitting on the telephone wires over the bridge. I didn't know telephones still had wires, but here they were in Wrightsville Beach, and cor- morants sitting on them, settling down for the night. There were enough wires to score for a full orchestra and if you used the birds as notes it would have been the *Sea Symphony*– I could hear it singing in the wires–

> *Of sea-captains young or old, and the*
> *mates–and of all intrepid sailors,*
> *Of the few, very choice, taciturn, whom fate*
> *can never surprise, nor death dismay . . .*
> *Suckled by thee, old husky nurse–embodying*
> *thee,*
> *Indomitable, untamed as thee.*

Just about sums us up, really.

What do you call those birds? I asked the young lady who was helping us moor.

I don't know, she said, as if it were a topic no sensible person would explore. Ravens? Blackbirds? Grackles? Spackles?

NEXT MORNING THE CORMORANTS HAD GONE fishing and Jean, the sister of Oriental Bev with the shark's teeth, showed us round Wilmington, fifteen miles up the Cape Fear River, with her husband Eddie.

Old wooden houses, classical public buildings, the sun, the river, the university campus, and outside the city long suburbs with large plots and fast food. Then we drove back to Wrightsville Beach and the coast—stilted houses and condominiums and the dunes and the crashing sea. What are condominiums? I asked.

Apartments, with lots of rules, said Eddie.

That afternoon Jean and Eddie sailed with us to Carolina Beach. We were glad of their help on the tiller as thanks to the young man in the rubber dinghy and his dog my right shoulder didn't work any more.

Jean's right leg didn't work very well either. She had gone out of her back door and a fox had jumped her from the top of the garden shed and bitten her twice, very hard. Her muscles were damaged and she had to spend a lot of time making sure she did not get rabies.

It's a savage land, I said—it was the chiggers got me.

Eddie and Jean handled the *Phyllis May* well, which is not surprising as Eddie had been a pilot in the navy and the couple had recently qualified as sea captains—We were hoping for jobs taking boats down the Intracoastal, but people say we are too old—they are looking for kids who will blast along it in ten days.

The north wind and the current joined in on our side and we were blown down the lakes and cuts at over eight miles an hour, with dunes and the Atlantic to our left, and soon we arrived at Oceana Marina, Carolina Beach.

Over the road was the ocean. The houses at Carolina Beach are on ten-foot stilts and look a bit peculiar but mock not, stranger, because from time to time a hurricane sends the ocean over the dunes and across the road, spreading hell and destruction.

RIGHT, SAID MONICA—A RUN FOR JIM. JIM SMELT the sand and pulled past the stilted houses and over the dunes to the edge of the bounding main, which bounded pretty high after days of wind.

We played the Game.

You can't play the Game just anywhere—you need plenty of space and not many people, because of the screaming. The wind carried Jim's cries past the surfers but few looked round as they spun and rolled in the high metal waves with the ridges of chalk that fell and thundered. Jim yelled and yelled and I could barely resist his strength. Monica was fifty yards away, now a hundred, and I bent and let Jim slip.

Jim hit the sand hard every ten feet. He was not bounding—he ran in horizontal flight. His ears were back and he looked straight ahead.

Like all great sprinters he did not fight for speed—he took power from the air, his blood, his muscles, his balance, his

SEA OF GRASS | 179

will: each step hurling him faster, relaxed between strides—into the zone, into the place where sportsmen sometimes go and they always say it was easy. Forty miles an hour, and for Jim today it was easy. He started to slow down as he passed Monica and stopped a hundred yards on and stood grinning and drifted back and Monica pulled his ears—my beautiful, my boy.

The surfers rose and swept and fell and the metal sea threw itself up and fell shattering and the sun was cold and the wind blew foam across the beach in sacksful.

My beautiful, my boy.

WE'VE HAD AN E-MAIL FROM MARGARET OF Atlantic Yacht Basin, said Monica—

There is one thing I meant to mention to Terry after I saw his awful bug bites. Fire ants are prevalent down south and they are dreadful. They get on your ankles, but the first one doesn't bite right away or the second one. They wait until a bunch of them get on you and then they all attack at once. Stings, itches, blisters—they are fearsome creatures and they have been known to kill small animals.

It says here in the travel guide that insects and animals get worse the further south you go, I said. And it's not just the fire ants. There are bees, hornets and yellowjackets, as well as mosquitoes, chiggers and ticks. Ticks carry Lyme disease and Rocky Mountain spotted fever. There is no cure for Lyme disease and Rocky Mountain spotted fever can be fatal. Ticks are everywhere. It says your pet is often the one who carries the tick to you.

Great, said Monica. I won't be able to let Jim have a run or stroke him.

It says the black bear can kill you, I said, and an alligator will attack anything that moves. And remember that gentleman on his jetboat on the Intracoastal in Florida and a stingray jumped out of the water and stabbed him in the heart? And what about that report in the *Daily Telegraph*?—ten people hospitalized last year after attacks by sturgeons.

> Mrs Poirier, who had her jaw wired shut for eight weeks, lost her memory and ran up medical bills of £66,000.
>
> 'It was like 1,000 razor blades hitting me at once when that fish jumped.'

You would think the fish would stay in the water where they belong. And pythons are eating all the pets in Miami and one was found last year with a half-eaten alligator in its jaws. The alligator was six feet long. It must be true—it's in *The Economist.*

What are we supposed to do? asked Monica.

The book doesn't tell you what to do, I said.

WE WERE GETTING USED TO BANGING ON THE roof—this time it was one of the young men from the marina, with a fine silver fish for our dinner. A bluefish. Watch its teeth, said the young man.

Pardon, I said, and the fish sank its teeth in my finger to the bone.

My God, I said to Monica—look at it—it's a piranha. If we fall off the boat they will strip the flesh off us in seconds and our skeletons will fall grinning to the bottom of the cut. In the book they didn't even mention the stingrays or the piranhas.

What about the foxes? asked Monica. If you don't get to a hospital in forty minutes you die mad and foaming at the mouth. They didn't mention the foxes. What about the snakes that float on the water like a moccasin and kill with a single strike? What about the burrs that Jim gets in his paws and when you pull them off they stick in you like teeth? Even the vegetation attacks you.

This book is a disgrace, I said—it doesn't mention half the things that get you. It's a whitewash job by the tourist people—you never see an American on the bank or in the woods. The countryside is full of death. The tourist people know it but they won't tell. And they never say what to do, because there is nothing you can do.

Yes there is, said Monica. We can head back north as fast as we can, and then go home.

That day there was a tornado in Wilmington. Houses on top of cars and cars in trees. Nine people were killed. There was six minutes' warning.

AT OCEANA MARINA WE LAY ON THE OUTSIDE pontoon and a dolt in a powerboat rushed by and his wake threw us up and the pontoon came up as we went down and went down as we came up and the drawers opened and the cupboards emptied and Jim ran shivering to his kennel and our mooring ropes snapped.

Over there under a great bridge Snow's Cut led to the Cape Fear River. A cabaret of pelicans glided and swooped and dove. Pelicans even *dive* slowly.

I stood on the pontoon repairing the mooring ropes and worrying about currents. Snow's Cut and the Cape Fear River were known for bad currents and poor markers, and the Cape Fear River was many miles wide and full of big ships. Brent and Michele had insisted on coming to pilot us— The currents are terrible, you will be swept away—so I knew we would be safe but when the captains had gone we still had eight hundred miles ahead and the tides are stronger the further south you go.

I tried to tighten a rope but I couldn't pull the boat in against the tide, which seemed to be going faster and faster.

I heard a hissing and I looked up and there was a band of brown in the water a hundred yards away, and it was foaming and kicking up waves. It was coming to get me. It hit the pontoon, which jumped and rejumped, and it carried on under me and poured like a waterfall over the line of rocks which made a breakwater behind us, then more water came and more, dirty and threshing and fast, and I walked along the pontoon and the current was moving quicker than I could walk. My engine would have no chance against this.

The currents worry me more than the animals and insects, I said to Monica.

That's the answer then, said Monica, to the wildlife problem. The currents will sweep us out into the Atlantic, and turn us over and drown us then the alligators won't get us or the foxes or the ticks. I don't want to be eaten by a reptile or die foaming at the mouth or covered with spots. I will end my days under the glassy cool translucent wave, with the dolphins, and a bit of dignity and romance.

What about the piranhas? I asked.

BRENT AND MICHELE MADE SURE THE CURRENT was with us, and we rushed down Snow's Cut on to the Cape Fear River, which was white silk—on its seaward rim five miles away great ships and little ships and daymarks, like scratches on your retina, mirageing in the early sun.

Brent stood on the back counter and told me again about the daymarks. These green triangles and red squares on poles are very important, because without them you lose the channel and run aground, or lose direction altogether and sail out into the Atlantic. You keep the red ones on your right and the green ones on your left except when you are going upstream or is it downstream, at which point they change. If you don't know if you are going upstream or downstream I suppose you look at the daymarks but of course that wouldn't help unless you were already sure which way round it all was. Sorry not to be more definite but I hope that helps a bit, because one day you may have to sail down the Cape Fear River, which reaches from one side of the world to the other, and as I say the currents are strong. To my delight Brent got confused about which side of the daymarks to go, but I think he got straight pretty quickly, though I wouldn't know.

Brent showed me the lines of foam where the currents met, and how when we crossed into the new flow our speed changed. The surface of the water tells you what the wind and the tides are doing, as the clouds demonstrate the currents in the sky. I imagined the deep tides shearing across each other, felt the power, remembered the sea at our windows in Pelican Marina, and felt afraid.

My God, what's that? A great ship frothing towards us out of the sun, changing shape in the slippery light like Omar Sharif on his camel. I had forgotten what it feels like when you are on a tiny vessel and a big ship is coming your way. The more scared you get the more it seems attracted by the vibrations of your terror. Even if it misses us the wake is sure to sweep us under. She's going over there, said Brent, she's military, and she passed to our left and she was not that big and hardly moving and I was glad Brent had not realized how frightened I was.

It was Monica's turn on the tiller and she sailed on a quarter of a mile from the shore, and after a while she turned across the tide into the South River, and followed it through the yellow marsh grass which stretched for ever on each side, jigsawed by creeks and patrolled by shrimp boats.

AT SOUTHPORT I SAT IN THE BOW, DRINKING A bottle of the excellent India Pale Ale our gallant captains had left—an undeserved gift. A cruise ship docked nearby. It was full, as is normal for cruise ships, of the recently dead and those soon to cross over the river—not the Cape Fear River, but the one that is muddy and cold and chills the body and not the soul. They came down their gangplank, carrying those who had crossed over since their last docking, or wheeling them in chairs to their final rest, and wandered into Southport. Mercifully they did not notice the *Phyllis May*, being occupied with the next step they had to take, which would so very likely be their last.

The captain of the ship walked along the quay. He was an American, a big chap. I am John, he said, I like your boat. He shook my hand. We are two hundred feet long, he said, and forty feet wide, but there is plenty of room for us on the Intracoastal. About three years ago I had forty narrowboaters from England on board together with a dozen Yanks. It was a cruise on the US canals organized by one of your British waterways magazines. The Brits all started drinking at ten o'clock in the morning and then gathered speed during the day. They were a grand lot–the Yanks were horrified.

DON CAME ALONG THE PONTOON WITH A BOT-tle of wine–I'll pick you up tomorrow morning.

Don was a mild and friendly man, slightly built, who had been on the boat alongside when we arrived at Portsmouth in June. His home was here in Southport, three hundred miles down the track. He was our age and had been a pilot in the navy.

Tomorrow morning was Sunday and he took us to the Episcopal church, with his new wife, Pat. He introduced us to Rhiannon. These are writers, he said.

Rhiannon was middle-aged, a bit of a looker, tall, well-dressed, a touch arty. Her eyes were grey.

How interesting, she said–and you folks are from England.

Her voice was soft and flat. Yes, I said.

How interesting–and you write books. What sort of books?

We told her.

How interesting—where are you going next?

We told her.

How interesting—where are you going after that?

We told her. Her eyes seemed to glow. She turned and there was a whirring and her eyes followed her head round later than they should. I thought I could smell smoke. Her shoulder jerked and she walked away—I'll just *die* if I don't get that recipe, she was saying—I'll just *die* if I don't get that recipe.

She's a robot, explained Monica. You can tell by their eyes, and everything they say follows logically from something else, or if a fuse goes they talk absolute nonsense. Real people talk a sort of half-nonsense all the time—the robot people haven't worked out yet how to copy it.

The minister came up. He was one of those cheerful little guys who get fat but you know he is still a ball of muscle. He had been in the special forces in Vietnam. He shook my hand and I was afraid he was going to throw me over his shoulder. We didn't talk for long but I liked him a lot. The US has little to fear if it can keep the Episcopal ministry on side. During the service he asked any veterans in the audience to stand and a quarter of the congregation stood.

After the service a tall thin woman—You are on a boat?

Yes, I said, passing through you know.

Oh well done, said the tall thin woman. She was wearing a twinset and pearls and her tall thin husband had white hair and a tweed suit. They were both quite old.

Where have you come from on your boat? she asked.

Portsmouth, Virginia, I said—you are English?

Goodness yes—English, oh yes indeed.

They explained they had lived in the US since the fifties, the husband working for a British conglomerate. They sounded like the Queen and the Duke of Edinburgh.

Where do you live in England? asked the lady.

We told her. Oh well done—do you know the Lichesters of Lichfield?

No, sorry, I said.

Do you know the Barchesters of Barlaston?

Sorry, said Monica, but have our card, with the website on it about the book.

Oh well done, a card. A card—well done.

They went away.

That couple are professional English persons, I said to Monica—they have an act you could take on the road.

They have been on the road for fifty years, said Monica.

AFTER CHURCH DON BOUGHT US A FINE SEA-food lunch looking over the Waterway and lest we shame him by dying of hunger on his territory before nightfall he followed up with dinner at home.

Don and Pat lived in St James Plantation, which is a gated community. It took ten minutes to drive from the marina to the community gate and ten minutes to drive from the community gate to Don's house. St James Plantation has three golf courses and a marina, and soon will have a bigger population than Southport. Don explained that the Carolinas are attracting a lot of people from the North because of the climate and the price of property, and gated communities are popular and the properties sell fast.

Their house was open plan—lots of wood, lots of space. Jim

roamed around the polished floors and rugs and found land-
fall in a corner. That photo is me, said Don, and the alligator
is six feet long. I blasted it with a shotgun and it didn't die so
I shot it in the eye with my revolver.

Don gestured that we should hold hands round the table
and he said grace, and included a prayer for our journey. A
good dinner, good wine. What do you think about the place
of the African-American people round here? I asked.

Different races are made different and have different ways,
said Don. There are a lot of black single mothers. Most of our
crime is done by black people—most people in jail are black,
and it costs a lot to keep them there. You British used to hang
people in public in your colonies until quite recently. We
should bring back public hanging right away.

You know that's not going to happen, said Pat.

SIX HOURS' BOATING FROM SOUTHPORT—PLAIN
sailing on a sunny morning. The canal was fifty yards wide
and in the sky Don and Pat on the high bridge waving—they
had come to check we had not starved in the night.

Today we would sail out of North Carolina, but the great
sounds, the captains, the seas of grass, the dolphins, the
beards on stools, the German shepherd, the kindness of
strangers, would stay in our memory, in colour with stereo-
phonic sound.

And what did you make of North Carolina, Terence my son?
Towards what conclusions did your self-obsessed and drink-sodden
brain struggle, what glint of understanding dawned of this great state
the size of England of which you have seen but a skimming, but the
rind?

I can offer this—one Sunday we left built-up and military Virginia and drove south. As we crossed the border we came on roadside sheds and shops and markets that seemed to say Look you are in North Carolina it is different here, a bit looser, more of a holiday place. In North Carolina there are waterside palaces with quays and fifty-foot boats and there are trailer parks with dinghies. There are forests and sky, seas of grass, the shining ocean—and talking of the shining ocean here we are sailing across the blue estuary of a river, tiny by North Carolina standards, but wider than the Thames at Greenwich, and the air is cool and the ospreys wheeling and the gulls like risen souls and on our left the Atlantic, which has calmed and blazes white as eternity.

The tide pulled under me but I held between the sandbanks and pressed towards the cut on the other side of the estuary and the electric beetle at my elbow crossed the red line into South Carolina, and we crossed with it.

Brent and Michele had warned us that Barefoot Landing was a funny, vulgar place.

Yo ho ho for Barefoot Landing.

Eight

IT'S CALLED
BEING FRIENDLY

South Carolina

*Santa Claus Is Coming to Town – The New Work of
Giants – The Lowcountry – We Don't Care How You Do
Things Up North – Message in a Bottle – Verdurous Glooms
and Winding Mossy Ways – Three Generations at
Thanksgiving – Bum on the Road and Wind in the Hair*

BAREFOOT LANDING IS T-SHIRT SHOPS, OUTLET
shops and restaurants. I like outlet shops though I don't seem
to have any luck with them. Once I became the only man in
the civilized world with a flesh-coloured T-shirt that reached
down to his knees. Then there was the business shirt made
out of deck-chair material.

Not far from us in Stone there is an outlet village off the
motorway, but I can never find the way in. An outlet with no
inlet. But say, are you listening—it's November, and Santa
Claus is coming to town!

He came thirty feet up and twelve o'clock high, with
Dancer and Prancer and Donner and Blitzen and Rudolph,
bobbing and jingling. The sleigh did a half-circle and landed
ten feet away. Ho ho ho, said Santa. A dozen pretty women
fell on him and they all danced, including Dancer and
Prancer and Donner and Blitzen and Rudolph.

We were in the Alabama Theatre, Barefoot Landing,
watching the best show we had seen since the Lyceum,
Crewe, thirty years ago, and you should have seen the girl
who played Robin Hood in that one.

The audience had trooped in busload by busload, holding

on to each other. They became a field of cotton, a thousand white heads row on row. The comedian appeared as a sly slow-talking southern lad and Monica and I thought he was exaggerating, though he wasn't. He mocked the old folk for their Toyota Camrys and how they would stop before turning off a main road. He mocked them for their windcheaters. The old folk laughed and laughed—they enjoyed the attention.

The Christmas Show was two and a half hours and we did not want it to end. Dancing and music, some of it to do with Christmas. One of the dancers was just like Jim the way he jumped and hung there, with his long face and stricken eyes.

The country music, the soul, the bluegrass fiddle—well-fed people with jobs entertaining well-fed people with pensions—but like the songs of Wales the music drew its power from old hunger, and looked to a better land over the river.

BAREFOOT LANDING IS AT THE NORTH END OF Myrtle Beach, which is an Atlantic leisure city—a linear city with forty miles of beaches—the Grand Strand—and fourteen million visitors a year. The south end of Myrtle Beach was dim gift shops and a rotting funfair and dying clubs: lovely and tacky and flapping in the wind and shut. The north end was exploding—hotels, hotels, hotels, golf courses, fifteen hundred restaurants, and on the waterfront concrete, concrete, scaffolding, steel, piles of gravel, trucks, cranes.

We decided not to interrupt Myrtle Beach in its fury, and left wishing we had come ten years ago. The Atlantic thundered on and the waves had not been developed and the sand was still free to all, and sometimes to dogs, and the Atlantic will be there when this new work of giants lies desolate.

• • •

BUCKSPORT LANDING ON THE WACCAMA RIVER is famous for its sausages. The trees were white and bare and the Waccama was black because it was made of tea so it all looked like the set for *The Creature from the Black Lagoon*, which like the Waccama River was in black and white and three dimensions.

Five Good Ole Boys came along the quay. In fact they were Young Ole Boys: camouflage and denim, hatted and fat. One of them was African-American. We had turned up in their lunch break. They wanted to know about the *Phyllis May* and we told them. She's a real neat boat, said the Young Ole Boys, and Is that a greyhound?

Why are all the trees dead? I asked.

They ain't dead sir—they're cypresses—at the first frost they go brown and the leaves fall off—here is one of the leaves, see, like a feather. In the spring they pretty up again.

Why do they call this the Lowcountry? I asked.

Because it's low, they explained.

Jim's thighs bunched up and his ears grew to their full height and turned like radio telescopes. A whippet is one of those animals with focusing ears. He rose on his back legs ready to leap the twenty feet off the boardwalk and into the marina garden to seize the marina cat, whose existence was an unendurable insult. He screamed and screamed—he is six years old now, and at the peak of his strength, but he has always been a good screamer. Stop it, Jim stop it, said Monica—poor cat.

Let him go, ma'am, one of the Young Ole Boys suggested.

Goodness, no, said Monica—he'll kill the poor cat, or the cat will scratch him and scar him for life.

Jim screamed some more and nearly pulled her off the boardwalk.

Let him go, ma'am, said another of the Young Ole Boys—round here it's permitted.

DON HAS COME THROUGH ON THE E-MAIL WITH some tips about the Deep South, said Monica, so we know what we are getting into.

That farm boy at the gas station did more work before breakfast than you do all day at the gym.

We all started hunting and fishing when we were seven years old. Yeah, we saw Bambi. We got over it.

We don't do hurry up well.

No, there's no Vegetarian Special on the menu. You can order the Chef's Salad and pick off the two pounds of ham and turkey.

Tea—yeah, we have tea. It comes in a glass over ice and is really, really sweet. You want it hot—sit in the sun. You want it unsweetened—add a lot of water.

We eat dinner with our families. We pray together before we eat (yeah, even breakfast). We go to church on Wednesdays and Sundays and we go to High School football games on Friday nights. We still address our seniors with Yes, sir, and Yes, ma'am, and we some-times still take Sunday drives around town to see friends and neighbours.

So every person in every pick-up waves? Yeah, it's called being friendly—understand the concept?

No, we don't care how you do things up north.

Bucksport Landing was a wharf with a chandlery and a restaurant, looking over the black Waccama. The famous sausage was full of herbs and very good.

Leila and her mother came to join us at our table. Leila was two and blonde. Monica and I cuddled Leila and missed our grandchildren. Are you part of the marina family? Monica asked Leila's mother.

Yes, in a way—the boss is my stepfather. I am divorced.

My God, I thought, divorced with a daughter of two.

The boss was a thin chap of a certain age who seemed to do everything that was done round here. He came over and took off his apron and told us about the chap who went out fishing on the Waccama with his dog. A light plane came over. A bottle dropped from the plane, and in it there was a message—*Your dog has fallen off the boat*. The plane led him back and circled round until they found the dog.

Then there was the chap who advertised for a female companion to go to Florida on his yacht and no one replied. He put in another advertisement saying he was leaving at nine o'clock on Tuesday, so there. Eight ladies turned up and he took them all on board. Two left the boat at the next stop and others dropped off along the way and when he arrived at Florida there were only two ladies left, who decided they fancied each other and went off together.

WE STAYED A COUPLE OF DAYS IN GEORGETOWN alongside the main street with its coloured houses and shops and left in the arms of high tide and banged down Winyah Bay with the wind against the tide and after an hour we turned into a cut and it was sunshine and trees and eagles and the wind at our backs and we turned right and here we are at McClellanville.

We moored to a rotting quay and watched the shrimp boats coming in. Each boat had attendant pelicans sailing behind an inch off the water or sitting on the back talking to the sailors. One pelican was smoking a pipe. What does the cry of the pelican sound like? asked Monica.

It's not so much a cry, I said, it's more of a low laugh.

To reach the quay we had to climb up ladders so greasy that we put old T-shirts on the rungs. We hoisted Jim up in his life jacket and went for a walk, Jim pulling and sniffing and pursuing his mission of pissing on the whole of South Carolina.

McClellanville was founded in the middle of the eighteenth century. In 1989 Hurricane Hugo arrived and they found the shrimp boats three miles inland. But McClellanville is still here—wooden houses, dirt roads, trees trees trees—twisted and bloated and corky and branches veiled in Spanish moss, branches growing out and down as if to grasp you off the pavement and carry you into the sky. A plaque says one of the trees is a thousand years old. In McClellanville the mayor is a tree.

The dull evening light did not reach the ground. We stumbled through verdurous glooms and winding mossy ways. Monica told me about a plaque in the church in Georgetown, from the Civil War, for an officer of twenty-eight. *His afflicted mother mourns the loss of her only son but resigns herself to the will of God.*

In the South the memories hang from the trees like moss, like photos of the dead.

An old wooden chapel lit from inside like a lantern. A lady

on her knees fixing flowers to the pews for a wedding. Where y'all from? she asked, and we told her.

If you want a lift anywhere, she said, y'all just come and ask me—I'll go to the supermarket or anywhere you want. Y'all just come and ask me.

They are so generous, said Monica—it's been the same all the way—piloting us across the dangerous bits, airplane flights, dinners and lunches and parties and barbecues, buckets of shellfish, bottles of wine, trips in cars, work on the boat, moonshine, T-shirts, pork scratchings, drinks without number, friendship, advice—and they never want anything back.

Mon, I said, it's just what that French chap de Tocqueville said—*As long as you are staying with a Southerner, you are made welcome, and he shares all the pleasures of his house with you.*

Good old de Tocqueville, said Monica, got it dead right—when did he say that?

Eighteen thirty-one, I said.

IN THE SOUTH YOU CALL YOUR ELDEST BROTHER Bubba. We had met Bubba at Atlantic Yacht Basin. He was a fit chap in his fifties and his wife, Jeanie, was younger and small and pretty. Jim leaped into Bubba's four-wheel drive with a single bound.

Bubba drove us for an hour into Charleston. He owned a company that put up signs, and he pointed out his white and blue signs, proud against the winter trees along the highway.

Three generations at Thanksgiving—twenty seats at the table. We linked hands and Bubba's brother-in-law gave thanks and prayed for his family and for peace and for a safe journey south for his visitors. I thought What have we done that people are so kind—we brought a boat and a dog to America—was it that big a deal?

A buffet—turkey, ham, stuffing, cranberry fool, sweet potato in a meringue pie, asparagus, carrots, crème brûlée, lemon pie, marshmallows—the lot. Iced tea. Beer and wine but only Monica and I seemed to drink it.

Jim lay next to Bubba on the sofa. Jim was so pleased to be asked. In America he was left behind too much—not like France, where he could go anywhere.

One of the family was a sixteen-year-old girl. It is now widely accepted that Edgar Allan Poe died of rabies, she said.

I suppose he went out of doors and the chiggers brought him down and a fox got him, I said.

Bubba's brother Robert was an optometrist. He enjoyed the mid-century American masters—Fitzgerald, Steinbeck, Hemingway. Like others I had met, he had not heard of Raymond Chandler. I asked him about his favourite American poem and he explained people didn't read much poetry in the US.

Bubba's mother told us it had snowed on Tuesday and it never snowed in Charleston and if it did it never snowed in November and she had not seen anything like it and she was eighty-four. I did not tell her what Monica and I do to the weather.

Bubba's nephew, who was nine, told us about the Civil War—a quarter of a million soldiers killed, he said, and that was just on our side.

With twenty people from the same family I expected argument, conflict, threats, perhaps violence, but this was an undefiled Thanksgiving—expected, pure, loving.

It was a Norman Rockwell painting. That's me in the corner, the big chap holding a beer, and there is Monica on the sofa showing our photo album and everyone is looking really interested and Jim is snuggled up to Bubba but the painting is not about us; it is about celebration, and freedom from want. It is about family, about America, about happiness.

And suddenly they were all gone—in England everyone would have been drunk by now and would have stayed half the night arguing, but the Americans don't do things that way. They vanish, sober, into aery nothing.

IN FEBRUARY I HAD LOOKED DOWN AT CHARLES-ton Bay from thirty-five thousand feet and today with a bit of luck we would arrive at that bay and cross it at sea level and sail up to Charleston, on the point where the Ashley River meets the Cooper River. We were going to stay a couple of weeks—Charleston is Mile 475 on the Intracoastal—we had been haulin'. McClellanville to Charleston is forty miles, and Bubba came to help us drive the boat.

Monica and I always spend an hour on the tiller and an hour off, so we don't have to hold a board meeting every time we change over. I decided Bubba would have the first hour and went up on the back and showed him how to drive.

First you start your engine by turning a key deep inside the engine room, and you climb out on to the back counter. Then you pull a little flap thing which is a sort of a safety catch—now when you drop into gear the engine will be connected to the propeller, which is very important because (*all together now*)—

The engine bone's connected to the Gear bone
The gear bone's connected to the Shaft bone
The shaft bone's connected to the Prop bone
Oh hear the word of the Lord!

There is a handle just here at your left hand called a Morse handle, but that is to confuse the Germans—it has nothing to do with Morse code. You push the Morse handle down and the gears engage and the propeller goes round and round and you move forward. The more you push the handle down the faster the propeller goes and the more noise you make. Pull the Morse handle back—here is the clever bit—and the gears disengage and the propeller stops and keep pulling it back and back and the gears click in again and the prop goes round and round the other way and you go backwards, though not in any particular direction.

The tiller is more tricky. It's too late to do anything about the front of the boat, which has already arrived, but you can have some effect on the back of the boat by pushing the tiller in the direction you want the back to go. The boat swings on its centre point and keeps on swinging until you find your new direction or hit something. Of course the propeller is not helping—always walking the back of the boat to the left in forward and to the right in reverse.

That prop, that prop's gonna
Walk you round
That prop, that prop . . .

(*Look, that's enough, Terence my son.*) Just a quick point finally—if you get near the shallows the banks drag your stern in and you need the strength of a man possessed to get back into the channel but we don't want to upset ourselves with all that.

A blue day, a new day, the cut fifty yards wide, small waves chasing us, yellow marsh grass to the sky. Sometimes houses and jetties, all fully stilted. Now and then a boat coming from behind: always slowing, always waving—Bubba in full cry with the Morse on the metal and the engine roaring and the boat shaking and the tide behind us and the beetle scampering along the little screen at eight miles an hour.

I gave up trying to enforce our steering regime—like Brent, Bubba is not an easy man to get off the tiller. These chaps are used to the four-storeyed plastic boats they call trawlers—to them driving a narrowboat is a Frog-eye Sprite instead of a Ford pick-up—bum on the road, wind in the hair, a girl and a pint waiting at the end of the afternoon, and you are eighteen again.

What do you call those birds, Bubba? I asked.

On the Intracoastal there is hardly a post without a bird drying his wings, hardly a rail without a row of diving fowl having a chat, never a stretch of water without a half-submersible looking at you—Oh, he's up-ended, never to be seen again.

I don't know, said Bubba. Maybe loons.

Out into Charleston Bay, out and out—Where are the daymarks? I asked.

Forget it, said Bubba—I live here, let's rock and roll!

Straight across the bay, against the tide. Something was going on under the water, which was pooling and swirling and then the fins, the black fins cutting the waves towards us, and turning and coming in again, and the grey bodies flexing and rolling—two, three pairs. The dolphins are happy and they make you feel good too.

Charleston on the skyline—Charleston where the American Civil War began. Just behind us a small island—Fort Sumter. The fort was flying the Union flag and the rebels began to bombard it. After a day and a night Major Anderson surrendered to save his men. The Civil War didn't continue in a spirit of mercy and good sense, alas.

Coming at us all the way from Charleston the line of foam where the rivers meet—thump—Look how she has suddenly slowed in the current from the Ashley—look how the water is brown not blue!

Charleston was just there on White Point but it took forty minutes to get there, and another twenty to push up the Ashley River to the left of the point and arrive at the James Island Connector, which is the bridge that connects the James Island bone to the Charleston bone. Bubba handed me the tiller to take the *Phyllis May* under the flyovers and into our mooring because I am the steering man, the righteous one, the one who never fails.

There were three flyovers and so many arches and I chose the wrong arch and there was no room and as I turned the current was like a wall and Oh my God here we go I've lost it we will be smashed against the pillars but I got in somehow and you won't tell anyone will you?

Nine

EVEN IN ARCADIA

South Carolina

Jim Hit Him Before He Reached the Ground – The Beautiful Hunley Most Like to a Fish – It Effulged with Chrome – Don't Forget the Diver – Old and Mad and Busy and Joyful – A Satisfying and Well-Balanced Meal – They Never Found the Gorilla – The Mine Dropped Off and Started to Tick – Even in Arcadia – We're Not Going to Die – The Marina of the Damned – Ready to Run Across the Room and Dive out of the Window

I ALWAYS LIKE TO CARRY A LOT OF MONEY WITH me when I set out into the world and Monica, without my ever catching her at it, does her best to reduce the amount I can lay my hands on. This evening I managed to liberate twenty bucks and set out into Charleston for a pint with Jim. Bubba had gone—no use asking him out for a pint because he drinks nothing but iced tea, disgracefully sweet. Anyway they don't have pints over here and they don't have pubs and there are not many bars and they are dark and full of drunks and don't allow dogs. A hopeless mission—an old chap and his whippet driven by memories of how they did it at home a long time ago, a long way away, and the beer is no good so why bother.

Under the vaulting flyovers and across car parks and there was a door in the wall and behold a bar. I went straight in with Jim—they can always throw us out. The bar was dark and squalid and everyone was drunk, though it was but six o'clock—the other side of American temperance. There was no draught beer. I asked for a Samuel Adams and got the usual reply—Sorry sir I was sure we had one somewhere but we don't—and I settled for a Red Stripe, which comes from

Jamaica and is rather like beer. No one seemed to have noticed Jim.

You are English! said the lady in a black business suit on my right. We went there last year, didn't we, Ethel, we went to the Lemon Minister, and Wark. You know Wark? And the Swolds, with all the fields and the cows and the walls—we liked the Swolds. We quite liked Wark, but we liked the Swolds more. Didn't think much of the Lemon Minister.

Is there somewhere I can get a pizza? I asked the barman. Can you order one in?

Yes, sir, said the barman and picked up the phone. An hour, he said, it's Saturday.

Oh dear, I said.

Next to me was a tall man with raggy blond hair, about thirty. Follow me, he said. You can't take that bottle outside so here is a paper cup. Come on, they'll put the beer on my tab.

In the car park there was a black pick-up. Jim and I got in—the cab was full of lead pipe and spanners and I had to sort of put Jim in my pocket. I'm Ed, said the tall man with raggy hair.

I'm Terry, I said, like Teri Hatcher, who used to be Lois Lane in *Superman*, but I'm straight.

Ed drove me to the centre of Charleston and left me outside a crack den. I have a call to make, he said—I'll be back. It's been a privilege to meet you.

The crack den was derelict, shattered, with a pile of pizza boxes on the counter and foxed posters of Marilyn and Marlon and Elvis. There were wrecked tables and chairs. I ordered a pizza and bought a beer, which turned out to be a sort of draught lager, and sat down. Jim lay down on the patched concrete floor. Jim doesn't lie down on concrete floors but he lay down right in the middle of this one and people walking round him stopped and petted him and he closed his eyes.

I began to realize what was going on—Jim had got the joke before me.

I didn't need to go to the restroom but I went because I had a theory and needed to check it out and there was sparkling porcelain and towels. All the filth and decay was deliberate—this was a sophisticated pizza restaurant and bar in the middle of downtown Charleston and I loved it.

Ed returned. Let's go—your dog must meet Hunley.

Hunley was an uncropped poodle rather bigger than Jim. He looked like a black retriever. He came out of the car like a rat from a drainpipe and Jim hit him before he reached the ground. The noise was terrible. It is very hard to separate two dogs fighting even when they are on leads but Ed and I managed it. When we pulled the furious creatures apart, to our surprise both were alive and unhurt. Ed put Hunley in the front seat on a short leash and I did the same in the back with Jim, where we sat on a heap of electric plugs and wires and Jim and Hunley growled in close harmony as we drove.

I call him Hunley, said Ed. I bought him because a poodle is a good boat dog and they are supposed to love water. He wouldn't go near the water so I chucked him in and he sank. That's why I call him Hunley—after the submarine.

IN EARLY 1864 THE UNION WAS STILL BLOCKAD-ing the coast and the war was going badly for the southern states.

As night fell on 17 February a terrible machine came out of Charleston Harbour. On the 1,200-ton *Housatonic* Lieutenant Higginson was called from his cabin–

> I went on deck immediately, found the Officer of the Deck on the bridge, and asked him the cause of the alarm. He pointed about the starboard beam on the water and said 'There it is.' I then saw something resembling a plank moving towards the ship at a rate of three or four knots; it came close alongside, a little forward of the mizzen mast on the starboard side. It then stopped, and appeared to move off slowly . . . it was entirely awash with water, and there was a glimmer of light through the top of it, as through a dead light.

It was the submarine *H. L. Hunley*, named after its inventor, who had drowned during its trials. The *Hunley* stuck a harpoon into the wooden side of the *Housatonic*. The harpoon was attached to a mine and as the *Hunley* backed away the mine blew off the starboard stern of the warship and sank it and killed five sailors.

The *Hunley* and its eight-man crew never returned to base.

In 1997 the submarine was recovered from the sea outside Charleston harbour. The salvage crew had expected a machine stuck together from old boilers, but the *Hunley* was beautiful, most like to a fish. She was made from three-eighths of an inch steel, and she was forty feet long, four feet wide and four feet high. She was powered by cranks operated by hand and there was no evidence that fresh air could get in when she was underwater.

I thought of the Italian human torpedoes in the Second

World War, and the British who came on the *Tirpitz* from beneath.

Death should be proud to take such men as these.

ROBERT THE OPTOMETRIST, WHO LIKED THE American prose masters, had called with one of his motor cars. Jim was in the back seat and Monica was next to him, and I was on the front seat with Robert among the levers and the silver.

It was a 1951 Buick Roadmaster—the one with the mouth-organ smile, and fake supercharger vents down the side. It was not in a fifties colour—nothing so vulgar—it was thirties apple green, two-toned. The '59 pink Cadillac Eldorado is the very Marilyn of motors, but for style give me a '51 Roadmaster—ninety-three on the Swansboro Scale—no, make that ninety-five. This is the very Marlon—it bulges with muscle and it effulges with chrome. It has white-walled tyres and windows that sink sideways, leaving you in an unglazed summerhouse. It gives you the fifties message before Elvis, before James Dean—*Look we won the war and the thirties depression has not come back—in fact I have plenty of money, though you personally may have very little, and I have a car that might not be very graceful but it is solid and helps keep things the way they are and as far as I am concerned they can stay that way for a very long time.*

Of course things were not that way for long, and we must all thank God they were not, but Robert's '51 Buick is still that way—spotless proof that if you want to make something beautiful it helps to have taste, it helps to have sensitivity, but you should above all have confidence, know where you are heading, be sure you are right.

We drove to the Battery Park and Robert, who was born in Charleston, found a parking space and took Jim for a scream. There are a lot of trees in Battery Park, and a lot of squirrels. Back to the car, with Jim exhausted—and there was an African-American gentleman of a certain age having his photo taken against the car. The black guys love it, said Robert.

We agreed that there is only one thing worse than gongoozlers, and that is having no one take any notice of you.

Robert plucked the fruit of fifty years' living in Charleston by finding a second parking space and we marvelled at the eighteenth-century coloured wooden houses, narrow-fronted, balconied: and the public buildings with their pillars, and we strolled under the trees. It was a South Carolina November day, like the best English July day you ever remember. Robert told us that in 1951 even a Buick Roadmaster did not have air-conditioning and Goodness it can get hot in the summer.

We walked down the long tourist markets full of grass baskets, cypress bowls and semi-precious jewellery, and I bought a T-shirt with *Frankly My Dear I Don't Give a Damn* on it and nearly bought a three-foot-high copper frog but Monica stopped me.

More African-American people—Man, that is the best car! I love the car!

How do the races get on in Charleston? I asked Robert—up in Virginia there are a lot of mixed-race couples in the malls and a lot of African-American soldiers but people don't seem to mix so much round here.

Now that's not an easy topic, said Robert—I'd rather write to you about that one. And he did—

Overall, blacks and whites in Charleston get on very well. When problems do arise, it is often not so much related to skin colour as it is to cultural differences. These differences, oftentimes associated with family, political and work values, can add to the division. Many folks in the US have become resentful of anyone, black or white, that places an undue economic burden on government indigent programs that cause the politicians to raise taxes.

Next day I asked an English expatriate—What is the proportion of African-American people in South Carolina?

About 30 per cent. There are no problems—people have had hundreds of years to get used to each other.

Do the races mix?

No, they lead separate lives.

ALL NIGHT LONG THE WIND WAS HOWLING AND half hid under the concrete flyover the *Phyllis May* swayed and the rigging on the yachts rang like bells. A dull morning and low clouds rushing over and rain. It was one of those days that are hot and cold at the same time—windy and sweaty. When we went out of the boat it rained and when we stayed in it stopped and we stayed in and got depressed.

Our rubber visitor spent the morning under the boat, scraping: his bubbles gargling and rolling up under our windows.

You had a lot of barnacles, he said, pulling up his executioner's mask—and grass too, and you are being eaten away. Your propeller is changing colour. You have rust on your bottom. You are on salt water, which is a very fine conductor, and the water is full of electricity, from other boats, from marine installations, or generated by the ever-present forces of nature. Your sacrificial zinc anodes under the bow and the stern go first because they are lower on the periodic table and then your prop goes and then you go. Your anodes started a foot long and now they are the size of tennis balls. Only your anodes have saved you from electrolysing away into a handful of fizzing rust.

What can we do? I asked.

There are two boatyards not very far away. They will draw you out and look at your anodes and your bottom. It is possible that you will need English anodes and they won't have those.

At the time of writing, and I would guess at the time of reading, neither yard has rung back.

We mustn't let the buggers get us down Mon—we'll e-mail Pete and Karen at Canal Cruising in Stone, and go for a walk with Jim.

OUT INTO THE DAY THAT WAS TOO HOT AND TOO cold at the same time and through filthy vacant lots past the big hotel. Oh my Gard, said the uniformed doorman—what a pretty little dog, and what a lovely colour, like a little deer.

He pulled Jim's ears and then he went inside and came out with a box of lemon biscuits which he gave us and we thanked him and wished him well and walked on.

I thought you are supposed to tip the doorman, I said to Monica, not the other way round.

This is the South, said Monica.

A mile later a park by the river. A pier, with a courting couple and an African-American fisherman from Central Casting. Under the trees dozens of tents and camper vans and bikes—a group sitting round, men and women, all ages. Excuse me, said Monica, is it a race?

No, said the dominant male, a large old man in a camping chair—we are cyclists. That's the beer wagon—get a beer, sit down. You folks from England? Why is your dog so thin?

The group explained that they came from all corners of the United States to ride their bikes—not race them, just ride out together round a course maybe thirty, forty miles long. Then they come back to their campground and drink beer. You are a club? asked Monica.

No, we aren't a club—we just turn up to the events that are organized. This lady came from Seattle, I came from California. The events are usually organized very badly.

The large man showed me his motor home—it was one of those that goes out at the sides like a bellows and it was like your front room but bigger, with a steering wheel in the corner. He showed me his bike, which was a pedal version of the ones in *Easy Rider*—you sit down low with your knees up and the handlebars out in front. I rode this one from Miami to San Francisco last winter, he said. We have a tandem too like this and my wife and I ride together—she is a new wife—my first wife died eighteen months ago. I am seventy-four.

We chatted a long time with these people and they were so happy they made Monica feel happy too and they made Jim feel happy and he lay around and they petted him and they made me feel happy because one of the taps on the beer wagon gave forth a liquid very like beer. These people were not rich—they were mad and busy and joyful—they were the best.

When we got back to the boat there was an e-mail from Karen—she had taken advice of Brian at the other boatyard who knew about such things and they thought we had a good chance of making it to the Gulf of Mexico just before we fizzed away into half a pint of Diet Coke.

MONNIE HAS GONE TO THE MALL, SO YOU AND I CAN dine together in Charleston, gentle reader, my dear old chap, and how kind of you to join me. I will show you a typical American dinner—it's not the same as back home you know.

Jim can't come. Don't look at him—it will spoil your evening—the betrayed eyes.

We'll go in your car. It's only a hundred yards but there are no pavements and there are the fire ants and you can get arrested for walking on the side of the road with a funny accent.

Here we are—next to the fourteen black pick-ups. See that shed—the rusty one with smoked windows? Up those wooden steps with the dirty carpet and the people waiting in line. It's six o'clock—we've left it a bit late.

Inside already—you can't see? You must have poor night vision—take my hand and come over here by the T-shirts.

Hi, my name is Ellie Mae and I will be looking after y'all. Our specials tonight are shrimp and grits and she-crab soup. Can I get y'all a drink?

I'll have a bottle of Palmetto Ale, please, Ellie Mae—that's the local IPA, isn't it? My friend will have the same.

Something the matter? Oh, I see. Relax, man—they are all like that—they are students working their way through college and yes they are gorgeous but I would have thought the fires had died down a bit by your age. Calm down—she's coming back.

Here are the drinks and the iced water—are y'all ready to order yet?

Yes Ellie Mae, I'll have the shrimp and grits and a house salad and collard greens, and my friend will have the ribs and a salad and fried green tomatoes.

Balsamic vinegar dressing, Italian, basil, thousand island, vinaigrette, Greek, ranch, creamy dill, or blue cheese? And are y'all having another drink?

One basil, one ranch please, and two more beers.

See how they hustle drinks—I had eight glasses of white wine here one night with no effort at all. But most people drink water or Coke or, God forgive them, iced tea. The calorific value of a bottle of sweet tea is the same as a pint of London Pride—a narrow choice, eh? Take you a while to make your decision about that one—could lie awake all night, har har.

Look old man, if you don't mind me saying, you can't just pick up your beer and drink it—the bottle can freeze to your tongue and medical attention is expensive here. Put it in your armpit for a few minutes first to warm it up.

Here's the bread—those brown balls under the rolls are called Hush Puppies. You remember Hush Puppies—the shoes we all wore in the seventies. When they went out of fashion they were shipped to the US and ground up and fried. They wash them first but they still taste a bit leathery to me.

Here we are—yes, that's all yours—you haven't been given the buffet for a wedding by mistake. Don't panic—you are not expected to eat it or anything—you take it home in a box.

Just pick the fried bread from off the top of the salad. And have a couple of those slices of green tomato in batter—each is four hundred calories. That will make a satisfying and well-balanced meal. I shall eat half of my collard greens—cabbage with lumps of fat bacon—and I will manage a shrimp. The shrimps are the size of gerbils. The grits is corn porridge by the way. It will solidify into a cake by tomorrow morning and I will slice it up for breakfast.

Now the waiters are going to do the Macarena—they do it every twenty minutes to show they are having a great time. It's noisy but it will be over soon and you don't have to join in. Here, have half one of my gerbils. No, hands off the pork ribs—Jim likes those.

Our bill already—lovely thank you Ellie Mae—my friend will pay. How many different parties on average would you serve at this table in an evening? Ten? Well done, Ellie Mae. Yes it was lovely—can we have the big box please?

That's right—at least 15 per cent tip—we don't want to be beaten up by her boyfriend in the car park. They don't pay her anything of course, but she counts on a hundred dollars a night. Now hold on to me and feel your way round this corner.

Quite sure you don't want a T-shirt? You won't find them like that in Tunbridge Wells, with the shrimps riding surfboards and playing guitars.

Be very careful here on the stairs. Watch the carpet, it's torn—
Too late!

Oh my God what a mess. You've spilt Jim's pork ribs all over the place. How do you expect him to eat them now? And look at you—food all over you. Go over there where no one can see you and I will sort this out.

Ellie Mae my child—I will come by tomorrow about this time for a chat. I may be able to help you in your career.

. . .

WE HAD FIFTY MILES TO GO FROM CHARLESTON, and you can't do that in a narrowboat on a short winter's day unless you have a full crew and get the ropes off early. Put this on first, said Robert, and tied on to the tunnel light a Christmas wreath of pine branches and a red velvet bow.

Under the flyovers and across Charleston harbour and into the cut—broad, blue, jettied: houses thinning slowly. Faster than top speed—the tide was with us.

I was on the tiller and Bubba and Robert were hanging on the grab-rail. We were brought up here, said Robert. We used to go water-skiing down these stretches. You can't now, it's *No Wake, No Wake*—all jetties and houses. We lived here a long time—we knew everyone.

I tried to follow what the brothers were saying over the noise of the engine.

That's where that girl, said Bubba.

They say she very nearly, said Robert.

Actually she did, more than once—I should know, said Bubba.

The pistachio ice cream, said Robert.

It was strawberry. And it was in Barefoot Landing, so it doesn't count.

Her brother, said Robert.

Oh my God her brother, oh my God.

County Judge now, said Robert.

They never found the gorilla, said Bubba.

Or the piano accordion, said Robert.

Sometimes it's best, said Bubba, just to let things fade away.

Inside the boat Jim was lying on his back with his legs in the air, his paws bent over, grinning. He loves having friends on the boat—more pack power, and more chance of getting your tummy tickled.

Six hours later and we were on St Helena Sound, a great water, where the Edisto and the Combahee flow into the Atlantic and I was on the tiller again, and the sound stretched smooth into the ocean and into the sky.

As always on a calm day at high tide there was a sense of abundance. This is America—be astonished at the waters—we have rivers that dwarf the Rhône—we have two oceans. We have Arcadias of forests. Marvel at the marshes and the yellow grass—we have thousands of miles of marsh and yellow grass. Be charmed by the people—we are three hundred million—we are multitudes.

In 1776, when the population of America was only three million, Thomas Paine published his book *Common Sense*—

America doth not yet know what opulence is; and although the progress which she hath made stands unparalleled in the history of other nations, it is but childhood, compared with what she would be capable of arriving at, had she, as she ought, the legislative powers in her own hands.

Hit the bullseye with that one, Tom. Tom Paine's books were burned in England by the public hangman, and books don't get much better than that.

BEAUFORT, SOUTH CAROLINA, IS A DIFFERENT place to Beaufort, North Carolina, as you might expect, and further to clarify matters it is pronounced *bewfoot*.

Beaufort waterfront is beautiful. The trees, the old houses not too tall, the main street just there, the shops. On our left a walk along the bay between the palms—yellow grass, white boats, the tide rising. The evening was short and night the usual surprise and the street lamps had been coiled with lights so they looked like candy walking-sticks.

Heads down, here come the gongoozlers—three Young Ole Boys and a Young Ole Girl.

Oh my Gard, oh my Gard—you're here, you're here! They told us you were coming! It's the replica, the replica! It's come! It's come! Nearly submerged—that's so authentic—that's real neat! Now where does the mine go at the front? Where is the conning tower? Shouldn't she have *Hunley* on the side? Didn't know she had windows! Did she really have flowers on the top?

We normally dive at dawn, I explained, and spend the day at ten fathoms, but I brought her up this afternoon so the citizens of Beaufort could have a good look at her, and to clean the windows and water the flowers. The mine dropped off and started to tick and it's just underneath the pontoon where you are standing.

Oh dear, I guess they told us wrong, sir and ma'am—do forgive our poor manners—but she's a real cool boat, just the same—Gee she's so thin. Y'all take care now—is that a dog? She looks like a little deer.

AT NIGHT JIM WAITS FOR US ON OUR BED IN THE cabin. We kick him out but before dawn he creeps back and we are too sleepy to push him off. Every morning he comes five minutes earlier. This morning I woke up and tickled him behind the front leg and he groaned quietly, as he does when he is very pleased. I rubbed his chest and felt his heart beat.

I made breakfast, and turned on the radio, and it was Lowcountry Radio—*The Dick and Wally Show.*

I was so excited, said Dick or Wally. My friend took a chance and it came off. It must have been two hundred yards—you could see the jerk and then it sort of rolled and then it was away into the trees. Nice antlers, a real good one. We laughed and laughed just with the pleasure of it. The fresh air, the sport. I love nature—it had been ages since I shot anything.

Wish I had been there, said Wally or Dick, it must have been magic.

Then this doe, said Dick or Wally—looked like a doe, about a hundred yards, and I hit just behind the front leg to get the heart and it sort of hopped into the bushes but we found him and he had little buttons on his head. I didn't flinch at all when I pressed the trigger—that was the best bit. It is so easy to flinch and you miss and you feel bad and you have let yourself down. We were flying, man, we were happy—you should have seen him hop!

I thought What have you got to flinch about—you are not the one who will be shot and left to blunder round in pain until you die, so some bastard can get pleasure from you.

At dinner that night a man in a tartan shirt talking loudly to his friend—It's the spray that gives it away, the pattern—you can tell if you have hit them in the chest or not, or in an artery. I look on the trees, but you can often see the blood on the ground, or on the bushes. I make my own cartridges now, got more power—you can tell by the blood.

I suppose there are Dicks and Wallys everywhere, said Monica.

Even in Arcadia, I said.

TO GET TO HILTON HEAD WE HAD TO CROSS Port Royal Sound and Port Royal Sound is five miles wide. Sure we had managed the Bogue Sound on our own but that was more a case of running along the shore—Port Royal Sound is an estuary like the Cape Fear River and the widest crossing we had tackled without a pilot.

To get to Port Royal Sound you have to go ten miles down the Beaufort River and then you go on to the heaving main and you can be swept out to sea and if the wind comes up against the tide you can be turned over. As my old rowing partner Dai Morgan in Llandaff would put it—One slip boyo and you're buggered—literally!

We laid the chart on the table and studied the thirty-mile route and went online and checked the tides and the weather. There would be a slight risk of rain and winds of five to ten miles an hour. I didn't know what winds of five to ten miles an hour meant—they sounded pretty fast to me.

Like your girlfriend blowing in your ear, said the chap in the next boat.

When we left town the afternoon was still, and we wove down the Beaufort River through cuts and narrows in the yellow grass. The river became wider and wider and when it was a mile wide it stopped and Tits Magee faced the endless white waters of Port Royal Sound, his heart pounding, his resolve evaporating because he could not see the daymark or where he was on the chart and the beetle on the GPS said we were crossing Jermyn Street. Call me a scaredy-pants but I do so much like to see the other side before I set out to sea in a canal boat.

We might pause, gentle reader, as poor Tits faces the terrible crossing and bring you up to date on some matters from Virginia which must have been troubling you. Yes thanks, my hernia operation worked fine, and the heart doctor prescribed a tablet and it has fixed my palpitations though no doubt it will be destroying other vital organs—I know what goes on in the pharmaceutical industry.

But here I am for the moment alive and scared and far from shore and looking into the sun for the pole and triangle of the next daymark, far away and thread-thin and fading and I've lost it and it was probably something else anyway. I would blame Monica but can't think of a reason and she has gone below. But she just pointed at the chart and said There you are as if it was easy.

I could go on into the nothingness and keep hoping and that might be best. Let's try to work out what the GPS is showing—use the magnifying glass and look closely into the hood—and think man, think. And keep the tiller going straight—look where the sun is—you have wandered forty-five degrees—you'll finish up in the Gulf Stream. The GPS screen is clearer now—so that is where we are! Now the chart—you will be a long way back from where you think because you always are and the narrow bits are broad and the broad bits go to the end of the world—Oh look over there! I think I can see my daymark again! It is! It is! It's the mark! The mark! Now relax, you were never in danger because you kept so cool.

There's the next mark as well! It is! It is! Now we won't die! We aren't going to die!

Out and out into the five-mile sound and there are no day-marks any more and the magenta line showing the Intra-coastal Waterway has gone from the GPS screen but the water is smooth and look—that black blur over there. If I head for that I am bound to hit the other side somewhere and then I can run along it. And I can see some sort of headland—that has to be the entrance to Skull Creek. Why don't I just head for that? That's why the daymarks have run out and there is no magenta line—you can just sail towards the headland. It's all so simple really—it's a lovely day and you just sail towards the headland, out across the shining sound, and here come the dolphins!

EACH NIGHT AT HARBOUR TOWN YACHT BASIN on Hilton Head Island cost us two bucks fifty a foot. Harbour Town is a gated community, and like Portmeirion village in North Wales it was designed around a concept.

Portmeirion is bogus Italian and seizes you and flies you out over the Dee estuary, dizzy with the fun of it. Harbour Town is fifties American and clean and tasteful like Singapore or Switzerland, and makes you feel death is too much to hope for.

There is a red and white candy-bar lighthouse and gift shops and a circular boat basin from a Mediterranean tour catalogue and the blocks of flats they call condominiums like slabs of cheese around the basin and among the trees. The basin is full of million-dollar powerboats and cruisers and sport-fishers. One white plastic cruiser in the middle of the basin was a hundred and twenty feet long. It was called the *Passion for Excellence*. Once a day, for reasons not revealed to us, it would go out into the sound for an hour, with a grinding of bow thrusters—*Passion for Tupperware*, I said to Monica, har har.

The *Phyllis May* docked next to a sixty-foot sport-fisher—no one on board. No one on board any of the boats. We walked along the pontoon and looked back and the marina staff were running tours to the *Phyllis May* in a little boat. Six gongoozlers were standing up in the boat in a row, quite still, as if this was their last chance to see something so strange and if they moved it would open its wings and fly away.

I felt sorry for the Harbour Town gongoozlers—one day something arrives from the world outside, where things are dirty and make no sense but can be so beautiful you just want to look and look and wonder what else you have lost.

We walked to the beach and a notice told us to cooperate with the ecological plans for the area and clear off, so we walked down the side of a golf course. It said in the book the golf course was one of the finest in the country, and indeed Kidderminster's best could not have woven the grass on those greens.

The Harbour Town mosquitoes are trained in laboratories by men in spectacles to bite writers who don't like Harbour Town, and when we got back to the *Phyllis May* I had been bitten twelve times on each forearm and twelve times on each leg—three nights' sleep broken and the scars still there two weeks later. The residents of Harbour Town would have laughed like anything if we had told them but we spoke to no residents of Harbour Town and we heard no one laugh.

. . .

I LAY AWAKE SCRATCHING, LOVELY GEORGIA ON my mind.

Tomorrow we cross the state line, Monica had said, and we go up the Savannah River, which is deep and full of ships. The thing is not to get run down by a container ship.

I remembered that sailboat skipper we met in Beaufort– when he sailed out on to the Savannah River he had his radio on the wrong channel and forgot to look over his shoulder. The container ship sounded its siren and he looked round and saw it coming on him, fifty yards high, fifty yards away.

Now wherever he is he keeps his back to the wall and moves from one foot to the other, ready to run across the room and dive out of the window.

Ten

RAINING ALL OVER THE WORLD

Georgia

With a Sad Sweet Song – I Think It Is Titanium Slag – She Had Antlers on Her Head – Bunch of Crooks – The Death of the Ball Turret Gunner – Now She Is Like the Rest – Only the US Army Can Save Us – Eight Thousand Acres of Trees – Now That's What I Call Hospitality – A Sour and Plangent Bellow – Pretty T-shirt and Silver Sandals – Dreadful Things at Three in the Morning – One Day at a Time, Sweet Jesus

I SAT AT THE TILLER, LOOKING OVER MY SHOUL-
der too often but otherwise in a contemplative mood. It
would soon be dark and the container ships seemed to have
knocked off and so had everybody else, including the pelicans, who had gone down the pub. The grey river was a mile
wide, with a terrible shore—ragged machinery hundreds of
feet high spilling noise and steam, hung with lights like
Christmas in hell. But when we came on Paris from the rear
three years ago in the *Phyllis May* the City of Light had looked
savage, unbuilt, infested with pirates; so the jury was still out
on Savannah.

I had always wanted to go to Georgia, and I knew it would
be a rainy night when I arrived—that it would be raining all
over the world. Maybe I would be in time for the midnight
train.

Our younger daughter is called Georgia—after my father,
but with a sad sweet song in mind. 'Georgia on My Mind' was
written by Hoagy Carmichael, and so were 'Stardust' and
'The Nearness of You', not to mention 'Heart and Soul'.
Yes, I know he wrote 'My Resistance Is Low', but show some

forgiveness, it's Christmas. Did you know his real name was Hoagland? You don't care? That information won me a beer in the Handlebar in Beaufort–my God what's that?

A huge tug coming right at us–hold right, Darlington, it's a wide river–there you are he's given you fifty yards. A hoot, a hoot! He hooted me! I have been hooted by a huge tug! He said hello! He likes me!

I remembered that time on the Birmingham Main Line Canal when we had just bought the *Phyllis May*. A railway runs alongside the cut and a long train came up behind me and as he passed the driver hooted, and he waved. For a moment on one bright morning I was accepted among the oily engineering aristocracy and their lovely old machines. I had never been welcomed again into that brotherhood, until the tug hooted me in Savannah.

We are moving fast with the tide behind us and here comes Savannah up on that hill and here comes the wharf–here it is–look at that fool–NO I CAN'T COME IN THAT WAY–the dockmaster doesn't know what he is doing–you don't come in with a strong current behind you and try to force the back in unless you plan to go straight into that glass-fibre freak just downstream and out the other side, and there goes a million quid.

Chuck him the bow rope, Mon, and ask him to get it on a cleat and hold the end of it and fall silent and show some respect and let me dock my boat my way–the current will sweep me right round and I will come in as neat as that Jeff Goldblum landing on the butter and we will be safe in Savannah, which looks a very strange place indeed.

• • •

THERE IS NOT A LOT OF POINT TAKING THE trouble to read books that tell you what a place is going to be like. How can you contain a city in a book—the stones, the wood, the tiles, the parks, the people, the memories? You can try for the ambience, the spirit of a place, but you bring most of that with you anyway.

I expected Savannah would be small, quiet, rustic, low-built—squares, benches, old folk. Dear me I was mistaken.

We were ten feet below the street—above us a row of coloured brollies along the railings, and under the brollies a row of white faces. Behind these a market with wooden roofs, and a cobbled waterfront: buildings worn and tall and various like old Bristol, the lights of the restaurants and gift shops vivid in dusk and rain.

We took Jim for a walk along the river, and the Savannah, wider than the Thames at Westminster or the Rhône at Lyon, poured by offering lumps of driftwood, and disappeared into the rain under a bridge hung from webs of white silk. The rest of Savannah was hiding on top of a hill. But first, an oyster bar on the waterfront.

I'll have some of that Bobbitts Double Best, I said, pointing to the illuminated sign four feet long over the bar.

We don't sell that, said the barman.

I suppose the sign is to confuse the Germans?

Or anyone else, said the barman.

Certainly confused an Englishman, I said.

That beer's no good anyway.

Thanks for the advice.

We do a draught Sweet Water IPA.

Tell you what—I'll have some of that draught Sweet Water IPA.

Good choice, said the barman.

Oysters are eaten a great deal in the South. They are bigger than European oysters. On the Intracoastal Waterway they surround you in heaps: on every post, every mudflat, every rock. They hang on to the bottom of your boat and breed in your cooling system. The Americans mix the shells with plaster and build walls and houses and pavements from them, and sometimes they just put them on their gardens. They fry their oysters in batter, and grill them, turning them into chewing gum. They sometimes eat them raw and they taste as if they had died fairly recently, but as an Englishman I prefer to be present at the time.

But these oysters were superb and I said so and the barman brought me another IPA and filled this one much nearer the top.

By our side a pale gentleman in his forties. He was enjoying his oysters but he said that where he came from, horseradish sauce was not served with shellfish, and that seemed to him very wise.

Gregor was first officer on a boat in the port—thirty-six thousand tonnes—a handy size, he said. She was carrying titanium slag. At least he thought it was titanium slag. The crew was Polish, apart from the Indian who did the dirty work. The ship was owned in one country and registered in another and managed in another. Gregor worked for an agency in Cracow. In a day or two his ship would be off round Florida and up the Mississippi to pick up some more titanium slag—at least he thought it was titanium slag.

You had a lucky escape with that Bobbitts, said the barman. We wouldn't sell that rubbish here.

• • •

SOMETHING TERRIBLE HAPPENED TO AMERICAN cities after the Second World War. It was a rotting and a giving up as trade went out to the hypermarkets and malls along the suburban highways and law slackened its grip downtown and property values collapsed. To us the derelict alleys and the vacant lots and the shacks and ruined warehouses still look awful. Elizabeth City had been chaos.

But update this desperate story—now there seems to be a realization that waterfronts are good places to invest, and a remembrance of the brief history which Americans love so much, and an urgency to catch the whole mess before it hits the ground, and an optimism that we can save this place. Nowadays you can look at a waterside city like an ancient statue. It might have a head and a shoulder and a foot missing; it might be stained and rough, but in your mind you can put it back together in its balance, its grace.

Out of the boat and up the ramp and into the covered market. Geoff the hot-dog man came out from behind his kiosk and fell upon Jim, and Marcia on the coffee stall cried out— The little deer, the little deer! Jim licked her ears as she bent down. She had antlers on her head. She put a pair on Jim and they posed together for a picture, Marcia with more enthusiasm than Jim.

Let's climb those steps on the wall and have a look at Savannah, I said. My God, Mon, hang on to me, these open iron rungs give me the vertigo. Watch Jim—don't let him run up—if he falls between the steps he will slice himself in two.

Now we were looking across a moat to the second-floor

back of the old waterfront buildings–tall and stained, with bridges to more gift shops. We turned to cross a thin park, and then blasting traffic, and we were in Paris. The traffic was Paris, and the height of the buildings was Paris, and the trees were right if you lose the Spanish moss.

Over the road the golden dome of the town hall and in a wooded square the Greek pillars of Episcopal Christchurch, then the main shopping street, with clothing shops, restaurants, empty windows. Half a block away rotten alleys: stained multi-storeys. It was raining all over the world.

WE FOUND A NARROW AWNING AND JIM SET-tled under a table. A gentleman sat down at the table alongside. He was youngish, rather roughly dressed, with an earring and long hair. My father was in England in the war, he said. He was a navigator on the Flying Fortresses.

My God, I said–they were losing 70 per cent of their crews.

He was never attacked by fighters, said the youngish man, but he said over the target was the longest thirty seconds of his life. The flak was terrible. I was an accountant, with Deloitte. You know when Enron the energy company and Arthur Andersen went down it devastated Chicago–thousands and thousands out of work. Arthur Andersen employed a hundred thousand people, and Enron twenty thousand.

Bunch of crooks, I said, Arthur Andersen.

Oh yes, said the youngish man, but it was Enron, of course, that did for them. Andersen were Enron's accountants and they went down with them. Kenneth Lay was the Enron Chief Executive.

He died just before he was sentenced, I said. Only sixty-four, but it is hard to grieve for thieves and liars.

It was the right move by Kenneth, said the youngish man, in the circumstances. As it happens I too have had business problems–I had an excellent business model but I couldn't support it with enough cash. It is all a question of cash, you know, as now when I was planning to buy a cup of coffee.

You would like me to buy you a cup of coffee? I asked.

Sure, said the youngish man.

Delighted, I said.

I took out the wad of notes in my back pocket and gave it to him. It was four dollars, and I wish it had been more.

What a nice man, said Monica.

THAT NIGHT I WAS ON MY MOTHER'S LAP, UNDER the stairs. The engines roared in and out and the bombs whistled and the earth flinched. My mother was afraid. The gas from the meter smelled sickly. The stairs were not much protection and with any luck we would have died quickly.

One and a half million civilians were killed by bombing in the Second World War. Most were women and children under five. *Did heaven look on, and would not take their part?*

The individual terror and suffering was as great for the boys and men who dropped the bombs. Randall Jarrell the poet was an instructor in a bombing school–

> *From my mother's sleep I fell into the State*
> *And I hunched in its belly till my wet fur*
> > *froze.*

> Six miles from earth, loosed from its dream
>   of life,
> I woke to black flak and the nightmare
>   fighters.
> When I died they washed me out of the turret
>   with a hose.

MOST OF THE TIME WE HAD BEEN ABLE TO SEND and receive e-mails from our laptops. Jim has had a letter from seven whippets in France, said Monica, and a picture.

The picture showed three generations of brindled and white whippets. Three dogs at the front, standing square, ears half folded, looking slightly off-camera, attentive, proud, and three bitches a little smaller, ears less tidy. Right at the back a small face peeping over another dog: looking at the camera, ears down, anxious.

Monica replies to the letters we get for Jim, because I keep forgetting I am a dog.

A second letter to Jim—

I'm Simon, the little whippet hiding behind the others on the left in the family photo we sent you. I can't believe that we have had a message from such a very famous literary whippet—we will keep it for EVER and EVER.

My daddy and some of my half-brothers and sisters are also quite famous because they are all show or working champions. I'm not famous because I had a very difficult birth and was deprived of oxygen so I'm a bit different. People think I am still a puppy but I will

be nine in January. I look at things my own way and
prefer to stay at home when my family go out for
walks. Here is a picture of me in my football jersey–I
am very good at doing things with my ears.

The picture showed a skinny little dog with long legs
standing not quite steady, holding a soft toy in his mouth. His
ears were in full flower. Simon had been chosen for the
Christmas card, and he didn't seem to mind, though he had a
strange and puzzled look. It was enough to break your heart.

In Colombey-les-Deux-Églises, General Charles de Gaulle
lies next to his beloved daughter Anne, who had Down's syn-
drome. When she died he said *Maintenant elle est comme les
autres*–now she is like the rest.

MONICA AND I BROKE OUR FAST, AS WE DO
once a year, on a bag of macadamia nuts and a glass of
whisky. As we got off the boat it was hot but it was raining, so
I was wearing my Breton sailor's cap and yellow oilskin coat,
and Monica her waterproof jacket, and Jim his orange rain-
coat that he keeps trying to jump out of.

It rained and rerained, and then rerained again. This was
no patter puffing the dust and tapping the bushes, this was
rain, man, real rain, white as surf in the air and clear and
sparkling where it flushed and rampaged over our ankles.

Only the US Army can save us, said Monica, and Colonel
Frank Williams III came along the waterfront in a white car.

It is a privilege to meet you, yessir, said the colonel, and
your dog there in the back, what a well-behaved dog. I have
rarely seen such a fine and well-behaved dog. A happy

Christmas to y'all. We are now going down Interstate 95—the route to Florida.

Colonel Frank Williams III was a tanned, strongly built chap in civvies, and he smiled a lot, and seemed rather shy. He seemed also to be calling me sir and that made me feel odd because he was a colonel and I have never been considered officer material. But this was the South and perhaps everyone calls everyone sir. Perhaps he calls his soldiers sir. Perhaps he calls the waiter sir—and I am sure that if you tried to mug him he would address you with the greatest respect before he struck you down.

An hour later we turned off the road on to a track and then off the track and into a forest. We were in the alternative world of Tree, where there was no importance attached to air, or light, or space—what mattered was bark, and muscular limbs five feet thick, and a foot of leaves on the ground and all the air extracted and replaced by hanging moss and hot rain. This was a place you had not seen since your mother told you that fairy tale from another country, where there were witches.

A long low white bungalow, a dog hullabalooing in the porch, Martha, the colonel's wife, blonde and smiling, and someone who no doubt would have been Frank Williams IV were she not a beautiful young woman called Laura.

Jim walked into the sitting room, pissed on the Christmas presents, and threw up on the hearthrug.

YESSIR, SAID COLONEL FRANK WILLIAMS III. Your friend Colonel Mac and I worked together a lot. He told me he was a Stone Master Marathoner. He organized getting hold of the property we needed to do our jobs and I was artillery. It was a terrible place—I was cold every day. And the Bosnians and the Serbs and the Croats—such poverty, and such hatred. They would be friendly together during the day and set bombs at night. Yes, I missed home a lot. Now I run the army programme in Georgia for disadvantaged young people—we have a high success rate and 20 per cent join the army. I have done that for twelve years and will retire soon. We are pleased to have Mac's friends here—we like to have visitors for Christmas Day.

Martha was a gentle lady, though in her bosom the pioneer flame still burned. When she and Colonel Frank were first married they lived in a waterside house (it is hard not to live in a waterside house round here) and were much troubled by rats. One day Martha opened the drawer in her dressing table and a rat ran out. She picked up her husband's service revolver and shot it between the eyes with a single round.

Soon we will go across to my father's—Frank Williams Jr, said the colonel. But first, do go and check out the dock on the creek—it might help break your journey.

I went out with Monica and Jim and realized this was not just a lost residence in the woods—fifty yards from the front door were creeks and the yellow grass. Jim raced and jumped among the leaves and twigs on the wet lawn. That dock would be lovely, said Monica—we can break our journey here and it will help make crossing Georgia possible. I have been so worried—the marinas are too far apart—we are slow and there are not enough daylight hours. And you leave all the planning to me and sit drinking IPA all night.

I don't have a planning mind, I said. I am an artiste—I am divergent.

Degenerate you mean, said Monica.

Colonel Frank came out—How many acres have you got here? I asked.

Seventy, sir, he said.

My God, seventy—that's quite a plot! I suppose you could sell some of it for development and make a lot of money.

Yes, but then it has gone. There is the island as well of course—and some other land.

How many acres do you have?

Eight thousand, said Colonel Frank.

FRANK WILLIAMS JR LIVED FOUR MILES AWAY. Christmas lunch was rather like Bubba's Thanksgiving because there were about twenty people and it was a buffet. In fact it was very like the Thanksgiving except this was Georgia, among the woods and the creeks and the yellow grass, and the atmosphere was formal, even dynastic. The event turned peacefully around Frank Williams Jr, white-haired, benevolent, seated central to the action. Jim slept in a corner and got up now and then to do some fawning.

The live oaks with the moss are mainly around the houses, said Frank Williams Jr. The rest is pines. I look after it all. When there is harvesting or replanting we send for the paper company and they do it. When I was eighteen I was in the Third Infantry Division. We landed in North Africa and went through Italy, and then we landed on the French Riviera and headed north and I was wounded at Colmar. I was lucky—they fixed my knee and I played tennis for forty years. I will never go back to Europe—most of my buddies were killed.

There was no turkey in the buffet, but there were shrimps that looked like stage shrimps and crunched and melted, and dips from the dip-shop that had won the known universe dips competition for the last five hundred years. The pecan pie was treacle tart with roast pecans on it. That pecan pie will always have a place on the buffet table of my memory.

They are so hospitable, I said, so kind.

Yes, said Monica, even when Jim misbehaved.

Anyone can be hospitable to easy guests, I said, but when you walk in and piss on the Christmas presents and throw up on the carpet and they are still kind and welcoming, *that's* hospitality.

GEOFF THE HOT-DOG MAN AND JIM WERE wrestling in an ecstasy of farewells and Marcia came over to join in from her coffee stall. We had to leave the River Street mooring because a party of boats was coming and our last few days in Savannah would be spent moored under the Westin Hotel, the five-star cliff over the river. They should give us the bridal suite for that price, I said to Monica.

We had a cup of coffee and waited for the tide to go slack, and finished the box of cream doughnuts the dockmaster had given us, and the pecan loaf from Marcia. The dockmaster may not have known much about docking narrowboats, but he knew his doughnuts. Geoff the hot-dog man had given us nothing but love, but that is worth a few doughnuts, even cream ones.

The tide slackened. We looked to see if any container ships were on their way. They are taller than the houses and longer than the streets and as they go by there is plenty of time to read the names—*Bremen Express, Ym Tiansin, Safmarine Houston, APL Turquoise, OOCL Los Angeles*. Their bridges are nine storeys high, and there are fifteen hundred containers on the decks. From time to time they give out a sour and plangent bellow, like the devil farting.

I love to start the engine and get moving again, even for a few hundred yards, and we swung out from the wharf and wrote an S in the river and moored against the pontoon under the Westin Hotel, next to an empty sport-fisher a hundred feet long.

Jim was allowed in the Westin, and we walked the polished floors and the carpets among the Christmas trees with their bows and lights and settled in the bar. The hotel has more than four hundred bedrooms but today it seemed almost empty. The public areas were wide—block-like corners and square spaces and flat quiet colours. Nineteen forties, early fifties, I explained to Monica—same vintage as the Buick Roadmaster—I'll check the year with the barmaid.

The hotel was built seven years ago, said the barmaid.

Post-modern, of course, I said to Monica—can deceive even an expert. But very nice. Bit of a change from McClellanville, with the slimy ladder up to the wharf, and the lavatory in the paint shed.

I HAD BOUGHT A BLAZER WITH BRASS BUTTONS and a pair of flannel trousers and Monica wore jeans and a pretty T-shirt and her silver sandals and we arrived with some panache at the hotel restaurant on the second floor. We had a gin and dry martini at the bar and the barman asked me if I would like another and I said Yes and drank it and felt I had been hit over the head.

The barman looked like Louis Armstrong's fat grandson. I

am from New York, he said, but all my family came from Georgia.

Is there any racial tension around here? I asked.

Well yes, said the barman, certainly there is—a lot of tension. There are more and more Mexicans and they are after the jobs and they don't even try to speak English.

We went to our table by the big window looking over the Savannah and our bottle of wine arrived and our lamb took a long time and we drank most of the wine as we waited. I don't remember much about the rest of the evening, but we got down the gangway to the dock without incident and I took Jim for his last walk without fetching us both into the river. None of us had much trouble going to sleep.

ON A BOAT IT IS USUALLY THREE O'CLOCK IN the morning when the really dreadful things happen. I awoke in mid-air, and Monica too had slipped the surly bonds of earth. Together we landed on the bed as it was coming up on the rebound. Mercifully Jim had not yet crept in among us.

You develop a technique for dealing with wake—the first hit is always the worst so you wait, saying to yourself I am still here so I will get through the next one. But this wake was not dying—it bounced us and flung us and shook us and the ropes snatched and the fenders groaned and the water thumped and rang under the hull.

I'm scared, said Monica.

I was scared too. We pulled back the curtains and the tide was running out but the river was smooth and it was empty. Then the rocking started again and the *Phyllis May* was trying to roll right over and Jim was whining and the drawers and

cupboards were opening and there was a rattling and a ringing that we had never heard before. My God, I said to myself—we are going down in calm water—a submarine has come
up the Savannah and is pushing us over!

The far side of the river was smooth, but now and then a
slight breeze seemed to stir up a tiny swell that rolled towards
us in a line, not six inches high. When the first wave reached
us the effect was small, but each wave was arriving just at the
moment to build on the last and increase our roll so it was
like one of those bridges that is torn apart because the soldiers marching across forgot to break step.

The rattling was my new tin pelican, McClellan, who is
five feet long and flat and hangs on the wall outside the heads.
When disturbed McClellan rings and crashes like an iron
gate falling on concrete. So in times of trouble, McClellan,
like Jim, adds greatly to the confusion. Slowly the boat settled, and McClellan and Jim fell silent.

I know we are on a boat, said Monica, and boats move, but
I like to know why they move.

It's like my grandfather, I said, and the sailor.

My grandfather Billy Lewis had two favourite stories and
one of them was about a sailor.

During the First World War Billy was a nightwatchman at
the dockyard. He was sitting in a submarine in the dry dock
with a rating from the ship's company. Pembroke Dock is
about as far west as you can get in Wales, and it can be pretty
windy. Suddenly a gale arose and the submarine began to
move on its blocks. It bumped and jerked and the sailor
turned white and began to tremble.

Are you scared? asked Billy Lewis. A hero who has ven-
tured out against the Hun in a leaking sardine tin? A mariner

who has plumbed the darkness of the oceans, and weathered Atlantic storms and the terrible currents and towering waves? A man like you—scared by a bit of settling down?

I don't mind it rolling about when I am at sea, said the sailor, it's just that I get scared when it does it on dry land.

MONICA WAS SPENDING A LOT OF TIME LOOKing at charts and tide tables and weather forecasts.

Now we've got to go down the rest of Georgia, she said, and there is nothing there, only wilderness. There are these huge rivers—the Savannah, the Little Ogeechee, the Satilla, the Altamaha. And there are these huge sounds—Wassaw, Ossabaw, St Catherine's, Sapelo, Jekyll. There is one sound after another, and because the rivers are always making sandbanks you have to practically go out on to the Atlantic to get across. When the sounds are emptying the current won't let you go up them and if the wind comes against the tide they throw up huge waves. We might bash through with our new scuppers and the board inside the front door but do you think you could handle the tiller? The first six-foot wave would dislocate your shoulder.

I squeezed my shoulder—Oh dear, I said—I thought the Albemarle was supposed to be the worst bit.

Then between the sounds there are the bendy rivers and lakes and creeks and corners and half the time you are going the wrong way—there is no sense in it or direction, said Monica, and you can get lost and starve to death.

I knew it was like a jigsaw dropped on the floor, I said. I didn't realize it was such a big jigsaw.

We'll get carried out to sea, said Monica, or get lost and

murdered like that film *Southern Comfort*. And the marinas are too far apart. And there are the fogs.

It's only fifteen miles to Isle of Hope Marina, I said. We just have to go down the Savannah River and a few creeks. One day at a time, sweet Jesus.

The Westin seemed not to notice our leaving and we were too far away from Geoff the hot-dog man and Marcia on the coffee stall over the river to wave goodbye but we waved anyway. I looked back at the bow of a container ship under the cobweb bridge and saw it move and went cold but it wasn't really moving. I put the pedal on the metal and the *Phyllis May* hurried on down with the tide at ten miles an hour and the wind hard in our faces.

There were white horses, and cascades from the bow. But the fetch on the Savannah was not enough to brew up big waves and when you are heading straight at the weather the tiller does not swing or fight with you or dislocate your shoulder.

Solid as a rock, I thought, dear old boat. She'll need to be solid where we are headed. I squeezed my shoulder again and looked back with regret to Savannah on its forty-foot bluff. It wasn't quite raining.

Eleven

TREASURE ISLAND

Georgia

We Need a Qualified Sea Captain and a Professional Weather Forecaster – Meanest Armadillo in the Whole Damn Town – Treasure Island – Leroy Was Here – Written in the Wind – The Snakebird – Fresh Transfigurings of Freshest Blue – The Sad Discussion of Sin – Drunkenness of the Deep – Rickover's Final Defence

———

THE ISLE OF HOPE MARINA–DEEPEST GEORGIA–
big wooden houses, magnolias, curtains of moss.

This one could go either way, said Monica. We have to go
across Ossabaw Sound, which is three miles wide. There is a
warning for small ships off the coast. The tide will be running
down the Bear River, and the wind will be five to ten knots
against it. There is a risk of thunderstorms. We can't leave before ten because of the tides and we have forty miles to go
and there isn't enough time before dark. And we will have
Colonel Frank with us. We don't want to be responsible for
breaking the line of the Williams dynasty, when they were so
nice about Jim and the Christmas presents.

We know a five-to-ten-mile-an-hour wind is not much on
its own, I said, but that's about all we know. Against the tide it
might throw up huge waves. The forecasts are all different,
and wrong, and change all the time. If we had a powerboat
with a thousand horsepower we could just blast our way
through. But we have a forty-three-horse engine and twelve
inches of freeboard and a manual tiller. We could ring Frank
and cancel. But we are never going to learn about different
conditions if we stay in port. We'll lose our nerve and never

make it to Florida. We know what to expect–a bumpy ride and a late arrival, and I think we should go, and if we run into trouble I will take the responsibility. Never let it be said Tits Magee hid behind the skirts of a woman.

We are going a river too far, said Monica. To be safe we need a qualified sea captain and a professional weather forecaster on board, not two useless pensioners and a terrified dog. And look outside–you can hardly see across the marina.

JIM HAD DECIDED THAT LYING ON THE SOFA and being stroked by Frank's other beautiful daughter was a good enough way to spend a morning.

There is an occluded front said Becky, and a 23 per cent chance of precipitation. Fog will clear from all areas shortly and brighter weather will follow with winds of four miles an hour. You know in the studio I can't see what is on the screen behind me–it is all green.

How do you know what to point at? asked Monica.

I check on the monitors at the side, and the producer is talking into my ear, said Becky.

Jim groaned blissfully.

You're on first, Frank, I said, but I'll take her out, because I am the righteous one, the one who never fails.

I reversed off the pontoon and the current caught us and Frank ran down the gunwale and pushed me off the expensive cruiser I was about to destroy.

That was to demonstrate that great care is required, I said–that even the best steersman can make mistakes. Now this is how you hold the tiller. Are you familiar with boats?

I have my captain's papers, said Frank, and I used to command a seventy-two-foot ferry.

I went below and Jim was still lying on his back being stroked. I turned for comfort to my leather armadillo, Leroy—the meanest armadillo in the whole damn town. I had bought him for my grandson but Leroy and I had bonded before the time came to hand him over, and to split us up would have caused unnecessary suffering. Leroy was the name I originally chose for Jim, but Monica wouldn't let me.

The *Phyllis May* drove into the warm wind and bounced and banged. Colonel Frank on the tiller was rapt—she holds her course so well, he said, and she's so solid.

Look, said Monica, over there is the Moon River, like in our song. It is supposed to be the actual Moon River, wider than a mile.

I know where it's going—it's going our way, I said.

Becky left our Huckleberry friend asleep below and came along the gunwale to take the tiller and steer us out into Ossabaw Sound. Her slim arms held firm as we pounded for mile after mile, and her blue eyes were on the horizon—no doubt seeing occluded fronts hidden from mortal folk and calculating the chance of precipitation.

There wasn't room for me on the back of the boat and I went down to have a nap, but the Atlantic was only hundreds of yards away on our left and I looked anxiously through the front window, riding each wave, checking the electric beetle on the computer screen in the galley, accomplishing nothing but feeling that I was on the scene. After all I had made the decision to set out today, so I was in charge really.

In order to find somewhere to moor for the night we had to

go off the Intracoastal Waterway and up a river for six miles. The river was full of shoals and I went up on top with Frank in case he needed some quality back-up.

This GPS of yours is grand, said Frank.

I was pleased—praise for my little global positioning screen from a man who fired artillery and must be able to read maps and compasses and things and know where he is all the time.

You could cruise at night on this, said Frank. I love the colours.

Nevertheless Frank decided to go up the river the old-fashioned way using daymarks and compass settings, and to my great satisfaction he got lost in the shoals and had to reverse and turn right round and go a different way and we made it to the marina seven minutes before sunset.

In Georgia there is none of the lingering shadows lark, none of the duck-egg skies, none of the red fish netted in the trees—the sun is there, and then the sun has set, and if you haven't found safe landing, tough luck.

Don't worry, I said—you haven't demoralized the crew. It shows them that great care is required, because even the best steersman can make mistakes.

The colonel smiled, but not very much.

We had come six hundred and fifty miles of our journey.

NEXT MORNING MONICA EXPLAINED THAT WE had to cross St Catherine's Sound, and it was four miles wide, the biggest sound in Georgia, and the current would be against us. What's the wind speed? I asked.

Four miles an hour, said Monica.

Let's boogie, I said.

Our crew had gone home and I set off in a rush of spray down the brimming river, determined to do better than the colonel.

Each time I turned the boat the little beetle on the GPS screen turned and hurried back into the white deep-water channel. I would not have needed to look at the river, but there were crab-pot buoys in my path every so often–Don't want one of those round your prop, the colonel had said.

Hey, it's like a video game, I shouted to Monica–I'm having a great time!

Monica had a great time too, then a couple of hours later I took us on to St Catherine's Sound. A bloke on the dock had said the water here ran at six knots, and I didn't believe him, but I went through my usual performance of losing the markers and panicking in the face of the limitless waters and the Atlantic waiting on our left, but you can't stay scared when you ride on melted air and the sun is warm and the current is only a knot against you and the dolphins are sucking great breaths and jogging alongside for company.

Jim slept below–I had taken him out chasing squirrels before breakfast and he had treed half a dozen of them, running flat out and disappearing and coming back rolling his eyes and gasping–Look, I'm having a great time!

Here we are–this is the creek–and a couple of miles along it Creighton Island–the colonel's island, three thousand acres of forest.

We tied up to the dock and went up on to the walkway, a hundred yards long, over the marsh grass and into the woods.

It's Treasure Island! said Monica.

Palms, creepers, live oaks, pines; above the trees the hawks soaring. A hunting lodge. Behind it a sunny field and two fine black bulls.

I'll take Jim for a walk, said Monica. It's winter and there shouldn't be too many insects and things.

We found other buildings by the waterside, said Monica when they came back, and Jim ran off. Then I heard a commotion and he was chasing a piglet. It was brown and hairy and the size of a hot-water bottle and it was squealing. He got it by the scruff of the neck just as I caught him. I was terrified in case a sow came out for us. Frank said they reach three hundred pounds and have tusks.

You horrible animal, I said.

Jim grinned and rolled his eyes. He was having a great time.

NEXT DAY JIM AND I WENT FOR A WALK TO SEE the island. Along a track, across clearings bigger than four cricket pitches and into the jungle and we were at the waterside. Jim vanished and I worried lest the hogs took their revenge. But he came back and I petted him and he set off again.

A fearful commotion—Jim was somewhere in the dry undergrowth and I could see creatures rushing about—the hogs, I thought—he's at it again. Then a little face appeared at my feet, little pointed ears, a spotted body, a hooped tail, little yellow eyes looking up at me—Can you advise me what the hell is going on?

My God, it's Leroy!

Jim was chasing Leroy's mate, who leaped into the air and

fell sideways into some scrub, then he came back for Leroy. I thought Leroy might roll up, but he put on a fair turn of speed and with Jim hard behind vanished in the same direction. An armadillo is not a graceful creature. Leroy looked like a rugby ball bouncing into touch.

They would have been a bit crunchy, Jim, I said.

Back towards the dock and there was Jim standing by the door of the hunting lodge.

Jim has many expressions, and this was the abandoned whippet, the dying whippet, the whippet that none has ever loved, the whippet that gives so much. He was right by the door—Here is a house, on an island where there are hogs and armadillos to chase. We used to live in a house before we started going around on that damn shaking boat. We did the same things every day and we were happy. It's all so simple—I have worked it out—we can live right here, in a house, in a house.

NEVER HAVE LAND AND WATER MORE RELUC-tantly parted than in Georgia. They lie in a lascivious embrace, and the late sun turns the water to silver and the grass to gold.

There is my island, shouted Frank, and slipped sideways and down three hundred feet—an armadillo manoeuvre, written in the wind. And there was Creighton Island, and the dock and the *Phyllis May* the size of a louse, and the field where Jim chased the armadillos, and all the trees like moss.

The water lay languid in curls and whirls and swirls and meanders and wanders, and the grass was engraved with runoffs and runnels and funnels, and every ten miles a sound leached into the Atlantic, releasing water from land and bringing resolution, relief.

Colonel Frank turned round in the pilot's seat.

Happy seventieth birthday, Monica, he said.

PIGGLY WIGGLY IS A SUPERMARKET CHAIN AND I had bought one of their T-shirts. It was pink, with a drawing of a pig on the front, and a slogan on the back *I'm Big with the Pig* and it was too large for me. I looked terrible. I bet I'm the only Englishman wearing one of these, I said.

You are the only man in the world wearing one of these, said Frank Jr.

We had spent the night at Frank Jr's dock and now he had come down on his walking sticks to wave us goodbye. Waterside houses commonly have docks, with walkways on stilts striding a quarter of a mile across the marsh grass. Frank Jr's house had a proper stone causeway. You are not allowed to build causeways any more, but Frank Jr's house had been there a long time.

Steve was joining us for the day. He was the business partner of Colonel Frank. According to southern custom he had brought gifts—satsumas from his mother's tree in Florida, and grapefruit from his own trees, both with leaves still attached, and bottles of mosquito repellent made from lemons. As well as these citrus tributes Steve had brought two bags of ice and a sack of aromatic cedar logs. We put the logs on top of the boat and they smelt too good to burn.

Monica had worked out that if we left at nine the rising tide would bear us forty miles to a marina near Brunswick, and float us off if we went aground. We waved and set off down the creek.

Mud and oysters and a metre above us the yellow grass— the cosy sweaty smell of the mud. I love warm smells— tobacco, mud, a baby's hair, plaster in old houses, chip shops, cedarwood, Jim.

Jim was below and not shivering. Maybe he knew it was a calm day and Steve would make sure we got there alive or maybe he is getting used to the boat after five years or maybe he has just given up. I think he would have liked to come out on the bow but the currents are strong and although these are saltwater creeks there are alligators.

Steve was slim, maybe fifty, with a soft voice—not a stage Southerner like many, but a normal chap you could under- stand when he spoke. I realized that I would probably not keep him off the tiller unless I drugged his coffee, so I settled on the gunwale beside him. I can honestly say, said Steve, I have never seen anything like the *Phyllis May*; I could never have imagined anything like her, and she's great.

Frank Jr took us to lunch yesterday in Darien, I said—real southern buffet. Drove us all the way, and he's eighty-four. He has *Third Infantry Division* on his baseball cap. In Virginia Norwood Thomas had *101st Airborne Division.* If I was a war hero I would wear a hat like that. Frank Jr knows everyone in Darien of course. Then he came along to the boat later with a pretty blonde lady. She brought us a pecan pie. I bet she made the pecan pie I had on Christmas Day—I have never tasted a pie like that in my life.

The lady is late sixties, seventy, said Steve. She is not in Frank Jr's age group.

Gaolbait, I said—he ought to be ashamed of himself.

This is the area of *Gone with the Wind*, said Steve. But there are no slaves or rice fields any more, it's timber and shrimping. I hope you got some good photos of shrimp boats—the industry is dying—there are too many imports.

I got some great photos at Oriental, I said, and I bought Monica a painting of a shrimp boat for her seventieth, with the clouds, and the reflection, and the yellow grass and the trees—oh while I think of it—there's a sandbar round the corner, Steve, just under the water. Yesterday I was chugging along the deep bits on the GPS and Monica said—It's a shoal! I said Don't be silly, the GPS says we are in deep water. Then I saw the sand and banged the boat into reverse. The tide was dropping and we could have been there all night. The GPS is fine, but it is not the real thing.

Yes, it's a nasty bar, said Steve. But if you know which way the tides run, ninety-nine times out of a hundred you know which side of a point the sand will be. But everyone runs aground. I ran aground a while ago, but I was on a rising tide so I just sat there for a couple of hours.

A couple of hours? But your boat only draws a few inches. How fast were you going when you hit the sandbar?

Forty-five miles an hour, said Steve.

Monica saw an otter on the bank this morning, I said.

Yes, and there are mink. Otters are the worst—make a terrible mess of a boat. These creeks are full of fish—the trout are very tasty. There are alligators but they are tucked up asleep in mud-holes in January.

What are those birds? They are a sort of a big hawk and they are everywhere circling around—they look just like the red kites in France but their tails are not forked.

Buzzards—they ride on the thermals looking out for food.

And that is a cormorant, just there, I said, as the cormorant disappeared.

Yes, and we have the anhinga, which is similar but lower in the saddle—they call them snakebirds because you can only see the necks.

I love the pelicans, I said. Their big heads and beaks back on their shoulders, and their satisfied smile.

We were reaching the mouth of the creek and a sixty-foot sport-fisher came out of the Intracoastal Waterway on our left. Be careful, said Steve—they'll turn you over—they don't care.

They are too busy taking pictures, I said. We have been lucky so far. Perhaps they think we are very fragile and will go straight over and drown and sue them—you go fishing a lot, Steve?

Yes, off the coast. You saw my little boat, with the outboard. Frank Jr lost a son in a boat like that—he was twenty—Colonel Frank's brother. And his two friends. Never found them—never found the boat. It was a fishing competition in the ocean but it was cancelled because of the weather but the boys never heard of the cancellation.

God how awful, I said, how awful, and I thought of the wind in eight thousand acres of trees, and the family, waiting.

FOR FIVE HUNDRED MILES WE HAD NOT TIRED of water, grass and sky. I like Georgia best of all, I said to Steve. It is more remote, less houses, more space, and more bluffs and trees. I love the loneliness.

Terry, over there, in the forest—see the digger? That forest will be a housing community soon. Georgia is being invaded again from the north. The baby-boomers are retiring, and there is twice the population in the US compared with fifty years ago. A lot of people made money in the eighties, and everyone dreams of a waterside home with a dock.

I couldn't live here in the summer without air-conditioning, I said. But the winter is lovely.

The winter kept on being lovely and the grass and the trees were January pastels and the wind was warm and the alligators lay snug in their beds and the cormorants peered and plopped and the hawks wheeled and the *Phyllis May* rumbled along and twisted a translucent wake that unfurled to foam and spread to ripples and reached for the bank but the Waterway was broadening and broadening and the ripples swam away and drowned.

Out on to the Doboy Sound—the light, the light.

A ragged black line a mile away—a little crowd of pelicans chatting to a crabber and following his boat. Steve passed close by and greeted the crabber and the pelicans and we pressed on, swimming on air.

> *Then the sea*
> *And heaven rolled as one and from the two*
> *Came fresh transfigurings of freshest blue*

IT WAS WINDY ON OUR OUTSIDE MOORING ON St Simon's Island and there was frost on top of the boat. We were grateful that our air-conditioner turned into a heat pump when it ran backwards.

We had spent a couple of days lounging around in the marina and now we were impatient to get to Florida. There it

was supposed to be warm and the coast had been put back together and you didn't have to keep sailing out almost into the
ocean. Go the back way round St Andrew's Sound, said
the dockmaster—it cuts out the worst and it's bumpy today.

I put on my woolly jacket, and my yellow oilskins, and
my life jacket and my gloves, and wished I had brought my
Russian hat with the flaps. We splashed out into the wide waters, and after a few miles sidled into the creeks—the back-
door route for small boats and cowards.

There were new hazards here—corners where you could
scarce turn a sixty-foot boat, shoals and needle-eye entrances,
but you were deep into the winding waters and safe from
the waves and the currents and the cold sun was bright on the
best of the best of Georgia.

Monica joined me on the back. See that white bridge back
there in the sun? I asked. It's over the Brunswick River and
it's named after the poet of Georgia—Sidney Lanier. He was a
bit of a William McGonagall, but he loved Georgia, and it's
great to think he was appreciated.

> Oh what is abroad in the marsh and the
>   terminal sea?
> Somehow my soul seems suddenly free
> From the weighing fate and the sad
>   discussion of sin,
> By the length and the breadth and the sweep
>   of the marshes of Glyn.

When I was a boy Pennar Gut emptied in our windows
twice a day, but at high tide it filled and we dove from grassy
banks and walked on grass in the sea. In Georgia the tide was

filling the creeks and flowing into the marsh grass, covering it to the knees, and sometimes only the tips of its fingers showed, and sometimes it was buried in silver and blue. Yellow grass and water and the encircling sky, and you drowned in space and light. Over the marshes Lanier's white towers in the sun—yes, there is something else in the world, something that will not melt or sway, something that can reach out of the flatness and prove the third dimension and stop you driving into the grass in an *ivresse des profondeurs*, like a diver taking off his mask, drunk on nitrogen, never to be seen again.

Thank you very much and that's enough of that sort of thing, Terence my son. Just look ahead—the creek has broadened and you are going back out into St Andrew's Sound and do you know what those tiny white woolly things are two miles away? Those are white horses, Terence my son. You are going out into white horses in a canal boat. You know what that makes you, Terence my son?

I jammed my elbow into the corner by the grab-rail and settled in and we came nearer and nearer to the open water of the sound and then the wind and white horses set on me, shouting and shaking and crashing—Oh my God that was a thumper—she hasn't rolled like that before—I hope Jim was in his kennel or it would have slung him across the boat, and poor Mon—now, gently, loosen your armlock on the tiller and let her come round with the wind behind and she is doing her trick of riding the waves as if they are not there. Oh, yes, you yacht, you overtaker, flourish your camera, you are in the presence of one to whom fear is a stranger, who before this day sinks into the west with its sad discussion of sin will have sailed all along the coast of Georgia in a canal boat, contrary to reason and good practice.

But of course, there were still the nuclear submarines.

• • •

MONICA WAS VERY WORRIED ABOUT THE NU-
clear submarines. Some fool had told her that as they went
down Cumberland Sound in their sailing boat a nuclear submarine had risen from the depths and it was a mile long and
going like hell with a wake like a row of terrace houses and it
had nearly sunk them. Since then Monica talked a lot about
nuclear submarines, particularly late at night when she was
tired, and wouldn't listen when I said there were really not
that many of them and they were probably all broken down
under the North Pole.

Anyway this was it—here she was at the tiller and going
down Cumberland Sound, and she had lost her way.

The man who developed the Nautilus nuclear submarine
programme, which saved the world from destruction by not
destroying the world, was Admiral Hyman Rickover. One of
our gongoozlers had been a naval officer and he was inter-
viewed by Admiral Rickover for a job. It seems Hyman
Rickover was brilliant to the point of genius, but very eccen-
tric. He loved straight talking, but like all of us he had his
limits. We are an élite force, said Rickover. The world depends on us for its safety. When the survival of the very
world is at stake there are no short cuts—my men do no short
cuts.

Yes they do, Admiral, said the officer, all the time, and I
take short cuts along with them.

Hyman Rickover threw him out.

Rickover looked at the next candidate across his desk and
suddenly—Make me mad!—he shouted.

The officer walked across the room and picked up a glass

case containing a four-foot model of a Nautilus submarine and dropped it on the floor. The officer got the job.

I was sleeping peacefully when Monica throttled back and sounded the horn twice. When you make arrangements to summon each other in an emergency you don't expect anyone to wake you up, and the boat seemed steady so I went up on top in a bad mood. I'm lost, said Monica, and that is the mile-long quay for the nuclear submarine, and some sailor is on the VHF saying *Phyllis May are you familiar with these waters* and telling me to keep away and go to the port side of the green buoys—that's the left, isn't it?

The guardian of Admiral Rickover's heritage repeated his request and I took the tiller while Monica found herself on the chart. All the numbers on the daymarks had been changed—Rickover's final defence against an enemy desperate enough to penetrate to his very gates.

Now we were crossing St Mary's Entrance, where the submarines slid out into the Atlantic to their fearful duty. But no *Nautilus* lurched from the deep, and we passed over the magic line into Florida, the sunshine state, and near senseless with cold turned into our marina at Fernandina Beach. Opposite us a paper mill as long as Wolverhampton, with tattered towers and ladders and columns which smoked and roared and stank.

I've come on Floridas you won't believe.

Twelve

I'VE COME ON FLORIDAS YOU WON'T BELIEVE

Florida

Down Nassau Sound We Did Roam – He's Coming in on the Grab-rail – The Small Hairy Dog Began to Sing 'Moon River' – Plastic Lawn Deer – Like a Truck Falling on You – In Defence of Their Eggs – America's Worst Defeat – The Failing Theme Park – You Jump out of the Capsule and Whizz down the Wire – Nothing Happening Out There Today – The Careless White Bone, the Excellence – He's a Shoplifter as Well as a Scrounger and a General Thief

---

On the Phyllis May
One sunny winter's day
Down Nassau Sound we did roam
Drinking all night
Not feeling too bright
Well I feel so broke up
I want to go home

ACTUALLY WE STOPPED DRINKING AROUND MID-
night, and I didn't have much of a hangover, considering. But
before we sailed this morning Monica looked at me in a
funny way. Are you sure you are all right? she asked—do you
realize the lives of Jim and me are in your hands?

Such a lack of respect disturbs the natural hierarchy. What
happens if there is an emergency and the crew has to respond
without question to my curt commands? Monica will argue
and Jim will run away and hide and we'll all go down, each
blaming the others.

It started yesterday afternoon in Fernandina Beach with a
noise like a cannonball rolling across a sandy kitchen table—

side thrusters bringing a big boat into the next dock. (The noise is caused by the propeller in the thruster tubes forming tiny vacuums–it's called cavitation–I won't tell you again.) Then there was a banging on the boat and a man shouting– I'm coming aboard!

I didn't argue because he was big and old with a Breton sailor's cap and an English public school voice, though I suppose I could have had a go at fighting him off with a broom.

I am David, he said–the captain of the seventy-five-footer that has just come in. I went to Portsmouth Grammar School–it's not a grammar school of course–the headmaster was the chairman of the Headmasters' Conference and it is a public school of some standing. What a fine canal barge–and you are a writer! Come over for a drink before dinner–bring your wife. My God that dog is thin.

The big white boat had more galley than we have at home and four staterooms plus quarters for the crew. The bed in the main stateroom would have slept the whole ship's company and Monica and Jim and me. There was a cinema screen in the main saloon. In the engine room there were two turbo diesels, both six hundred and fifty horsepower, and plenty of room to walk around them, holding a gin and tonic.

From the bridge the bow of the boat curved up magisterially but you were high enough to get a good view forward. The wheel had a thin wooden rim and shiny spokes and you spread your arms and embraced it like a woman. Unlike the tiller on the *Phyllis May* it probably had great influence on where the boat went. There were dials and screens and lights, and things that went beep.

This is Jack, said Captain David. Jack was huge and bearded with big white teeth–he was nearly as old as Captain

David. David and I are the crew, said Jack–the owner is Rob. What will you have to drink?–we have most things.

A slim man in his late forties with a ginger moustache came on to the bridge. Hello, he said, I am Rob and this is Lila. Lila was blonde and looked as if she had come out of a yacht catalogue.

So you are a writer, said Rob, and that is your painted boat from England. That is indeed a fine boat–a piece of England come to the South. I see there are logs on top to keep you warm in England, where it is very cold. I am familiar with England–I have been there many times. I have relations there–in fact I have my own coat of arms.

I have often wondered what you do with a coat of arms, I said. Do you put it on your letterhead, and on your car bonnet, and on your tableware?

Sure, said Rob, all of those places. And I am a Knight Templar.

Good heavens–a Knight Templar! I thought they had died out or the Saracens had got them. Do you have to go on quests? I mean to kill dragons, or giants, or rescue maidens, or free Jerusalem, or find the Holy Grail?

It's a secret order, said Rob, and I have only just been elected. No doubt my instructions are on their way.

Lila sat by Rob on the bench seat with her legs under her and looked at him rather as Jim looks at me when he sits in the chair next to me when I am writing. She stroked Rob's thigh.

Captain David and I talked about the English rowing scene fifty years ago and he told me how he went to Sandhurst and Monica talked about our adventures. Let's all go to dinner, said Rob.

On the way to the restaurant I walked with Jack. It has been eleven days since I had a woman, he said.

Oh hard luck, I said, hoping that was the right thing to say.

Fernandina Beach is like Stone—very pretty and most of the buildings are restaurants, but there is more space in Fernandina Beach and the main streets are hung with lights, even in January when the gift shops are full of half-price Santas.

I am a Washington lobbyist, said Rob over the collard greens. It's not about influencing legislation—that is a long-term business—it's about getting things through the system. I used to work with a firm but now I work for myself. My clients are big companies, and on my website there is a picture of me with President Bush.

Do you get fixed fees or do you get commissions from results?

Both—this boat is part of my business—a good place to schmooze people. Get them on the boat and they are on your side.

Rob and Lila came back on the *Phyllis May* and we drank a bottle of Sauvignon and talked about Life and Business and Dogs and I read them the bit about the youngish man in Savannah who bummed a cup of coffee and about his father the navigator and the death of the ball turret gunner and how the fighters used exploding cannon bullets that could cut a plane in half and how I was bombed and how I gave the bum four dollars and four thousand would not have been enough and I wept for the pity of it and because of the drink but no one seemed to mind. I don't know what happened to Captain David but I guess Jack went to look for a woman.

When we sailed in the morning we idled the *Phyllis May* along the great white boat and back again and waved but no one waved back, but we had said goodbye last night so that's all right and here we are now on the South Amelia River and the water is getting bluer and bluer and the woods darker green and the *Phyllis May* is running like a watch. Her wake is green tourmaline with gold lights, fringed with lace.

So Rob is a Knight Templar–I have never met a Knight Templar before. I am sure he will be a *verray parfit gentil* knight, like Chaucer's knight in the *Canterbury Tales.* I wonder is Rob pure–knights are supposed to be pure, but perhaps since the sexual revolution they have relaxed the rules a bit. I believe the Templars are a Masonic order, like the Shriners, who are drunk all the time and run hospitals. The Templars must be the ones who get all the prestige commissions–I wonder what his first quest will be? Perhaps to find all the bums whose fathers fought in the Second World War and give them four thousand dollars, or find the place where all the lovely girls are kept who are sold from the catalogues with the big boats, and free them. That will be up some dark river, like the Waccama, and there will be alligators, and piranhas, and Dicks and Wallys who make their own cartridges. *Childe Robert to the Dark Tower came.* They didn't have a Middle Ages in the US so Childe Robert will have a lot to learn. Captain David is a bit old to be his squire–but of course Lila would be his squire, disguised as a boy–they liked a bit of that sort of thing in the Middle Ages.

My mind drifted away, drowsed by the engine and my hangover.

BLAARR! BLAARR!

Oh my God! A great white ship right upon me—she's running me down! Why don't I look behind more often? That siren—it's just not nice. She's too close—she'll force me into the bank and turn me over. I can't speed up—I'm flat out! How near can I get to the side? They are on me!

Oh it's them!

Monica took Jim out on to the bow and waved and Captain David slid the plastic monster past us, with Jack at his side saluting, and Rob waved and shouted. Lila took photographs and David floored the pedal and flung ahead and the wake splashed into the woods on each bank.

Perhaps Rob has received his instructions for his first quest, said Monica, and is on his way. The battle against evil is all but won.

NEXT MORNING WE SAILED FROM PALM COVE Marina, at mile 747, to run thirty miles down the narrow cuts and the Tolomato River to the oldest town in the US. St Augustine was founded by the Spanish in 1565, and has changed hands twelve times since, but we understood that at the moment it was in the hands of the Americans. St Augustine is not pronounced St Augustine, it is pronounced like brilliantine—if anyone pronounces brilliantine any more. You put brilliantine on your hair after the war, and it smelt awful and got all over your girlfriend.

Perhaps more to the point, it said in the book that to get to St Augustine you had to go across St Augustine Inlet, passing so near to the Atlantic that you are practically among the breakers. That's going to be bloody great, I thought—surfing the breakers on a board sixty feet long weighing seventeen tons, with a four-foot tiller arm—I could feel my shoulder going already.

But here we come into the sound—Oh it's not too bad—I can see the other side—a bit of current running in from the ocean on my left—oh I've lost her—no she's OK—just aim off and bang into it—if you let these head-on currents pull your bow round and get you broadside on you're done for.

Monica in the bow waving back at me, pointing and making the sign for dolphins. You hold out your hand in front of you and curve it up and down to suggest the flight of the beautiful creatures. If you like you can make a sucking noise too, though some might think that was overdoing it. You can practise at home, but make sure no one sees you.

And there they are—lots of little fins, going all ways, and then four little dolphins slid from the deep, lingered among us in mid-air and slipped away. Baby dolphins, baby dolphins, shouted Monica.

One more flight and some big fins. It was a pod, said Monica—they call it a pod, a family group. Oh the darlings, the little darlings.

The maternal instinct is very strong in Monica.

Now I can see the breakers—must be a quarter of a mile away—a boatyard and waterside houses on my left and a pelican just overhead. Pelicans are beauties in their ugly old way—white, brown and black heavily textured feathers, white and yellow domed head, yellow eyes. Their feet are black rubber like a swan—why has this one got his feet down? Oh, he's coming in on the grab-rail!

As we sailed along I did most of the talking and the pelican nodded and smiled. Then I looked up from my GPS and he had gone. He saw you turning right to go up to St Augustine, said Monica, and he knew you were not going fishing in the Atlantic. He wanted a free ride and a free dinner.

It would be lovely if we could have a pelican, I said. They don't interrupt you when you talk and they are so relaxed and wise and they don't whine and pull on the lead and they can catch their own dinner and you don't have to take them for walks.

Good idea, said Monica—he could come into bed with us in the morning. Jim would snuggle up to me and you could snuggle up to your smelly old bird, all beak and feet.

MONICA AND I TOOK JIM UP TO THE QUAY FOR his late night walk, and on the way Jim went on to one and three-quarter ears. When he is asleep, which is nearly all the time, Jim's ears are folded back on his head. They are like that too when he is running. What little time is left he mainly spends mucking about, with one ear up and the other down. But when he is about to attack, both ears are erect, and pointed forward, and quivering. Jim's ears are hollow like flowers and you can see through them and they are very soft. Apart from the coiled and hurdling muscles of his thighs, Jim's ears are his best bit.

A chap appeared out of the dark with a small brown hairy dog. Good evening, said the chap.

Jim and the small brown hairy dog pulled towards each other, and then walked in a circle, sniffing. They did not wag their tails.

That's a nice little dog, said Monica. I used to have a nice little dog like that when I was a little girl.

Would you like to see him dance? asked the chap.

He held out his hand and made a circle in the air and the small brown hairy dog went up on his back legs and spun around. The chap made a circle the other way and the dog went the other way. Jim started to growl and his ears went stiff and began to quiver.

Would you like to see him jump? asked the chap.

He reached behind him on to his boat and took a long white stick and held it out and the small brown hairy dog jumped it one way and then the other and then went under it by mistake and the chap scolded him. Jim growled some more.

Does he sing 'Moon River'? I asked.

Sure, said the chap.

The small brown hairy dog cleared his throat and began to sing 'Moon River'. After a couple of hoarse notes he gave up.

He's got a cold, said the chap.

Poor little fellow, said Monica.

Jim gave a scream and went for the throat. He nearly pulled me off the dock and he was still growling when we got him back to the *Phyllis May*.

That dreadful little hairy dog showed him up, I said. Jim didn't like him because he was jealous. Jim won't dance or jump or sing. In fact he won't do anything.

He'll come when you call, said Monica.

No he won't, I said. He'll sometimes stop and let you come and get him, but only if he wants you to.

All that time and money in dog school, all those evenings we went with him and all that training and he's out of control, said Monica.

But he's beautiful, I said, and he loves us, and he's got the softest ears.

I don't like it when dogs do tricks, said Monica.

Just as well, I said.

Jim laid back his ears and grinned.

ONWARD, ONWARD–WHITE PELICANS ON THE Matanzas River–blue-white, electric white. And alongside them on the sandbar hundreds of little black and white guys, like tennis balls on feet. They would have been shoulder to shoulder, if tennis balls had shoulders.

When we passed waterside houses they sometimes looked Spanish, and some had big terraces boxed in with nets. No lonely mansions as in Georgia, but smaller plots, lower-rise houses, some condominiums–from formality to informality, to a summer place.

We were going somewhere that was so informal it wasn't there at all.

On the chart a grid of creeks led off the Intracoastal and we turned right and docked at Palm Coast Marina, mile 803, under a high quay in the middle of a building site–piles of dirt, muddy roads, the foundations of condominiums and houses and wharves. The pretty semi-detached houses across the cut were finished and occupied. The Village is just up the road, said the dockmaster, but it's not finished.

Henrietta came along the quay and looked at the boat and walked back to the door of the marina office. She wants her dinner, said the dockmaster, but we are out of shrimp. I'll get some later. Jim looked out of the boat and Henrietta fled under the bridge and into the sky. She's a dear old thing, said the dock-master, but she sure makes a terrible noise when she is cross—like a scream and a fart and a car crashing.

The cry of the Great Blue Heron, I said, is never forgotten.

We got lost in the building site but found our way to the road and walked with Jim along a jogging path by some woods, staying away from the ponds. Keep him on the lead, I said, then at least we will have a chance of pulling him back out of the alligator.

Car parks, piles of gravel, condominium blocks ten storeys high. I see no Village, I said.

We passed from the car park through an ugly gap in a tower-block wall and were in a space defined by the three blocks, the walls hung with balconies. It was a bit like a square in France or Italy, but it was a triangle. In the centre a rock band was doing a sound check and there were back projection screens above, facing three ways. Around the triangle were gift shops, clothes shops, and cafés and restaurants which reached out on to the central piazza. They were all full—it was Friday at five o'clock. We went into a bookshop and soon my T-shirt was dark with sweat. It must be an inferno in the summer, I said, and it's all fake—Disneyland, based on a European village square, in the middle of nothing but heaps of gravel and car parks and desolation.

It's rather nice, said Monica.

It's bogus, I say, and not nice bogus like Portmeirion. It's all kitsch—no style, no taste—look at those condominiums looming over it. Think of the heat—it's only February now but I'm drenched—you can't air-condition the whole thing. If you do you are back to a shopping mall. The Yanks get me down with their false environments—they are afraid of reality, in case it bites them in the bum, which of course it always does.

Dear old England, where you can go out of doors without worrying about chiggers and alligators and dying of heat or cold. Bring back the rude waitresses, the dirty toilets, the Saturday night teenage drunks like Babylon. All is forgiven–just take me back to Blighty and put me in front of a telly and I'll watch the cricket with a couple of mates and drink London Pride out of cans or we'll walk up Tittensor Chase with Jim and he'll find that rabbit he buried last spring.

You're tired, said Monica–we have been pushing along. You will finish your book soon, and we can go home.

We walked back between the ponds–the alligators come out at dusk, I thought. Now we are by the woods–and there in the woods eight deer–we were right on them–they were looking straight at us–you could see their eyes shining, the white hairs on their muzzles, the black around their eyes, their ears like Jim's. They seemed as tall as me, and so dignified, so still.

It's marvellous what they can do, I said. They sculpt them in clay, putting in every hair–takes ages–then they cast them in resin. They call it resin but it's just plastic. Plastic deer–like everything else round here it's all plastic; it's all a fake. Plastic lawn deer, part of the fake Village–garden ornaments from hell–fake, fake, fake!

The deer tensed and blinked, and leaped into the air, and rushed away, their white bums flashing.

FORCE ON, FORCE ON, TOWARDS DAYTONA Beach, down the Halifax River where the waters are half a mile wide. A short chop, and the wind behind us–just right for our long thin boat. The daymarks were not too far apart, and the banks on each side had houses and jetties. This was nothing to old Tits Magee.

Safe at last, I thought, south of the tides and the currents, and I hugged my fleece and my oilskin and my scarf round me, and my Australian bush hat, and tried to remember in which restaurant I had left my Breton sailor's cap. I must have looked pretty dashing, and it was a shame that there was no one much to look dashing for—the Waterway was empty and the sky was grey.

A funny noise I had not heard before—crackle, crackle—it was getting nearer and then I saw holes in the water. The rain was falling faster than you expect. This was rain from a bigger planet, rain with bigger drops that came faster because there was more gravity, and it came faster again, and thicker, and though there was no wind it whitened the water and filled the air and I could not read the chart on the roof or see twenty yards ahead.

Such storms pass quickly in the US—most tornadoes last less than ten minutes. Tornado One was touching down in Sumter County sixty miles inland. The winds reached a hundred and fifty miles an hour and pulled trees out of the ground. Six people were killed. Tornado Two hit Lake County, fifty miles away. It travelled twenty-two miles, destroying homes, cars, businesses and trees. It killed fourteen people. Tornado Three hit New Smyrna Beach, south of us. It didn't kill anyone, but it left five miles of destruction. If we had been a few hours earlier the *Phyllis May* would have been flipped out of the water like a hooked trout.

Those poor people, said Monica. Your friends or family killed; your house or your business blown away. Can you imagine the noise of it, the weight of it? It must have been like a truck falling on you, like a bomb.

Norwood Thomas rang—Are you all right? Steve and I have been worried—those tornadoes were so near. Those poor people. Take care—you will always be in our thoughts.

TERRIBLE, SAID TIM AND KIM. TERRIBLE. THE second worst in Florida's history. We have a quiet summer, apart from Ernesto, so all the forecasters are wrong about the hurricanes, but then in the winter the tornadoes get us. Those poor people. And we are in real estate, and it's bad for business.

I had called into the bar at Daytona Beach Marina for a quick one before dinner and Tim and Kim were settled in. They were in their fifties. Real estate, I said—that's interesting—so much development all down the coast.

There have been thousands of high-rise condominiums built in Florida in the last few years, said Tim. Business is not good just now but it will pick up. Kim and I work together—we have been married three months.

Everyone I meet is on a second or third marriage, I said.

It's because we have so much in America, said Tim. We get used to having what we want when we want it.

I'm not sure you have everything. What a savage land—I don't understand how the East Coast was ever settled.

Oh no, said Kim, it's really nice here.

But the boardwalks are still smashed up from last year's hurricanes, and you can be swept away into the sky at any moment, and you can't go out of doors in the summer.

That's true, said Kim, but we have air-conditioning.

And the wildlife attacks you. I was chiggered—it was awful.

Ah, the Red Bugs, said Kim. You paint yourself with nail polish and then they die and then you are all right.

A fish bit me. And there are pythons in the swamps, and lizards that run at thirty-nine miles an hour, and alligators. Death stalks you wherever you go.

There is some truth in what Terry is saying, said Tim. Look at that time when I dropped my mobile phone and bent down to pick it up and four banana spiders jumped out of the grass and fastened on to my neck. They were as big as my hand—like that.

He held out his hand in a claw. I had to go to hospital and have the poison drawn out by syringes, he said. It was in defence of their eggs—they were mother spiders.

He swelled up all down his face and neck and chest like a freak, said Kim. He was off work for six weeks.

Tim's phone rang—Oh, good, said Tim. You will be really happy. Lovely neighbours and the wildlife is wonderful.

I could see the eight scars on his throat under his chin—they were smooth and shiny and each was the size of a penny piece.

Tim put the phone in his pocket and looked at me. In defence of their eggs, he said—they were mother spiders.

MOSQUITO LAGOON, INDIAN RIVER—THE NAMES, the names. We are sailing through a pattern of islands and out on to Mosquito Lagoon. Mosquito Lagoon is big enough to appear on all the atlases, and the name had bewitched me. Now that I knew more about mosquitoes the romance had gone, but so had the mosquitoes because it was winter.

We were running down the west shore outside the islands of spoil from the dredging and there were two miles of water on our left and then the narrow strip of the Canaveral National Seashore and then the Atlantic.

A day from the big book of best days—the air was fresh and there was so much space, and all the birds and the water for ever, and a cloud or two, and the millions of fish beneath us, and the Atlantic just over the dunes where the merchant ships sailed along the coast.

In 1942 Admiral King, the Commander-in-Chief of the US Navy, did not believe in blackouts or convoy escorts. So the amusement parks blazed and headlights flashed along the East Coast and the merchant ships passed before the lights and the U-boats waited with their bows pointed to the shore. Along the Atlantic coast and on the Gulf of Mexico four hundred ships were sunk, at the cost of nine U-boats. Five thousand US, British and Norwegian sailors died—twice the deaths at Pearl Harbor. You could read a newspaper on the Outer Banks by the light of blazing oil tankers, and wreckage and corpses lay on the beaches and the blood of the dying tankers fouled the waves. It was America's worst defeat of the war.

The Royal Air Force and the Royal Navy lost 9 per cent of their number in the Second World War, and the British Army 6 per cent. The British merchant marine lost 17 per cent—thirty-three thousand men. We carried petrol, an old seaman told me one night in the Star. When that was torpedoed you stood no chance, and we all knew it. So the officers didn't call it petrol—they called it white oil.

The Admiral's folly became clear and at last the Battle of the Atlantic was joined—*everything happening elsewhere, on land, at sea, or in the air, depended ultimately on its outcome*, said Winston Churchill. The Allies killed three quarters of the forty thousand U-boat sailors—the worst toll of any force in the war. The morale of the U-boat force did not break.

Men like these deserved a nobler mission. Over the horizon, forty miles away, appeared the top of the NASA Vehicle Assembly Building.

THAT IS WHERE MY HUSBAND GOT TREED BY AN alligator, on the roof of his car, said our taxi driver on the causeway from Titusville.

In the wide grassy drain by the road a pair of eyes and a couple of nostrils turned with us as we passed. He had a flat tyre, said our driver, and got out of the car. If he hadn't heard the splashing the alligator would have got him. He jumped on to the trunk and then on to the roof and there was the alligator waiting for him to come down. He waved and someone stopped and the gator went away. You watch your dog—you can just be walking by a little lake and grab, and he's gone.

We drew up outside the Kennedy Space Center.

I expected a frontage at least as grand as a shopping mall. Inside I expected high ceilings, and light to see where you were going, and food better than a bad UK motorway station. I guessed there would be pompous music, but did not expect it to follow me around quite as much. The Kennedy Space Center comes on like a failing theme park, and those who reach for the stars had not painted their front door.

Robot Scouts, said a sign. We sat down with half a dozen others and behind a glass wall a little display appeared with lights and a videotape presentation, about some robots that went to the moon and didn't do much when they got there and some other robots that went to Mars and crawled around a bit.

But the rocket garden was great—rockets standing on end and a big one lying down, and then we got on a bus and went by the Vehicle Assembly Building. From Mosquito Lagoon we had seen it get bigger and bigger and take on a shape and move round to our left and wait for us and here we were. We saw the crawler track to the launch sites, and went into a big building and there was the back end of a Saturn V rocket.

Bloody 'ell, I said. Bloody 'ell.

The Saturn V rocket is three hundred and sixty feet long and weighs three thousand tons and the thrust cone of each of the five motors is as big as a squash court. One titanic rocket stage, then another, then another, then the tiny Apollo spacecraft with its little bow thrusters to land you on the moon like a butterfly. How did they feel when they went along the walkway into the capsule? asked Monica.

We went along that walkway too. And we saw how small the Space Shuttle is, and that it *glides* in to land, and we won't forget the picture of John Glenn on his last trip in space when he was seventy-seven.

We waited for the taxi. Look at the NASA mission statement in this booklet, I said—

> *To understand and protect our home planet*
> *To explore the Universe and search for life*
> *To inspire the next generation of*
> *   explorers . . . as only*
> *NASA can*

That's all a bit general for me, I said. Kennedy had a mission you could understand—to get to the moon by 1969. But why keep on shooting rockets into space—because the science will result in a better baking foil for chickens? The chances of life within our reach are too small. The numbers are wrong—it's too big out there. And there is no warp drive, and Lieutenant Uhura is not going to tuck us into bed when we beam up from another world where the air is so very like our own. Our home planet is the only one we are likely to get and maybe we should give it all our attention before it melts away beneath our feet.

YOU DON'T SEE THEM RIGHT AFTER THEY GET back, said our taxi driver, because they are sick. My husband is a fireman and a paramedic who goes into the shuttles to carry them out. None of them can walk—it's the space—their muscles have all gone weak. And before they go he hides in a bunker buried in the ground right up by the rocket and if it starts to go wrong he goes up there on the gantry as quick as he can and he has his one astronaut to get. He gets that one and they jump out together and whizz down a wire. If the rocket actually launches and then goes wrong they can abort the mission up to a certain point and the capsule comes down off Morocco. He has been out there training to pick them up.

He must be a brave man, I said. But he thought it best not to take on the alligator.

You bet, said our taxi driver. Look down there.

Down there was a twelve-foot alligator. Its head was hidden under the grass by the bank, a bit like an ostrich. I thought they were supposed to hide under the water, I said, not bury their heads in the bank and leave all their bodies out.

I guess he got a dog or something, said our taxi driver, so he's not hunting for a while, and he reckons he is big enough to lie any way he wants.

We were nearly back at the marina, where the condominiums frowned over the Waterway. Is Titusville being developed like the rest of the coast? I asked.

Yes, it's awful. Always pressure to sell our land and houses to the developers. When I came here it was not like that. At the time of the *Challenger* disaster in 1986 fourteen thousand worked here, and they all lived in Titusville, and ten thousand were laid off. Titusville was a ghost town. But now here come the condos.

INDIAN RIVER! WE ARE ON INDIAN RIVER! HOW often I had looked at the pictures of Indian River in books back home and been fearful because it is so wide. Now here it is and it's three miles wide but though there is a bit of a chop there is not much tide or current this far south.

Indian River isn't our destination—our goal is the Gulf of Mexico. Indian River takes us down the east of Florida to mile 988 on the Intracoastal and then at Stuart we turn right on to the St Lucie Canal and across the peninsula for 150 miles, crossing the killer Lake Okeechobee, the Big O, the mother of the Everglades, the great wet heart of Florida. If we make it over the lake we head for Fort Myers and then we sail out into the Gulf of Mexico with Captain Rob and then we can go home.

But turning to more immediate matters we have to get out of this marina entrance with dignity and we appear to have met some nostrils. Is Jim safe inside?

The nostrils were the front part of a fat leathery face which sank into the river, and then there were a few square yards of smooth water, as something colossal moved just under the surface, then a flipper; then a blunt tail swilled out, and the creature turned on its side. A manatee–the sea cow, that all the posters and ceramics and carvings try to show as cute, when the poor thing looks as if a drunk had started to mould an elephant seal out of clay and gave up before he reached the face. Manatees are peaceful creatures, which is as well because they can weigh three thousand pounds. I turned to bring the propeller away from the great beast and headed out on to the Indian River.

Under the central arch of the bridge and along the magenta line on the GPS into the chop coming on the south wind. Nothing happening out here today–Oh, what's that? A pelican had thrown himself into the water alongside us and come up gulping, and now there are pelicans in all directions, sailing along and diving.

A pelican does not dare the clouds, but he flies *wittily*. He has broad wings and most of the time he is inches above the water, smiling quietly, his head back on his shoulders, gliding the way you glide in gliding dreams. The wave effect keeps him airborne, but his flight goes slower and slower until finally he sits down, because you might as well–or he heads upwards, clutches his wings to his chest and dives as if he has had a heart attack in mid-air.

Over the shore the buzzards wheel, and here in the river on each daymark a cormorant holds out wings to dry.

Snakebirds peer out of the water, and the seagulls cry, and there is the rolling adagio of a pair of dolphins, and cormorants like arrows from the bow, and the pelicans gliding and diving and gobbling, or sitting with one yellow eye on the *Phyllis May*.

Nothing happening out here today.

INDIAN HARBOUR WAS A HOLIDAY PLACE. Through a fence between houses and condominiums and we were on the Atlantic shore—it was evening, and the ocean was calm, and the sky was grey, and we were alone.

We ran Jim on the narrow sand and then he stood with us panting and we watched the day fade on the Atlantic.

> *In the cloudy grey, in the timeless quietness*
> *One explores deeper than the nerves of heart*
>   *or nature, the womb or soul*
> *To the bone, the careless white bone, the*
>   *excellence.*

For nine hundred miles the ocean had been over our shoulder: filling the air with light, replenishing the lagoons, releasing the rivers. Now our prodigious companion was leaving us and we would miss his company. A few days of easy cuts and sheltered rivers and we would be heading inland.

We turned and walked back to the marina. I'm worried about that Lake Okeechobee, I said. It says in the books it's rough and it's nasty. It says if we are used to the waters of the Intracoastal we are in for a shock.

The Intracoastal was enough of a shock for me, said Monica.

It develops a short high chop that is a killer, I said. It's not an estuary or a sound like Albemarle or Pamlico—it's a sea—seven hundred and fifty square miles. It's half as wide again as the English Channel and it's flat on the edges—no white cliffs, no Cap Gris Nez—just water. Okeechobee is Seminole Indian for Big Water.

You've got to give it to those Seminoles, said Monica—they get to the heart of the matter. But don't worry, I am taking us round the rim. It's longer but much more safe. We're going round the rim. I am more worried about finding moorings on the way down—so many marinas were destroyed by Wilma last year.

HALF OUR WINDOWS LOOKED OUT OVER THE basin at the yachts and the pelicans and the other half looked over the blue Indian River, and the weather was June in February. Monica was working on the route and I decided to go for a walk around Historic Downtown Fort Pierce.

I clipped Jim into his life jacket and swung him up on to the dock. The hurricane damage had been repaired and the new boardwalks smelled sweet and woody.

Like other historic downtowns, Fort Pierce had been reclaiming itself for some years, though there were still vacant lots and shutters. It was late afternoon but the wide grid of streets was empty. A hallucinatory townscape of white walls, on one the Chirico shadow of a figure walking out of view. Inside the buildings I imagined Edward Hopper people—a man facing away over a desk, a woman in a slip sitting by a bed waiting for a lover who would never come.

I was looking for a newsagent and a bookshop and have you seen the muffin man? But as usual all the real shops were out of town, on the highway. Here there was a wig shop, a nail bar, a restaurant supplies store, a copy shop, a cigar shop, a day spa, a karate studio. There was a little café with a neon sign which said *Open* and tables outside so I could sit with Jim, but it was shut.

A railway line crossed the street and a train came through. As the last wagon went by the engine sounded its siren, with an hysterical and ominous plangency, two miles down the track.

Back at the harbour a gift shop—perhaps there would be a stuffed manatee for a grandchild, or a T-shirt with a coloured sailfish. We went into the shop and Jim snatched at his lead and I looked down and in his mouth there was a little brown dog of plush. I am so sorry, I said to the lady—I don't think he has dribbled on it.

The lady took it rather well though it was not easy to get the little dog from Jim's mouth. I wiped it on my shorts when the lady wasn't looking and put it back on the shelf. I bought a couple of postcards and the lady smiled as we went out and said Have a nice day.

On the pontoon I looked down and Jim had the dog in his mouth.

He's a shoplifter as well as a scrounger and a scavenger and a general thief, I said to Monica. It was really embarrassing—I went back but she wouldn't let me buy it and he had chewed the bloody thing. And it's probably me, but Fort Pierce is a loony place, deserted, surrealistic, hyper-realistic.

Things were going on round corners that I could not see and I kept feeling that something unbelievable could happen at any moment.

In the sky to the north a silver rocket flung upwards and curved overhead, and the winds took its white wake and turned it to a scribble and it climbed and climbed and the setting sun caught it and it shone like a star.

Maybe it's our good luck star, said Monica, for the Okeechobee.

Thirteen

LOOK FOR ME THERE

Florida

We Go Tomorrow – The Sound of Fear – Did You Make It Yourself? – Night of White Satin – You Put Your Left Hand In – Green Cheeks and Thin Black Legs – Cole Slaw Wrestling – The Dancing Dick – The Twelve-Foot Alligator – The Whiskered Death – Fat Man Come in Red Boat – Look for Me There – The Red Tide – The Long Pink Tongue for the Salty Bits in the Corners

AT STUART WE TURNED RIGHT AND LOCKED UP on to the St Lucie Canal, which sets out across the Florida peninsula towards the Gulf of Mexico. In the way is Lake Okeechobee, and before the lake the last refuge is little Indiantown Marina.

You look upset, I said to Monica. Something has gone wrong. Has Jim thrown up, or the gas run out, or your laptop stiffed? Share your problem with old Tel, and he will wrestle it to the floor and stamp on its fingers. For we are doing well, my little darling—we are poised, poised I say; quivering to throw ourselves like Caesar's legions across the lake—around the lake I mean.

I just rang the Corps of Engineers and the rim route is shut, said Monica—there isn't enough water so we have got to go across the middle.

Got to go across the middle? *Got* to go across the middle? Who are the Corps of Engineers to tell me what to do? How dare these brutish soldiers boss around a sophisticated mariner from a more advanced society on the brink of his greatest success? To hell with the Corps of Engineers—

they don't understand—this is the *Phyllis May* that can sail across a wet football field. We draw only two feet—we'll go round the rim regardless. There you are—problem solved—the industrial-strength mind of Tits Magee has smashed its way through.

The marinas on the rim were destroyed by the last hurricane, said Monica.

We'll anchor out, I said, on the rim route.

You must be mad—we have no dinghy and anyway as soon as we set foot on shore the alligators will eat Jim.

Jim can stay on board, and use the *New York Times*.

He won't, he'll burst, or die. He's a very clean dog.

I understand, you have had a lot of disappointment. Poor Mon, you carry all the weight of management while I sit in the corner at my laptop on the log-box, with my feet on Jim, writing my little book. But fortunately due to the soundness of my overarching project design we have plenty of time. We will do the direct route but we will wait for a really calm day. We can wait for a month if we need to—relaxing in little Indiantown Marina, being welcomed and loved by the good ole locals, with our finger on the pulse of the weather. And when we set out who cares we will be out of sight of land— who cares when the water is like a mirror, stirring only at the lazy splash of the pelicans and the slow dolphins passing with a smile and a sucking noise like a kiss.

They are throwing us out of this marina tomorrow, said Monica, because they are full and they need our space to lift boats out, and there isn't another marina. We are going to-morrow, and the weather forecast is wind ten to fifteen miles an hour and there will be a killer chop and rain and thunderstorms and we could be struck by lightning and it's too far to ask any of our friends to come down. We're on our own, and we go tomorrow.

Don't worry Mon dear—there will be an answer, trust me.

There is an answer already—we go tomorrow, and we go across the middle.

ALTHOUGH TOMORROW WAS COOL, AT FIVE o'clock in the morning it was 100 per cent humidity, so before we got the boat untied we were both wet through. Jim knew what was happening and was sitting in his kennel sulking, and Monica and I were trying not to quarrel. You have to try hard not to quarrel when you are frightened and sometimes we do not try hard enough.

Since I had accepted that we were crossing the middle of the lake there had been a sound in my head like a single note from a distant soprano saxophone, steady in pitch, but slightly ragged—the sound of fear. And my brain had fogged and it was not easy to remember all the jobs to do, or how to untie the knots in the mooring ropes, even though I had tied them myself. I sat on the rough concrete wharf, sweat running down my face and chest, trying to shuffle my bum across to the only point where I could stretch my foot down and touch the gunwale and get aboard without pitching into the basin, and I was thinking Once I was nineteen and full of promise, and this was what it was all leading to—this is how the Golden Welshman finishes up—a fat old man rolling round on a quay in the darkness, scared stiff, and ahead of him the limitless waters and the winds and waves and a desperate struggle that could cause him deadly fear and great physical pain and worse.

Monica came down the gunwale. Her face was strained—Look at the fog—that's all we want.

I switched on the tunnel light and it lit up the fog. But I could see enough to manoeuvre and got out of the marina rather smoothly for a man with a bad attack of the shrieking willies.

We headed west along the St Lucie Canal, black and smooth, an occasional car passing along the highway above us to our left, and the tunnel light wandering ahead into cotton wool. Daylight crept up behind in dark grey and white.

And so the *Phyllis May* and its little crew headed towards the terrible Okeechobee. The fog deadened the sound of the engine and my sweat dripped on to the engine-room hatch. The fog seemed to be getting thicker and I thought I could smell smoke.

A tree oozed by, full of vultures with black heads—strange fruit. The heads turned to watch us as we passed.

You could be in for a shock, Terence my son.

IN STONE I HAD SEEN THE ENTRANCE TO LAKE Okeechobee from the air by way of the Google Earth website. All very simple—a canal, and a tiny lock leading out of flat country on to a great water.

But that was the mock. The turtle proved to be a pair of siege gates—beamed and barred and sparred and overpowering and over there, and reaching away on each side a great bank—the thirty-five-foot levee a hundred and fifty miles long that kept back the inland sea, so it did not overflow again and kill us all.

Port Mayaca lock, said Monica into the VHF, Port Mayaca lock, narrowboat *Phyllis May* requesting lockage.

Fizz fizz squawk, said the VHF, *fizzy fart, wroosh wroosh spit,* and we eased forward into the throat of the lock. The gates began to open and through them was the lake, a white hole in the side of the world.

The fizzers and wrooshers–three Good Ole Boys–came out of their cabin as we passed the seaward end of the lock and stood thirty feet above us–Did you make it yourself?

As we are in America the query was without irony. No, I shouted, it's an English narrowboat–first one to sail in the US.

Now y'all take care out there, shouted the Good Ole Boys, and waved.

You bet your asses, Good Ole Boys, I thought. I wonder if they were trying to warn me? They looked as if they would have liked to tell us something.

It was eight in the morning and the sun had come up somewhere else and the fog had lit up and the water was smooth and white. On each side high poles and on each pole a pelican, following us sideways with his eyes, looking sad– they would have liked to go fishing but they couldn't see where to go.

Neither could I–there was no up, no down, no in, no out, no forward, no back, only the whiteness–the whiteness and the nostrils.

THE NOSTRILS WERE A FOOT APART AND THERE were black bumps a couple of feet behind them that I took for the eyebrows, and six feet behind that the tips of a dragon crest. Monica ran along the gunwale and got behind me on the tiller, lest she would be snatched off the boat and tossed into the air and caught square in the jaws and then the twisting and the drowning. I headed away and the nostrils sank into the lake, rather slowly.

I could still see the shadow of the lock behind me but ahead just cotton wool above and white satin below. On the GPS screen there was the beetle boat and the route across the Okeechobee marked with the magenta line, my tightrope across the inland sea. The beetle boat was square across the line—I was heading north instead of west. I had to get straightened up and moving before the wind came up and overwhelmed us—we needed action. I leaned on the Morse handle and the prop seized the water and I rushed on, round and round, in circles.

The trouble was that the beetle boat on the screen was ten seconds behind me—when I turned it turned too, but later. I suppose it had to send a message to its satellite in outer space and then wait for it to come back. And the screen was small—only four inches—a tiny coloured diagram of a large white world. I was overreacting to the image on the screen and the boat would touch a straight course and then head off the other way and I had to pull it back and I pulled too far and so I was crossing the line this way and then that and lucky not to lose it altogether. When I had used the GPS before I could always see something real to steady my hand—here when I looked up there was nothing—the lock had melted and I was adrift in whiteness, swimming through nothing.

I was scared but too busy to worry. I had to get control quickly—we would be lucky to get across at all if this went on—

I must be doing three times the necessary distance—and by the time we got into the middle of the lake the wind would have come up, and the Okeechobee would have us in its jaws.

I kept working with the tiller and the screen and by slowing my reactions I stabilized the path of the boat. We still wandered, but in slow curves, and were a little way out into the lake already. At least it's calm, I thought—let's take it one at a time—let's get to the first daymark, seven miles out. Monica came up from the saloon—You are on your way, she said—I can see you on my laptop.

All we need is a belt to break or dirt in the fuel or the GPS satellite to stiff I thought and we are buggered, literally. But what can I do—we are committed—we have to blast on and hope that this little screen keeps telling us where we are in our cotton-wool universe. I tried to get some more revs out of the engine. I hope Colonel Frank was right—he said you could sail at night with one of these, and that's what we are doing—sailing in a night of white satin—flying blind.

I wasn't frightened now but rather thought I should have been. The first daymark was more than an hour away but the time passed quickly as I worked the screen and the tiller.

I saw the mark sooner than I expected—we had visibility of a couple of hundred yards now, but since there was nothing to see I had not known that. Anyway there it is, bless its little red triangle. As I saw it my course stabilized—a few precious minutes of normal sailing.

Look at the chart—my word we are a long way out into the lake now—I hope it stays calm, I hope it stays calm. Perhaps the mist will keep the wind down—at least it shows there is not much wind about. The boat moved a few inches sideways and I nearly jumped off the back counter—it's the wind getting up, it's the killer chop—but the sea was almost still. We passed the daymark and were back in our white night.

This was the decisive part of the crossing—if we could make the next daymark seven miles on we would be into the system of marks leading us along the channel to Clewiston, and nearer to the shore with less room for the chop to build up. Keep the revs hammering—God bless the engineers of Bordeaux who marinized this engine, thank heaven for the little GPS—don't worry, don't let fear stiffen your reactions—every turn of the prop gets us nearer safety. Oh, I'm losing the course and heading south—back on the line, steady now, steady.

The lake was staying calm and I was beginning to feel we could make it, and began to enjoy the warm mist and the pearly water and the little beetle going ahead in tiny steps. Even the attack by flies did not affect my mood—or the ant-like creatures running over my jacket and across the GPS screen and shitting on it.

I was no longer surprised by American wildlife—I knew that every ecological niche was full of something dreadful—even the niche occupied by frightened Welshmen trying to cross an inland sea in fog has its special parasites and bearers of venom and disease, lying in wait—Here we are lads, here he comes—it's the Welshman on his boat—our time is here!

Have they flown out of the mist, I wondered, or did they lie in wait under the flower pots on the roof? There are all different sorts of them, but they are not biting me—oh goodness me there's the second daymark—we are two thirds across!

We had reached the marks heading into Clewiston, and Monica took over—You horrible old man, covered in flies—

where did all these nasty little insects come from? Look, they are running all over you—don't let them get on Jim, they might bite him.

I had been on the tiller nearly three hours. Now the mist cleared and the wind got up but we were near the shore, and soon Monica was steering us through the wilderness of marsh grass and into the open lock out of the lake.

We had made it—we had beaten the terrible Okeechobee, and we had done it on our own, and there was only the Gulf of Mexico left and even if we went down in the Gulf we would still have made the end of our journey. A great peace came upon me, and I looked over my shoulder for a last sight of the lake.

My God, Monica, I said, look at that!

A tower of cloud, a black and grey continent of cloud, wider than the Florida peninsula, more vast than the inferno when the oil tanks at Pembroke Dock went up in the war. Billow upon billow, each curve and eddy defined by the sun, bursting upward and upward—an Oppenheimer catastrophe moving across the lake towards us.

I am become death, the destroyer of worlds

CLEWISTON MARINA WAS A VERY RELAXED place, with mobile homes parked in rows in the grass and agricultural machines standing about and a little motel and notices saying *Richard's Rattlers*, and *Charlie's Worms*. There was a floating pontoon, and a Tiki Bar ten feet above us, and a café and a restaurant and a marine store and good showers and a dockmaster called Little Man. He was not that little but you knew he was called Little Man because it was in letters a foot high on his back and each time he saw you he would say They call me Little Man, and I'm having a great time!

Little Man had bright blue eyes and they were crossed like mine but you knew he was smiling in your general direction and he could tie a rope to a cleat by snapping his wrist from six feet away and I had never seen that before.

There was no wireless connection for our laptops at Clewiston but it seemed like our sort of place and we decided the world could do without us for a few days.

There were only seventy miles left to Fort Myers, and all the great crossings had been made. We marked our *traversée blanche* of the lake by singing an old Seminole chant, and dancing around the saloon with Jim, who howled rather out of tune.

> *You put your whole self in, your whole self*
>   *out—*
> *In out, in out, you shake it all about.*
> *You do the Okeechobee and you turn*
>   *around—*
> *That's what it's all about.*
>
> *Whoa-o—the Okeechobee,*
> *Whoa-o—the Okeechobee,*
> *Whoa-o—the Okeechobee,*
> *That's what it's all about.*

IT WOULD HAVE BEEN GRAND TO BREAKFAST next morning off the little silvery slippery guys around the quay, but I lacked the skill and anyway Charlie's Worms was shut. So an American breakfast to go from the café–fresh pancakes, eggs, crispy bacon, sausages, maple syrup, coffee. Here's your silverware said the old lady at the counter, giving me a plastic knife and fork in a paper napkin.

Carrying our meal back to the boat–there in the yard was a Great White Egret. She was tall and graceful, her eyes heavily made up with green, and thin black legs and feet that spread out to hold her steady, each spider toe six inches long. She was beautiful, and she was kinda eyeing me. I went closer but she backed away. No, I have had no egrets.

In the bar that evening Little Man was incognito–he had put on an embroidered jacket without sleeves and he came up to me on my stool and put his arm round me. Perhaps he felt we stood more chance if we faced as one the level gaze of a hostile world. We both coughed lightly in the haze and looked north, as best either of us could look in any particular direction.

I don't know what a Tiki Bar is supposed to be, apart from a bar, but it is usually a shed without walls, so we could see the whole expanse of the catastrophe in the sky from one horizon to the other. It's fire, said Little Man–forty thousand acres of it, up the north end of the lake. It's not meant, but it happens and it's part of the cycle of trees and vegetation and things.

I suppose our mist and fog on the lake was partly smoke, I said. We could have been lost or suffocated or eaten by ants. But the insects were fleeing the fire–that's why they were different types of little insect, and why they did not bite me. They were refugees. Always something new in the Land of the Free, plenty of surprises on the narrowboat *Phyllis May*.

It will take them a month to put it out, said Little Man. Did I tell you I used to be a cowboy?

NEXT EVENING IN THE TIKI BAR A BAND WAS tuning up, and after a while the lead singer and the two other guitars and the keyboards and the drummer set off into a tale about a Louisiana Saturday night, involving a single-shot rifle and a one-eyed dog.

It was not a tight band—more a group of well-meaning people planning to stay as far as they could in the same key. As most country tunes are based on a similar chord sequence and are at dance tempo, the band sounded better than you might expect. When we closed all the windows the music was at just the right level, with a slight intensification of the bass notes, which wandered around the beat and from time to time closed on it, arriving just before the drummer.

An ideal moment for a Dogfish Head IPA. To show that I bear no malice about the trash offered as beer in the Home of the Brave I would report that Dogfish Head IPA is as tasty a brew as has graced the inside of a brown bottle. It seems to be available only in the biggest supermarkets, and I haven't seen much of it south of the Carolinas. It should be sold by law in every bar and restaurant in the Union, and in every wig shop and nail bar.

They have cold rooms in the big supermarkets full of nothing but beer. I am often to be found inside them, showing early signs of exposure. One day I was pulling out a couple of cases of Dogfish Head 60—6 per cent. A geezer came up—Nothing wrong with the 60, he said, but the 90—that's the one.

He had five cases in his trolley and looked in good shape for someone who drank beer with 9 per cent alcohol. I bought a case and it was OK but the alcohol rather dimmed the taste of the hops, and two Dogfish Head 90s that night dimmed everything else and Monica had to wake me up to go to bed. You really don't need more than the Dogfish 60– the hops alone can give you hallucinations.

Anyway this evening I settled down with a free magazine I had picked up in the marina store, a 60 at my lips. The magazine comes from Tampa, Florida. It is called *Full Throttle*, and I commend it to you. It is full of young women with full breasts and empty eyes, lying on Harley-Davidsons, often backwards, and huge men in leathers with bald heads, and obituaries for bikers recently passed over to the other side of the carriageway. There were advertisements for lawyers, mainly lovely young women on motorbikes, who specialize in injury and wrongful death cases, offering in-home and hospital appointments. There are pictures of customized bikes– art at its most high–and tattoos with humming colours, and calendars of events including co-ordination with Hooters restaurants and biker church and treasure hunts and of course cole slaw wrestling, always a big one with the Florida Bikers.

And jokes–

A southern biker was visiting a Yankee relative in Boston over the holidays. He went to a large party and met a pretty co-ed. He was attempting to start up a conversation with the line–Where does you go to school?

The co-ed, of course, was not overly impressed with

his grammar or southern drawl, but being polite she did answer his question. Yale, she replied.

The biker gave her a strange look and took a big deep breath and shouted—WHERE DOES YOU GO TO SCHOOL?

I don't get it, said Monica, and then she did and laughed. Let's go up to the Tiki Bar for a drink and a meal, she said—Gulfstream Rose doesn't feel like cooking tonight.

IN THE BAR THE BAND WAS AT FULL THROTTLE and there was a Dancing Dick. He was tall and slim, with a seventies afro hairstyle and spectacles and a tartan shirt. He was white—everyone was white. He was jumping up and down on the spot and jerking his arms and kicking up his knees. He looked awful. There were others dancing but the Dancing Dick had centre stage. The funny thing was that he seemed to know what he was doing, and only an athlete could keep jumping like that for ten minutes. He had a partner some of the time, and each knew what to expect of the other. Most of the others on the floor were dancing like normal civilized people, but some were doing rather the same sort of dance as the Dick. My God, Monica, I said, I think he means to dance that way—it must be a local dance—do you think he is doing the Shag?

Shagging was an important part of southern culture (stop sniggering that boy) during the depression in the thirties, when there wasn't much else to do, and in 1984 the Shag was named as the official dance of the state of South Carolina. At the end of the set the Dancing Dick had gone, no doubt for a shower and a massage and some isotonic drinks and a bit of stretching and a day in bed.

One old big man and two young big men made room for us at the bar and I tried to attract the barman, who was talking to a girl a few feet away. After ten minutes I penetrated his consciousness and he came over—I'm off duty, he said, but I'll serve you.

Very kind, I said, and the barman smiled.

It is easier in some ways to live in a society without irony.

I am Burl, said the old big man. This is Merle, my nephew, and that is Carl, his friend. I worked in real estate with my father who became very rich. I can afford to come down from Michigan, where there is six feet of snow, and stay in my condominium here in Clewiston, and drink all night in the open air. I have been much blessed. All my life I have followed Jesus, and taken with thanks what He has seen fit to grant me.

Merle his nephew came to look over the balcony at the *Phyllis May* ten feet below. I'll call in tomorrow and have a proper look, he said.

No he won't, said Burl, he's drinking tonight. He won't be up all day.

Carl his friend was about twenty. He was as big as the rest of us put together and had a baby face and a camouflage hat. I've always wanted to go to Europe, he said. I've always wanted to go to Amsterdam. But my hobby is watching videos and I saw this film. In Amsterdam they find out you are American and then they drug you then they cut off your legs and cut out your eyes and torture you to death.

I've been to Amsterdam quite a lot, I said, and I must say I have never been tortured there myself.

But I'm American—there's the Iraq war—everyone hates us.

Sixty years ago the Dutch were starving, I said, and your air force dropped food. People haven't forgotten Operation Manna, and if they have you can remind them.

I understand you can have a good ole naughty time in Amsterdam, said Carl, apart from the torture.

They have cafés, I said, where they don't mind what you smoke.

I like a smoke, said Carl. I'm not a criminal or anything—some people think I am a wicked criminal because of my camouflage hat, but I'm just a guy who likes a joint after work. What about the prostitutes—I believe they are in shop windows?

That's true, I said.

How much would it cost to have a prostitute in Amsterdam? I'm afraid I don't know.

If I took five thousand dollars would that give me a good time?

Oh I think so, I said.

Oh I think so, said Monica.

I would take my mother, said Carl. We are always together. You must watch *The Hostel,* the film about the torturing. And have you seen *National Lampoon's European Vacation*? And *Deuce Bigalow, European Gigolo*? They tell you all about Europe.

After some time we attracted the barman, and paid. I'm still off duty, he explained.

Jolly nice of you to stay, I said.

It's a privilege to serve, said the barman.

The Michigan men and Monica and I took pictures with

our arms round each other. Nephew Merle seemed a little drunk. I owe it all to Jesus, said Burl.

Now I've met some English people I feel different about Europe, said Carl, and I shall be over to see y'all. I think you are very nice people and I am glad the Dutch won't torture me.

A GREY MORNING AS WE LEFT CLEWISTON ON the Okeechobee Waterway, for a short run following the side of the lake before we turned west towards Fort Myers. The hot wind was hard in our faces.

I had heard there were alligators on this waterway. And indeed the shore was covered in twisted bodies, brown and green and grey, tumbled over each other, but the bodies were lifeless and as we came nearer in the poor light they resolved into stones and logs and reefs.

Then we began to see the nostrils and the eyes.

An alligator looks very like flotsam but you can tell it is an alligator by the two sets of flotsam breaking the surface. One set is the nostrils, and the other is the eyes. They move together, as they are on the same ancient head. As you get nearer they sink slowly. The sinking is the worst bit—they are not frightened: just considering their next move. Where do they go? They are aware of you, that's for sure; they would like to kill you, no question; so they must be under the surface trying to find a way to reach you and organize a bit of twisting and drowning.

On the back of the boat Monica and I were inches over the water, with no protection—if an alligator could brave the prop he could swipe us off the counter like a crazed shoplifter. I could sense the reptiles' frustration—it had been a cold winter and they were starving—that is why so many are in the water hunting, not lying out on the bank. How can they get a meal out of this noisy monster hurrying by?

A parliament of vultures—the ones with the black heads. A hundred of them standing around and on a corpse as big as a horse—the chest empty, the limbs splayed in abandon, the soul gone to the marshes of paradise, where it could feast on boaters for all eternity, with two twistings and drownings a day. You can be sorry even for a killer reptile—he must have been a beauty.

We churned on and here was another big fellow. He lay facing the Waterway. He was not moving apart from his yellow eyes, which followed us. He was perhaps twelve feet long.

> What to say of him, God knows.
> Such violence. And such repose.

Oh my God!

The alligator hit the water in a ringing bellyflop and made for the back counter of the boat, his tail driving hard. Monica swerved and stepped as far as she could into the engine room and looked down for the jaws coming up for her legs.

The prop thrashed the water into yellow foam.

The *Phyllis May* fled along the far side of the cut, Monica pressing the Morse handle hard down for a few more revolutions and more foam and more noise. Rows of nostrils and eyes twitched and swivelled as she passed. Into the basin before the lock and the boat turned towards the gates which opened out to the west—the last gates before the Gulf of Mexico.

Thank heaven, said Monica—I think he's gone. Watch out we don't lock through with him or he'll have me off the back while we are waiting.

MOORE HAVEN ON THE CALOOSAHATCHEE Canal, the little town half blown and washed away.

Dinner was two catfish, a gift on the dockside from an old guy and his wife.

What bait did you use? I asked.

I had meant to be a fisherman myself on the Intracoastal but they don't let you fish in the marinas and I was too lazy to go somewhere else. But if he would tell me his bait I might have a go some time.

Night crawlers, said the old guy.

I did not enquire further.

Catfish are strong-tasting fish, enjoyed by many. They are grey, and white underneath and slippery, with a big head and whiskers and stiletto spines. The Intracoastal is seething with catfish and they have been around for millions of years. Under the skin the head is protected with a carapace, and although the fish was only a couple of pounds I could not cut through the backbone. Monica was dispirited by the fish appearing to be still alive after two hours, though I had bashed it most vigorously to release it from this world of toils and snares.

We were enjoying our catfish when my thumb started to hurt—in the angle where it joins the hand—the place where my grandfather had always told me that lockjaw started. The catfish had driven a spine into me as I strove to get it off the old guy's hook. It's not poisonous, he had said.

But the pain was so intense that there must be venom in the wound. It was not a normal puncture pain—it was too harsh. And I could feel it going along my thumb. I put down my knife and fork and explained my fears to Monica. The pain reached my wrist and now my elbow and as God is my witness *I felt it reach my heart.*

It's reached my heart, Monica, I said. I suppose it had to be—something in the US was going to get me in the end. It is the poison catfish, the killer of the waterways—the whiskered death.

Have some more mashed potato, said Monica.

WE WERE FAST AGROUND IN THE MIDDLE OF the Caloosahatchee River, two miles from Fort Myers. Monica had been at the tiller. Monica does not make many mistakes, so when she fouls up she takes it hard.

It's a very narrow channel, she said.

Yes, I said, and you are outside it.

I didn't mean to do it, said Monica—I was pushed over by another boat.

You sound like Tony Blair, I said. No one is questioning your motives. You know what they say—there are two sorts of boaters—those that run aground, and liars. These great rivers and lagoons are often inches deep. The Indian River is only three feet average. We are half a mile from the shore here, but look over the side and there is the sun shining on the bottom.

I spoke to the Towboat US chap on the VHF, said Monica. He said we would know him because he is a fat man in a red boat.

I looked through my binoculars, through which you can see as plainly as with the naked eye. There were the new condominium blocks at Fort Myers and our marina under the bridge two miles away, and the traffic on the Edison Bridge and under it an insect boat foaming our way. Fat man come, I said, in red boat. Can we have a chat about Jim while we are waiting?

The fleas have gone, said Monica. American fleas need American flea-spray.

Great, but I was thinking about what you said about finding him a pal. Perhaps we should ring Whippet Rescue when we get back.

He wouldn't be lonely when we went out, said Monica, and it wouldn't be so bad for them in kennels if there were two of them.

We'll call her Daisy, I said.

Jess, said Monica.

I'VE WRITTEN A POEM, I SAID TO MONICA, TO BE read at my funeral. I'm over seventy, and you have got to be realistic. We might be taken up in the Gulf of Mexico tomorrow—it could be the Rapture. The poem is called 'Darling'. It's for you.

> *Where the bow touches the water*
> *In the light on a black headland*
> *Look for me there*

> *I shall not lean on the tiller again*
> *Or hold you in the midnight storm*
> *But there are places where earth rubs up*
>   *close to heaven*
> *Look for me there*
> *Mist on the cut*
> *Ice talking along the hull*
> *The sunset canal incarnadine*
> *Darling—look for me there*

You've made me cry, said Monica.

AN ADVENTURE BEGINS AT DAWN WITH QUIET conversations on a runway or a platform or a quay, about things someone has forgotten to bring.

Captain Rob arrived on the beat of six thirty and I was on the back of the boat, hoping I had not woken the whole marina when I banged open the hatch. Marv from the next boat untied our line and I backed slowly into the basin and turned on to the Caloosahatchee.

In the saloon Monica was trying to reason with Jim. He didn't want to set out again—nine months of being chucked about in a buzzing tube is a long time. He shuddered and whined and would not be comforted. Jim had had enough.

But hang on Jimmy—this is it—the last adventure—the Gulf of Mexico. Soon we are going home.

The river was a couple of miles wide and a blue day arose and there was a breeze and I gave Captain Rob the tiller.

It is my pleasure to help, he said, in this grand endeavour.

Captain Rob was a grandfather, though he looked like a

beach boy. He had been a banker and decided he preferred to go fishing so he bought a couple of boats, eighteen and twenty-two feet long, and hung out his shingle, offering backwater fishing in the creeks and lagoons and rivers. There are lots of fish round here—one day he caught seventeen different sorts. For the first year he and his wife lived off peanut butter and now he was earning more than he did as a banker. Like our other gallant captains, he said he had never even imagined a boat like the *Phyllis May* and he would never drive anything so strange again and she tracks like a champion and bang bang look how she went over that wake the sweetheart.

Like Jim, Monica and I were tired and wanted to go home. We would always treasure our memories of the lovely Yanks and their enormous country but sometimes you just want to live in Lilliput and watch Wimbledon and go down the chippie.

But even a burned-out traveller could not resist the blue waters turning to green and the river two miles wide narrowing into islands and then broadening out towards the Gulf and the sun and the warm wind, and the Sanibel Bridge coming up with Marv and his camera. Marv had talked his way on to the centre span, where pedestrians are not allowed. Marv looks like Jimmy Carter, and the bridgekeeper didn't want to risk turning away a president.

At least the attacks by your wildlife are over, I said to Rob.

What about the no-see-ums I warned you about?

No-see-um.

And the giant lizards?

No-see-um.

Look at that, said Rob.

Under my feet, inches away from the side of the boat, two

dim shapes: muscular, eight feet long. They held alongside without seeming to flex their bodies.

They will be up in a moment, said Rob.

The dolphins were shining grey, and blew and sucked and I could see the blow-holes open and they rolled down again and held tight to the boat.

They're getting some good vibrations, said Rob.

We're giving them excitations?

Good, good, good, good vibrations, said Rob.

With our grey escorts we headed out to sea from the Sanibel Bridge, to where the waters widened and the waves chopped green and there was a smell of salt. The spray from our bow was flame, and the flakes of flame. I took over the tiller.

Where is the line? I asked. At what point are we actually in the Gulf of Mexico?

The line is at the Sanibel lighthouse over there to starboard. From then on you are in the Gulf of Mexico. Not far now—your boat is handling the waves well and the dolphins will make sure we get there. They are very clever, you know—they are trained to rescue people and fight alongside the marines. This pair has probably been sent by the CIA. They don't want a writer saying he went to the US and had a failure. Think back, I bet you have seen this pair before.

Thank heaven, I said, a creature that is on our side. You have so much savage and dangerous wildlife. I nearly lost my life to a catfish—I could feel my circulation collapsing—if I hadn't been a runner he would have had me. But all that's over now—they can't get me out here on the bounding main—ah the buggers, Tits Magee has triumphed—he has overcome—not the Virginia chiggers, the Hilton Head mosquitoes, the bluefish, the catfish, the alligators—nothing has stopped him, because his heart is pure. Your heart must be pure indeed if you are to survive the terrible broken coast of the eastern US—anything wrong, Rob?

Rob was coughing, a dry cough, as one who has put too much ginger on his melon, or has been covered in pepper by an enthusiastic Italian waiter. It's the Red Tide, he choked.

The Red Tide?

Yes, said Rob, gagging, it's a red algae. It is in the seawater. It is thrown up by the bow in the spray and we are breathing it in. It's an irritant.

He broke down coughing and I tried to answer and couldn't. We coughed and coughed and the *Phyllis May* drove out into the Gulf of Mexico, shouldering the green waves, foaming at the neck most like to a swan, throwing poison in the wind. Monica came up from below—Jim isn't well—he is gagging and coughing!

I could not speak but pointed to the GPS, which showed we were crossing the magic line, and Monica held the tiller with me.

We kissed and embraced and waved our hats.

We knew the Gulf of Mexico was there, though our eyes dazzled. We knew we had made it, though we could not say so. We knew the Sanibel lighthouse was behind us and the Gulf was under our flat bottom and those were the waves not of the Intracoastal but of a great sea, but we couldn't revel in it because we could hardly breathe.

The US wildlife had not stopped us, but it didn't give up easy, either.

. . .

ON THE FLOOR JIM WAS FIGHTING TO GET HIS whole body inside a bag of beef jerky. Cousin Ken's champagne cork went up with a merry bang as everyone shouted different instructions about how to open the bottle. Marv had already printed a couple of his pictures, and Captain Rob's wife, JoNell, who had shadowed us in a fishing boat, brought us shells harvested after the last hurricane—angel's wing, moon snail, buttercup, fig, olive, scallop, sand dollar.

Poor old Jim, said Monica, six hours of boating and then the Red Tide. But he has cheered up now we have stopped. Next week we fly home, Jim baby, and Andrew, our agent in Liverpool, will get the boat back to Stone. The St Christopher keyring Karen and Peter gave us at the boatyard has brought us a lot of luck. I wonder if Jim knows we are going home?

Of course he knows, I said—he knows everything before we do. Now excuse my coughs but on behalf of my dog, Jim, I want to say a few words. I want to say how pleased I am all this nonsense is over, so I can sit under the table in public houses as is proper in a civilized country and run on the common again and find that rabbit I buried last year and feel the grass between my toes and the ground firm so I can get my athlete's balance. And eat pork scratchings—the stone-hard greasy ones that nature intended as my natural food, for which she gave me my mother-of-pearl teeth and my nutcracker jaws and my long pink tongue to lick out the salty bits in the corners.

Well done, said Captain Rob, to the *Phyllis May* and its crew!

Everyone shouted Well done! Well done! and lifted their glasses and coughed.

I put my arm around Monica—We have been so lucky, and

everyone has been so kind, and I just want to say, while our friends are here, I just want to say to you, my Gulfstream Rose . . .

I began to cough, and everyone else began to cough.

Jim looked up and licked his lips. He grinned, coughed, and farted.

Dropping Out,
or How It All Began

AS I SAT IN ATLANTIC YACHT BASIN, GREAT
Bridge, Virginia, for three months in a heat wave, staring
death in the face, there was time to think about the path
Monica and I had travelled since we met, and how I had finished up an old man on a narrowboat far from home, trying
to write a book about a journey that was not going well—a
journey that was not going at all.

ONE SATURDAY IN 1959 I CRASHED THE CARDIFF
University Union hop and there was a girl in frilly red petti-
coats. When she came up to London to teach I asked her to
marry me. But you are a brutish businessman working for a
soap company, she said. I explained that I was really an
artiste waiting my hour.

Each day I travelled up to the City from our flat in a lit-

tered shopping parade. The trains were filthy and over-
crowded and too cold or too hot and I was hunched up writing stories in my lap for *Punch* and dreading another day at
Lever Brothers–

> Fear in the belly
> Fear in the brain
> Here we all go
> To work again
>
> Sweating hands
> Sweating feet
> Move along please
> Someone wants a seat
>
> Imagine that girl
> In a lustful pose
> Dull the ache
> With the Daily News
>
> Try and forget
> That here we go
> To a million desks
> All in a row
>
> Breakfast, dinner
> Lunch and telly
> I love my beer
> And I love my Mummy
>
> Come here Mummy
> Hold my head

> Why am I still aching
> Now that I'm dead

I was brought up with a three-hundred-degree view of Pennar Gut, with Pembroke Castle holding one corner and the sea flooding in from the other twice a day in hammered silver or mercury, and the clouds over Bentlass, where my grandmother was born, at the ferry. Now I was the Prince of Aquitaine, in the banished tower–

> These are the blues of the businessman
> These are the blues of the tired man
> My music the rattle of car and train
> Save me Lord from the telephone
>
> Hear me, people hear my voice
> I sing of trees and long soft grass
> All day I sit upon my arse
> Save me Lord in my tower of glass
>
> My boss is sitting on my back
> People all round me I don't like
> I eat too much and my belly aches
> Save me Lord from the diesel smoke
>
> New towers growing every day
> And there we'll all be filed away
> Until we go home in the usual way
> Give us strength O Lord to collect our pay

In eight years at Lever Brothers I heard no mention of the poor shareholders. We fixed our prices with our competitors, allowing us three men for each job, two-hour lunches for the Board, and freedom for the managers to go off every lunchtime and get drunk with someone from J Walter Thompson. The organisation was balanced so that no-one took any responsibility for anything. Promotion depended on how good you were at crawling–

> That's the fellow that's the chap
> That's the one we're putting up
> That's the laddie that's the boy
> The Sales Director's pride and joy

> His suits are tidy, not too neat
> He's always frank but still polite
> He's often right but sometimes wrong
> It's good to see him move along

> He worked for Roscoe and for me
> Got good reports from old J B
> That's the sort I like to back
> The new and better class of chap

> Nicely spoken never farts
> Took a good degree in arts
> I like the lad I like his views
> Oh I could kiss his soft suede shoes

I hung on because I did not want to quit as a loser, and was selected in 1965 for six months overseas experience in Canada. At the end of the attachment Monica and I drove from Seattle to San Francisco and strayed onto the grass of hippy paradise.

When we got back, You'll work only twelve hours a week,

said the Principal of the North Staffordshire College of Technology—plenty of time for your poetry.

In the wet North Midlands the winter sun hardly rose—

> Christ how green the fields
> And Christ how bright the flowers
> Be gracious to us Lord
>
> Send us a good morning
> (Christ how tall the clouds)
> God how the air is wet in our throats
>
> Drive us like leaves before thee Lord
> Let our work glorify thee
> Christ how light thy yoke
>
> Send us home (Christ how glad the cries
> Of our children) while the sun dies
> Like a red fish netted in the trees

Overhead St Michael fought the dragon each Michaelmas evening and the canals were stage sets for miracles, even the Annunciation. Look down there on the towpath, almost out of sight—do you see her?

> The canal has swallowed the clouds
> And lies immaculate under the warmth
> Of the sun and mists
> Hang from the sun in skirts
>
> All the dead brown laces and grasses
> Are drying out long time full blown

The ivy makes a crown
With soft green pearls

The girl wears it as she walks
High on the canal bank over the birds
And the toy cows there is no wind at all
To stir the gown

Of her gay visitor
Who speaks and smiles
Perhaps he kissed her leaving a word
That seemed to mean life or death

Here we were safe from the knife beneath the cloak—and far from the squalor and herds of London. The clouds from Shropshire sailed close over our roof—

The house shook at its moorings all
    night long
The wind tried the shutters
The rain crept under the doors
Outside in the garden the tree cried
Help and the moon fled
In tears of rain

The cat crouched in the cupboard
One eye open, dreaming of wolves
And Lucy in her cot
Sailed fast across the seas of heaven
Which she still sometimes revisits in
    sleep
Pursued by a hurricane of angels

Baby still slept bellyful
While the Jerry rain machinegunnèd
  the walls
And woke us to a quiet storm of love
That rose, outstripped the tree-stripping
  wind
Outwashed the rain
And sailed us clear to sleep again

Monica and I could start again, in our own way, in our own place, in our own time, on our own terms, and we could try our strength, and grow.

Perhaps, even, there were other things than poetry.

ON MONICA'S DRESSING TABLE WE STARTED OUR market research and consultancy firm. We learned how to get the big competitor interviews and write reports that scorned jargon and reached conclusions. We bought a big house for our offices. The international companies and the government discovered us and we travelled the world and the firm flourished and in the firm our children grew with us.

After thirty years we retired, and bought the *Phyllis May*, and Jim, and one day we decided to sail to Carcassonne.

By the way, Terry, said Monica, you told me fifty years ago you were really an artiste, so I said I would marry you. Did you say you had thought of a title for a book?

Quotations, References, Echoes

Chapter One: *Their Gods Are Not Our Gods–Staffordshire*
Ruth, Ch. 1 • Parker/Beck, *Captain Marvel* • Burroughs/
Hogarth, *Tarzan* • Patterson/Caniff/Wunder, *Terry and the
Pirates* • McKay/Ferrell, *Anchorman* • Moeller, *The Intracoastal
Waterway* • Maptech Chartkit, *Norfolk Va. to Florida and the
Intracoastal Waterway* • Larson, *Isaac's Storm: The Drowning of
Galveston* • Yeats, "When You Are Old" • Montand, French
film star • Avon Cosmetics, Skin So Soft • Traditional,
"Wayfaring Stranger" • Lamond, *Shanghai Express* •
Guantánamo Bay, U.S. Detention Center, Cuba • Reeves,
country singer • BBC News 16.05.06, "New U.S. Alligator
Killings" • Colorado State University, Tropical Meteorology
Project • Macaulay, "Horatius" • Marvell, "The Garden" •
Revelation, chapter 12 • Denny, *Granny Buttons* blog •
Carolina Country Snacks, Henderson, North Carolina, pork

products • Freshers Foods, Wigan, pork scratchings •
Sanctuary Records Group, *The Romantic Strings of Mantovani*
• Acrobat Music and Media, *The First British Hit Parade* •
King, Stewart, Price, *You Belong to Me* • Sony Budget, *The Best
of Johnnie Ray* • Columbia, *Johnny Cash, The Man in Black* •
EMI Gold, *The Best of Crystal Gayle* • BMG, *Ultimate Dolly
Parton* • Sony, *The Very Best of Kris Kristofferson* • EMI Gold,
The Very Best of Bobbie Gentry • Capitol, Glen Campbell, *My
Hits and Love Songs* • Warner, *The Very Best of Emmylou Harris*
• Bryant, "Love Hurts" • Cervantes, *Don Quixote* • Melville,
Moby-Dick • Stevenson, *Dr. Jekyll and Mr. Hyde* • Dalí,
Persistence of Memory • Housman, "Into My Heart an Air That
Chills" • Housman, "Loveliest of Trees, the Cherry Now"•
Fitzgerald/Nugent, *The Great Gatsby*

Chapter Two: *The Ice Storm–Virginia*
Hadley, *Epic to Epigram* • Lowell, "The Quaker Graveyard
in Nantucket" • Samuel Dana Greene, *In the* Monitor *Turret* •
Soley, *The Blockade and the Cruisers* • US Navy
Superintendent of Documents, Washington, D.C., 1968,
Dictionary of American Naval Fighting Ships • Leacock, "The
Marine Excursions of the Knights of Pythias" • Hume, *The
Virginia Adventure* • Donleavy, *The Ginger Man* • Blake, "The
Sick Rose" • Brendon, *Ike* • Summersby Morgan, *Past
Forgetting* • Genesis, chapter 6 • Cheney, Vice President,
when the U.S. redefined torture • Calley, leader, My Lai
massacre, Vietnam • Pompadour, saying • *Washington Post,*
27.06.06, "Floodwaters Wreak Havoc Across Area" • *Daily
Press,* 27.06.06, "10 inches of Rain Soaks D.C. Region" •
Wallace, *Sanders of the River* • Greene/O'Ferrall, *The Heart of
the Matter* • Audit Commission, report on North Staffs NHS

Trust finances/management 2004/5; Health Protection
Agency, report on hospital infections, 2006 • Anka, "My
Way"

Chapter Three: *Stand and Deliver–Virginia*
Virginia Pilot, 09.08.06, "Officials Warn Mosquito-borne
EEE Virus Is More Active" • Cook, *Beyond the Fringe* •
Andersen, disgraced accountancy firm • Lorenz, ethologist •
Dumont/Vaucaire, "Je Ne Regrette Rien" • Horton,
Hamilton, Carawan, Seeger, "We Shall Overcome"

Chapter Four: *The Village of the Damned–Virginia*
U.S. Department of the Interior Fish and Wildlife Service,
butterflies list • Madame de Pompadour, saying • *Virginia
Pilot, Washingon Post*, 03.08.06, weather reports • Eagle
Pointe, sales leaflet and event schedule • Columbia, *The Best
of Willie Nelson* • Capitol, *Kenny Rogers: 21 Number Ones* •
Columbia, *The Essential Kris Kristofferson* • Rounder, Alison
Krauss & Union Station, *Lonely Runs Both Ways* • Sun,
31.07.06, "The Rapture Has Begun!" • LaHaye and Jenkins,
The Rapture • Romero, *Night of the Living Dead* •
Romero/Savini, *Night of the Living Dead* • Woodward,
Carr/Walker, *Can't Stop the Music* • TV series, *The Bionic
Woman* • Newman, "Lead, Kindly Light" • Jefferson et al.,
American Declaration of Independence • Episcopal Church,
prayer book • John, chapter 6 • Deuteronomy, chapter 8 •
Williams, "Guide Me, O Thou Great Jehovah" • Dion, pop
singer • Bragg, arts commentator • Traditional, "All My
Trials" • Hosmer, " 'Thy Kingdom Come!' On Bended
Knee" • Newman, "Praise to the Holiest in the Height" •
Ward/Fincher, *Alien* • Pompadour, saying • Bennett,

Humperdinck, Williams, pop singers • Mancini, "Moon River" • Clough, "Say Not the Struggle Naught Availeth" • Porter, "At Long Last Love" • Danot, *The Magic Roundabout* • Milton, *Paradise Lost*, Book 1

Chapter Five: *The Terrible Sounds–North Carolina*
Football song, "Here We Go" • Stevens, "Nomad Exquisite" • Mitchell/Howard/Fleming, *Gone with the Wind* • Mew, "Pécheresse" • Unknown, *Beowulf* • Carroll, *Through the Looking Glass and What Alice Found There* • Roddenberry, *Star Trek* • Keats, "Ode to a Nightingale" • Genesis, chapter 1 • Williams, "Guide Me, O Thou Great Jehovah" • Plath, "The Bee Meeting"

Chapter Six: *Why Am I So Cold?–North Carolina*
Plath, "The Bee Meeting" • The Young Rascals, "Groovin'" • Gerry and the Pacemakers, "Ferry 'Cross the Mersey" • Ephesians, chapter 6 • Plath, "The Bee Meeting" • Cash, "I Walk the Line"

Chapter Seven: *Sea of Grass–North Carolina*
Morse, first telegraphic message, 1844 • Kennedy state funeral, 25.11.63 • Scheim, *The Mafia Killed President Kennedy* • Mann/Goffin, "Who Put the Bomp in the Bomp-a-Bomp-a-Bomp?" • Hosmer, " 'Thy Kingdom Come!' On Bended Knee" • Newman, "Praise to the Holiest in the Height" • Tennyson, *The Princess*, "Sweet and Low" • Genesis, chapter 1 • Proverbs, chapter 23 • Hammond/Warren, "Nothing's Gonna Stop Us Now" • Williams, *Sea Symphony* • Webb, "Wichita Lineman" • Whitman, "Song for All Seas, All Ships" • Margaret Barnes, e-mail to MD •

Howard/Renouf, *Adventure Guide to the Georgia and Carolina Coasts* • *Soundings* magazine Jan 07, quote from *Miami Herald* • Telegraph.co.uk 17.06.07, "Florida's Flying Fish Can Knock You Cold" • *The Economist* 02.12.06, "Snakes in Florida" • *Sun News*, South Carolina, 17.11.06, "Totally Destroyed" • Milton, *Comus* • Pasternak/Lean, *Lawrence of Arabia* • Traditional, "All My Trials" • Levin/Forbes, *The Stepford Wives* • Williams, *A Streetcar Named Desire* • Cornford, "The Coast, Norfolk"

Chapter Eight: *It's Called Being Friendly—South Carolina*
Bernard/Smith, "Winter Wonderland" • May, "Rudolph the Red-Nosed Reindeer" • Arnold, *Creature from the Black Lagoon* • Don Hill, e-mail circular about American South • Disney, *Bambi* • Keats, "Ode to a Nightingale" • De Tocqueville, *Journey to America* • Shakespeare, *The Tempest* • Traditional, "Dem Dry Bones"

Chapter Nine: *Even in Arcadia—South Carolina*
Ragan, *The Hunley* • *Tirpitz*, German battleship • Robert Brooks, letter to TD • Fonda, Hopper, Southern, *Easy Rider* • Yeats, "A Prayer for My Daughter" • Los Del Rio, "The Macarena" • Carmichael, "Georgia on My Mind"

Chapter Ten: *Raining All Over the World—Georgia*
White, "A Rainy Night in Georgia" • Weatherly, "Midnight Train to Georgia" • Cronenberg, *The Fly* • Miller, *Masters of the Air* • Enron, collapsed energy company • Arthur Andersen, collapsed accountancy firm • Shakespeare, *Macbeth* • Randall Jarrell, "The Death of the Ball Turret Gunner" • Lizzie Gill, e-mail as from Simon the whippet •

Roussel, *Charles de Gaulle* • Hill, *Southern Comfort* •
Kristofferson/Wilkins, "One Day at a Time"

Chapter Eleven: *Treasure Island–Georgia*
Mancini, "Moon River" • Croce, "Bad, Bad, Leroy Brown" •
Stevenson, *Treasure Island* • Stevens, "Sea Surface Full of
Clouds" • McGonagall, Scottish poet • Lanier, "The Marshes
of Glyn" • Rimbaud, "Le Bateau Ivre"

**Chapter Twelve: *I've Come on Floridas You Won't
Believe–Florida***
Traditional, "Sloop John B" • Chaucer, *Canterbury Tales:
Prologue* • Browning, "Childe Roland to the Dark Tower
Came" • Lowell, "The Quaker Graveyard in Nantucket" •
Mancini, "Moon River" • Williams Ellis, Portmeirion village
• *Daytona Beach News and Journal* 04.02.07, tornado reports •
Gannon, *Black May* • Jeffers, "Gray Weather" • Young,
Cruising Guide to Eastern Florida • Chirico, *Melancholy and
Mystery of a Street* • Hopper, *Office in a Small City*; *Summer
Interior* • Traditional, "Have You Seen the Muffin Man?" •
Nabokov, *Lolita* • Delta rocket launch, Saturday, 17.02.07

Chapter Thirteen: *Look for Me There–Florida*
Caesar, *Gallic Wars* • The Moody Blues, "Nights in White
Satin" • Meeropol, "Strange Fruit" • Oppenheimer, on
atomic bomb • Traditional, "The Hokey Cokey" • Williams,
"Louisiana Saturday Night" • Cianci, *Full Throttle* • Roth,
Hostel • Heckerling, *National Lampoon's European Vacation* •
Bigelow, *Deuce Bigalow, European Gigolo* • Wilbur, "Tywater"
• Leacock, "The Marine Excursions of the Knights of

Pythias" • Wilson, "Good Vibrations" • Stevens, "Nomad Exquisite" • Unknown, *Beowulf*

General Sources
Burns, *The American Civil War* • Cooke, *America* • Brogan, *The Penguin History of the USA* • Hamilton, *Against Oblivion* • Knowles, *The Oxford Dictionary of Quotations* • Lehmann, *The Oxford Book of American Poetry* • Nelson, *Anthology of Modern American Poetry* • Williams, *The New Pocket Anthology of American Verse* (1955)

Permissions

Jeffers. Used with the permission of Stanford University Press.

Excerpt from "Tywater" in *The Beautiful Changes and Other Poems*, copyright 1947 and renewed 1975 by Richard Wilbur. Reprinted by permission of Harcourt, Inc.

DON'T MISS

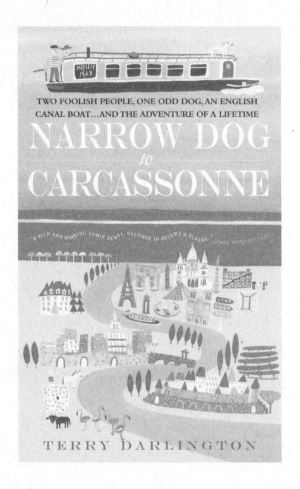